SIR THOMAS BROWNE

❁

At once it struck me, what quality went to form a Man of Achievement, especially in Literature....I mean *Negative Capability*, that is when a man is capable of being in uncertainties, Mysteries, doubts, without any irritable reaching after fact and reason.

JOHN KEATS, *Letter to George and Tom Keats*
December 1817

To

H·S·B

Love's not Time's fool

SIR THOMAS BROWNE

'A man of achievement in literature'

BY

JOAN BENNETT

Lecturer in English in the University of Cambridge and Fellow of Girton College

CAMBRIDGE

AT THE UNIVERSITY PRESS

1962

PUBLISHED BY
THE SYNDICS OF THE CAMBRIDGE UNIVERSITY PRESS

Bentley House, 200 Euston Road, London, N.W. 1
American Branch: 32 East 57th Street, New York 22, N.Y.
West African Office: P.O. Box 33, Ibadan, Nigeria

Printed in Great Britain at the University Press, Cambridge
(Brooke Crutchley, University Printer)

CONTENTS

FOREWORD

LIKE so many others I had enjoyed reading Sir Thomas Browne from the time when I first consciously enjoyed good writing, but in the course of years I became increasingly aware how imperfectly I understood him. A number of questions spurred me on to a further exploration of his work. What, for instance, was the nature and extent of Browne's scepticism? Was he exceptionally able 'to live in divided worlds', or was it common in the mid-seventeenth century to retain old beliefs (in, for example, witchcraft, or a Ptolemaic earth-centred universe) and yet to welcome, to advocate and to further the Baconian advancement of learning? Is Browne's work amusing to read because his ideas and the way he expresses them are strange to us, or because he writes humorously and is himself amused? Is the pleasure he gives to his reader due to the rhythm of his prose, his rich vocabulary and complex sentence structure, or do we enjoy his writings because they reveal a personality that delights us? These were among the questions in my mind when I chose my subject. This book is written in an attempt to answer some of them by studying his work in detail and relating it to some contemporary works that seem relevant.

I have not attempted a close analysis of Sir Thomas Browne's style although it is fully illustrated in quotations. To borrow his own phrase, 'I am naturally amorous of all that is beautiful', but the beauty of Browne's style has been admirably praised and I have little to add. His prose rhythms have been analysed and scholars have examined his rhetoric in relation to the history of prose style. In this area there is, I believe, nothing left to do and certainly nothing of which I am capable. My endeavour has been to find out what he thought and what the style expresses. To this end I have first tried to portray the man himself as we see him in his life and in his correspondence. After that I have examined each work closely, allowing him often to speak for himself, explaining where that seemed necessary and quoting contemporary comments where these are illuminating.

This book could never have been written but for the generosity of two great American libraries. In 1955 the Huntington Library invited me to work there for ten weeks and it was there that much of the preliminary reading was done. When the Folger Shakespeare Library gave me a Fellowship in 1961 I was able to continue the work which had made little progress in the intervening years. Doubtless I could have found all the books I needed without travelling so far, but these two libraries gave me the time to pursue my studies in ideal conditions, with all that I could need made easily available. I take this opportunity to record my thanks. I am especially grateful to Sir Geoffrey Keynes and to Messrs Faber and Faber for permission to quote extensively from their six-volume edition of the *Works of Sir Thomas Browne*. I am also indebted to a number of those who have written about Sir Thomas Browne or his background, whose names I have listed in my select bibliography, and I am obviously and very deeply indebted to the scholars who have established the text.

J. B.

CAMBRIDGE
December 1961

CHAPTER I

THE LIFE OF SIR THOMAS BROWNE

SIR THOMAS BROWNE was born on 19 October 1605 and died in 1682, on the seventy-seventh anniversary of his birth. He was twenty when Charles I came to the throne, thirty-four when the King was executed, and Charles II had reigned for twenty-two years when Sir Thomas Browne died. Yet there is nothing in his published writings to remind us of the Civil War. He seems to have pursued his studies, followed his profession and brought up his large family undisturbed. It would, however, be a mistake to conclude that he was a recluse who took little interest in public affairs. Letters to his sons after the Restoration clearly show both that he expected the boys (from the age of fourteen) to be interested in current events, and that he deeply welcomed the restoration of the monarchy and, still more, the restoration of the doctrine and ritual of the Church of England. During the Interregnum he followed his calling as a doctor of medicine and, doubtless, avoided disputes in accordance with his temperament and his belief. He had written in *Religio Medici* (in 1635): 'I have no Genius to disputes in Religion, and have often thought it wisedome to decline them, especially upon a disadvantage, or when the cause of truth might suffer in the weaknesse of my patronage.' But his own position is in the same work clearly set out: 'I am of that reformed new-cast Religion, wherein I mislike nothing but the name'—the name, he characteristically means, of Protestant. The same outlook is evident when he writes to his sons; he then uses the name, but lays stress on the relative unimportance of ritual differences. He writes to the fourteen-year-old Tom, then in France: 'Hold firm to the Protestant Religion and be diligent in goeing to Church when you have any Little Knowledge of the Language. God will accept of yr desires to serve him in his

Publick worship, tho' you cannot make it out to yr desires';[1] and, a few months later, 22 April 1661:

Honest Tom, [that is how he always begins]

I hope by this time thou art got some what beyond *plaist il*, and *ouy Monsieur*, and durst ask a question and give an Answer in French, and therefore now I hope you goe to the Protestant Church, to which you must not be backward, for tho there Church order and discipline be different from ours, yet they agree with us in doctrine and the main of Religion.[2]

In the same letter he tells Tom that 'Lent was observed this Year wch made Yarmouth and fishermen rejoice'. The letters to the boy of fourteen, as well as to his elder brother, recount items of news concerning Church and State, 'that you may not be totally ignorant of how affairs goe at home'. It is a fair conjecture that, albeit peaceably, Sir Thomas had himself followed the development of affairs with interest and that his sympathies had been with Church and King throughout the Civil War. But for his opinions and feelings in youth we have only conjecture to guide us. After 1635 we can deduce some things from his published works, and for his later years the correspondence is an illuminating guide; but the intimacy it affords begins only when his family is growing up and he himself is fifty-five years old. Concerning his own childhood we know nothing, except a few facts.

Thomas was the third child and first son of a silk merchant. He lost his father when he was eight years old and, in the following year, his mother married again. His stepfather was Sir Thomas Dutton, described by Sir Thomas Browne's daughter Elizabeth as 'a worthie person who had great places'; the adjective was either merely conventional or derived from her father's account of his stepfather, since Elizabeth was born fourteen years after Sir Thomas Dutton's death; Simon Wilkin, the admirable

[1] G. Keynes, *The Works of Sir Thomas Browne* (1931), vol. VI, Letter 2, p. 4. [Henceforward quoted as Keynes.]

[2] Keynes, vol. VI, Letter 6, p. 8.

nineteenth-century editor of Sir Thomas Browne's works, doubts whether it was deserved. His doubt is based on a letter reproduced in Thomas Birch's *Life of Prince Henry*, written to the Prince by Sir Edward Cecil and complaining of Sir Thomas Dutton's insubordination:

I am only unhappy in one thing, that the mutinous and unworthy carriage of Sir Thomas Dutton, whom your highness was pleased to favour beyond his merit, hath from time to time disturbed the course of the service; having even, at his first arrival here, braved me at the head of the troops, daring to tell me, to my face, that it seemed his majesty had given me a commission to abuse men, when there was nothing in question but the doing of the duty of a captain, which he ought not to dispute among us, seeing it was the first time that even [ever] he or his company came into the field among us: and ever since, in all meetings, he hath disputed my commission and authority so far, and with so much scorn, that, though hitherto, in respect to your highness, I have contained myself; yet seeing that now again, in a public assembly, he hath contemptibly spoken of my commission, and, upon base advantage, hurt Sir Hatton Cheke, his colonel, who took upon him the defence of it, I most humbly beseech your highness will be rather pleased to allow of that which justice here shall allot him; presuming that your highness's princely judgment will find it expedient that I be discharged of such a bad member, which, in the heat of his majesty's service, dare contest with me, and be content, upon any terms, to murder his commander.[1]

Birch adds that soon after the battle was won Sir Thomas Dutton, whom he elsewhere identifies as Sir Thomas Browne's stepfather, killed Sir Hatton Cheke in a duel and with this Simon Wilkin associates Sir Thomas Browne's verses:

Diseases are the armes whereby
wee naturally do fall & dye;
what furie ist to take deaths part
& rather then by nature, dye by Art.
Men for mee agayne shall clime
to Jared or Methusala's time.

[1] Simon Wilkin, *Sir Thomas Browne's Works* (1835–6), vol. I, p. lvii, n. 3. [Henceforward quoted as Wilkin.]

That thred of life the fates do twyne
their gentle hand shall clip, not myne.
O let mee never know the cruell
& heedlesse villany of duell,
or if I must that fate sustayne
Let mee be Abel & not Cain.[1]

The sentiment expressed in the verses is characteristic of Sir Thomas Browne; his stepfather's duel might well have suggested to him this line of thought. But the duel took place after the siege of Juliers in 1610, four years before Sir Thomas Dutton became his stepfather, when Thomas Browne was only five years old. It seems more likely that, if the verses refer to it, they reflect the stepfather's remorse rather than Thomas's impression of that time. The rash young man of the siege of Juliers may, after all, have become a worthy stepfather.

John Whitefoot, Browne's friend and earliest biographer, stated that 'he was defrauded by one of his guardians'. The facts relevant to this charge have recently been carefully collected by Dr N. J. Endicott, and assembled in an article in the *University of Toronto Quarterly Review* (January 1961). They show that in 1614 Anne Browne (now Lady Anne Dutton) relinquished the executorship willed to her and her brother-in-law Edward jointly. A court, whose business it was to protect the orphans, thought it safer to leave Edward as sole executor. There had been controversy between him and Sir Thomas Dutton, whom Dr Endicott shows to have been habitually in debt. Anne and Sir Thomas bargained with the court and settled for a payment out of the estate of £1542. 10*s.* 1*d.*, so that as Dr Endicott says 'they certainly got their share as stated in the will'. There were also unrecovered debts to the estate and its final value was uncertain. Eight years later, on 30 April 1622, Edward, now sole executor, owed £500 to the orphans. In 1624 and again in 1626, committees were set up to consider these affairs. No findings

[1] Keynes, vol. v, p. 191.

are known, but whatever they may have been, Thomas Browne had by this time received an excellent education. He was awarded a scholarship at Winchester College and remained there for seven years. In 1623 he became a fellow commoner of Broadgates Hall, later Pembroke College, Oxford. The Master of the College was Dr Thomas Clayton, Regius Professor of Physic in 1611 and Praelector in Anatomy in 1624. Browne's tutor was Thomas Lushington, 'a subtle divine and an eminent philosopher, an independant mind, with fits of unorthodoxy and irreverent speech'.[1] At the University, Browne was trained in the traditional disciplines of Logic and Rhetoric, Divinity and Aristotelian philosophy. Besides this, the University 'had recently added courses in Anatomy and Botany to the antiquated reading of Hippocrates and Galen, and clinical cases could also be studied in Ewelme Hospital, for which Dr Clayton was also responsible'.[2] In addition to all this, he acquired at the University or later, as he himself tells us, 'no less than six languages';[3] presumably Latin and Greek at the University and the modern languages on his travels. He took his B.A. in 1626 and his M.A. in 1629.

For a short while he practised medicine in Oxfordshire, then, in 1630, he began his travels by a visit to his stepfather in Ireland, where Sir Thomas Dutton was Scoutmaster-general. He then went to France and studied in the School of Medicine at Montpellier. Montpellier was partly Protestant, partly Catholic, and in the University students from all over Europe were gathered together. There was 'an active medical school of long standing and European repute, in which observation, experiment and logic were prevailing over traditional medical and religious authority'.[4] After a year at Montpellier Browne proceeded in

[1] Jean-Jacques Denonain, *Sir Thomas Browne, Religio Medici*, New Edition, with Biographical and Critical Introduction (Cambridge, 1955), p. vii.

[2] Denonain, *op. cit.* p. viii.

[3] *Religio Medici*, Part II, sect. 8. John Whitefoot tells us that he knew most European languages, Latin and Greek, a little Hebrew but no Arabic. See 'Some Minutes for the Life of Sir Thomas Browne' (1712), quoted by Wilkin, *op. cit.* I, xlv.

[4] Denonain, *op. cit.* p. viii.

1632 to Padua, 'celebrated for its teaching of anatomy and clinical observation, and for its early experiments in vivisection'.[1] William Harvey, after taking his Cambridge degree, studied at Padua under Fabricius of Aquapendente from 1599 to 1602 and Fabricius was still Professor when Browne was at Padua. He was one who, Professor Charles Singer tells us, 'made many contributions to the advancement of anatomy, most of which had physiological bearings. Thus, he was the effective founder of modern embryology and the author of the first illustrated work on that subject, in which he describes the formation of the chick in the egg.'[2] This is of interest because Sir Thomas continued to be especially concerned with this subject and made a number of discoveries in this field. My authority for this is Dr Joseph Needham,[3] who is less impressed than is Professor Charles Singer with Fabricius' contribution to embryology. Whatever the precise worth of that contribution, it is agreed by both experts that Fabricius was as much devoted to ancient authority as to experiment; he 'never shook himself free from Aristotle and Galen. This backward-looking habit prevented his work from being as important as it might otherwise have been', writes Professor Charles Singer. And for the student of Browne this double allegiance is of special interest. His own allegiance, when he explored natural phenomena, was to experiment rather than to authority, and in this he was, I believe, exactly typical of his own generation. He had been trained to respect both, and he rejected authority only when it was contradicted by experience. In 1633 Sir Thomas Browne went on to Leyden where he took his doctor's degree and where, Professor Denonain writes: 'as in England previously, he could witness the raging controversies between Arminians, Socinians, and the supporters of Protestant orthodoxy'.

[1] Denonain, *op. cit.* p. ix.

[2] Charles Singer, *A Short History of Medicine* (Oxford, 1928), p. 110.

[3] Joseph Needham, *A History of Chemical Embryology* (Cambridge, 1931), vol. 1, p. 136.

After his return to England, Thomas Browne practised medicine for two years at Shipden Hall, near Halifax in Yorkshire. There, between 1634 and 1636, he wrote *Religio Medici*, the work by which he first became known in his own time and which of all his works still gives the most delight. He was thirty years old when he wrote it and thirty-two when, according to Anthony à Wood, he 'was induced in 1637 to remove, after a residence of about three years to Norwich, by the persuasions of Dr Thomas Lushington, formerly his tutor, then Rector of Burnham Westgate, in Norfolk'. Others of his Oxford contemporaries, resident near Norwich, added their persuasions to the Rector's. In 1637 he was incorporated Doctor of Medicine.

In 1641, at the age of thirty-six, he married Dorothy, aged twenty, the fourth daughter of Edward Mileham, Esq. Six years before he had written in *Religio Medici*, Part II, sect. 9:

> I was never yet once, and commend their resolutions who never marry twice; not that I disallow of second marriage; as neither in all cases of Polygamy, which, considering some times, and the unequall number of both sexes, may bee also necessary. The whole woman was made for man, but the twelfth part of man for woman: man is the whole world, and the breath of God; woman the rib and crooked piece of man. I could be content that we might procreate like trees, without conjunction, or that there were any way to perpetuate the world without this triviall and vulgar way of coition; It is the foolishest act a wise man commits in all his life; nor is there anything that will more deject his coold imagination, when he shall consider what an odde and unworthy piece of folly hee hath committed; I speake not in prejudice, nor am I averse from that sweet sexe, but naturally amorous of all that is beautifull; I can looke a whole day with delight upon a handsome Picture, though it be but of an Horse. It is my temper, and I like it the better, to affect all harmony, and sure there is a musicke even in the beauty, and the silent note which *Cupid* strikes, farre sweeter than the sound of an instrument.

If we take this *au pied de la lettre* we may suppose that Browne married only 'to perpetuate the world', and chose Dorothy only because she was beautiful. When he wrote it he was endorsing what Milton describes in *Tetrachordon* as the 'crabbed opinion' of St Augustine:

> *It is not good for man to be alone.* Som would have the sense heerof to be in respect of procreation only; and *Austin* contests that manly friendship in all other regards had bin a more becomming solace for *Adam*, than to spend so many secret years in an empty world with one woman. But our Writers deservedly reject this crabbed opinion; and defend that there is a peculiar comfort in the maried state besides the genial bed, which no other society affords.[1]

This was clearly not Sir Thomas Browne's opinion in 1635; but how was it that he left the passage unchanged, when he prepared *Religio Medici* for publication in 1643? He certainly did not retain Part II, sect. 9, inadvertently. There had been two pirated editions and when Sir Thomas prepared his own he carefully revised his work. In this particular section he made several minor alterations to increase euphony or to convey a finer shade of meaning. For example, all the MSS and the 1642 editions read 'am resolved never to be married twice', which he alters to the more impersonal and more entertaining 'commend their resolutions who never marry twice'. Or again, 'not that I disallow of second marriage; as neither in all cases of Polygamie which considering the unequall number of both sexes, may bee also necessary', is modified for greater accuracy in 1643, and reads 'which, considering some times, and the unequall number', etc. Another interesting revision is the change from 'I wish that we could procreate like trees', which is the reading in all the MSS and in 1642, to the less drastic: 'I could be content that...'.[2] But while he carefully revised and reconsidered what he had written, he did not omit the now untrue statement *I was never yet once married.* He did not omit it, because it was essential to the pattern of sect. 9, which develops with unpredictable but inevitable sequaciousness out of its first sentence. From marriage he moves on to

[1] *Complete Prose Works of Milton* (New Haven, 1959), vol. II, p. 596.

[2] I am here indebted to the superb textual study of Jean-Jacques Denonain, *Sir Thomas Browne, Religio Medici, edited from the Manuscript Copies and Early Editions* (Cambridge, 1953).

love, from love to harmony, from harmony to music (with a characteristic aside on the controversial subject of Church music); from music which is 'a Hieroglyphical and shadowed lesson of the whole world' to poetry and man's natural inclination to rhythm, and all this about order and harmony naturally leads on to medicine, whose province it is to discern and relieve disorders. He reflects that he might, as a doctor, be expected to welcome these, but in fact: 'I rejoyce not at unwholesome Springs, nor unseasonable Winters: my Prayers go with the Husbandmans; I desire everything in its proper season, that neither men nor times bee out of temper.' So, by degrees, the paragraph moves to its unforeseen, yet perfectly consonant close, in 'the universal remedy'; 'for death is the cure of all diseases. There is no Catholicon or universall remedy I know but this; which, though nauseous to queasier stomachs, yet to prepared appetites is Nectar, and a pleasant potion of immortality.' The section is an artistic whole and, as such, he could not radically alter its opening lines. The mind travels in it from the inception to the close of life—from marriage and procreation to death and immortality. All the ideas in the paragraph are as interdependent as the verses in a stanza of poetry and while, like any work of art, it reveals the maker's mind, it must not be read literally as autobiography. No slight was intended to his young wife, just then expecting her first child, and we can be confident that none was taken.

Confidence that no offence was taken rests upon what we know of Dorothy Browne. The Reverend John Whitefoot, a close personal friend of the family, tells us that Sir Thomas 'had Ten Children by his Surviving only Wife, a Lady of such Symmetrical Proportion to her Worthy Husband, both in the Graces of her Body and Mind, that they seemed to come together by a Kind of Natural Magnetism'.[1] He is mistaken about the number of

[1] 'Some Minutes for the Life of Sir Thomas Browne', by the Rev. John Whitefoot, prepared at the request of Dame Dorothy Browne, 1679, printed in Browne, *Posthumous Works* (1712), p. xxxii. [Henceforward quoted as Whitefoot.]

children; there were in fact twelve, but this number includes a pair of twins, born in 1656, who died within their first year. There is reason to think that he was right about Dorothy's 'graces of body and mind', though one must not suppose that 'symmetrical proportion' meant equality of erudition or of mental capacity. Our only direct evidence about Dorothy, besides this tribute, comes from the references to her in her sons' letters; from her own letters to them enclosed with her husband's; and from our knowledge about the family which she produced and ministered to. Her character emerges as that of a warm-hearted, energetic, practical woman, deeply devoted to her husband, children and grandchildren and, like her husband, a devout Christian. It is unlikely that she was a learned woman. Her spelling is as erratic as that of the average middle-class woman of her day. This in itself is not conclusive, but it is noteworthy that Sir Thomas, though he admonishes Edward about spelling, never refers to or corrects his wife's. She was occupied with household management, care of her family in sickness and health and various helpful offices to her neighbours. She must have been long-suffering about her husband's addiction to experiments. There was the dead kingfisher 'hung up by the bill' to see whether his veerings showed the direction of the wind; chickens and mice weighed before and after strangulation to see whether their weight increased when the vital spirits left them; the toad 'in a glass included with many spiders' to test the belief that there is a natural antipathy between them. Then there were carcasses of peacocks, turkeys, capons, hares, etc., 'suspended freely in the air, and after a year and a half the dogs have not refused to eat them'. At all times the house must have harboured strange creatures, alive or dead, and she must have helped to maintain the conditions necessary to each experiment. Between 1643 and 1650 Dorothy bore a child annually; five more were born between 1650 and 1662 with only slightly longer intervals between them. Seven of the twelve children lived to be adults. During these fruitful years Sir Thomas Browne published *Pseudodoxia Epidemica* (1646), and *Hydriotaphia* and *The Garden of Cyrus* (1658), and he twice revised *Pseudodoxia* for the editions of 1650 and 1658.

There are no other recorded events until 1655 when he was called upon to testify at a Witch Trial presided over by Sir Matthew Hale at Bury St Edmunds. Thirty years before in *Religio Medici* Browne had written: 'For mine owne part, I have ever beleeved, and do now know, that there are Witches: they that doubt of these, do not onely deny them, but Spirits; and are obliquely and upon consequence a sort not of Infidels, but Atheists' [I, 30]. For Browne and for some others in his century belief in the power of the devil, operating through the agency of witches, was an essential part of belief in a spiritual hierarchy. Between 1660 and 1718 no less than thirteen works were published asserting the existence of witches. For many of their authors, as for Joseph Glanvill (priest of the Church of England and Fellow, as well as enthusiastic apologist, of the Royal Society), the motive for asserting witchcraft was to defend the Christian faith, since as Glanvill writes in the preface to *Philosophical Considerations concerning Witches and Witchcraft* (1666): 'Those that dare not bluntly say, *There* is NO GOD, content themselves (for a fair step and introduction) to deny there are SPIRITS or WITCHES.'[1]

In the first part of *Sadducismus Triumphatus* (1666) Glanvill expands this; he says that the Devil's influence is

> never more dangerous than when his agency is least suspected. In order therefore to the carrying on the dark and hidden designs he manageth against our happiness and our souls, he cannot expect to advantage himself more, than by insinuating a belief that there is no such thing as himself, but that fear and fancy make devils now as they did Gods of old. Nor can he ever draw the assent of men to so dangerous an assertion while the standing evidences of his existence in his practices by and upon his instruments are not discredited and removed.

[1] In the fourth edition the work was reissued with the title: *A Blow at Modern Sadducism*, and in the next edition of 1681 with the title by which it is now generally known, *Sadducismus Triumphatus*.

Glanvill's book is a work of propaganda whose object is to establish what he conceives to be the fact of witchcraft. Although Sir Thomas Browne never wrote a work of propaganda for this or any other cause (being by temperament an artist and a scientist, seeking in either capacity for truth), yet he shared Glanvill's view of these matters. In *Pseudodoxia*, a work which Glanvill knew and admired, Browne had said that the Devil: 'Endeavours to propagate the unbelief of Witches, whose concession infers his co-existency' [I, 10].

The many books in defence of witchcraft indicate a keen current interest in the subject. But they also indicate that belief was on the wane. Their authors knew that energetic, acrimonious defence was necessary if it was to survive. Nor was it in fact only atheists who doubted. As early as December 1642 Sir Kenelm Digby had written in his *Observations on Religio Medici*:

> I acknowledge ingenuously our *Physicians* experience hath the advantage of my *Philosophy*, in knowing there are witches, Yet I am sure, I have no temptation to doubt of the Deity; nor have any unsatisfaction in believing there are *Spirits*. I do not see a necessary conjunction betweene them, as that the supposition of the one, must needs infer the other. Neither do I deny there are witches, I onely reserve my assent, till I meet with stronger motives to carry it.[1]

And yet Sir Thomas Browne was not behind his times in believing in witchcraft. It was not until some forty years after his death that the belief, so terrible in its consequences, can be said to have become untenable, at least by sane and learned men.

Sir Matthew Hale, who presided at the trial on 10 March 1665, at which Sir Thomas bore witness, was learned, sane and notoriously just. Baxter, in his *Notes on the Life of Sir Matthew Hale*, gives us his character: 'He was most precisely just; in so much as I believe he would have lost all he had in the world rather than do any unjust act: patient in hearing the tediousest speech which any man had to make for himself. The pillar of justice, the refuge of

[1] Sir Kenelm Digby, *Observations on Religio Medici* (1643), p. 36.

the subject who feared oppression, and one of the greatest honours of his Majesty's government.' Yet he condemned the two women, Rose Cullender and Amy Duny, to be hanged, and there was no reprieve. The evidence of Sir Thomas Browne was a small factor; it seems certain that they were doomed in any case; credulity was too strong and not least that of the judge. There is an account of the trial in William Cobbett's *State Trials*, vol. VI. When first discovered this account had 'lain a long time in a private gentleman's hands in the country, it being given him by a person that took it in court for his own satisfaction'.[1] It is not a verbatim report, but it describes the evidence of the various witnesses and the behaviour of the three allegedly bewitched children. The part concerning Sir Thomas Browne is as follows:

There was also Dr Brown of Norwich, a person of great knowledge, who after this evidence given [about half-way through the trial] and upon view of the three persons in Court, was desired to give his opinion, what he did conceive of them: and he was clearly of opinion, that the persons were bewitched, and said, That in Denmark there had been lately a great discovery of witches, who used the very same way of afflicting persons by conveying pins into them, and crooked as these pins were, with needles and nails. And his opinion was, that the Devil in such cases did work upon the bodies of men and women, upon a natural foundation, that is, to stir up and excite such humours superabounding in their bodies, to a great excess, whereby he did in an extraordinary manner, afflict them with such distempers as their bodies were most subject to, as particularly appeared in these children; for he conceived that these swooning fits were natural, and nothing else but that they call the Mother [i.e. hysterics], but only heightened to a great excess by the subtlety of the devil, cooperating with the malice of these which we call witches, at whose instance he doth these villanies.[2]

The hysterical symptoms, rigid bodies, clenched fists, shrieks, etc., had been seen in court—the vomiting of crooked pins and nails (a common supposed manifestation of witchcraft) had been

[1] *Cobbett's Complete Collection of State Trials*, vol. VI (1810), col. 687.
[2] Cobbett, *op. cit.* col. 694.

reported. When the children were approached in court by the witches we read that they:

In the midst of their fits, to all men's apprehension, wholly deprived of all sense and understanding, closing their fists in such manner, as that the strongest man in the Court could not force them open, yet by the least touch of one of these supposed witches,...they would suddenly shriek out opening their hands, which accident would not happen by the touch of any other person.[1]

There were however present some persons sufficiently sceptical to suppose that the children might be counterfeiting; Justice Hale then ordered that the children be blindfolded and that, under the observation of Lord Cornwallis, Sir Edmund Bacon and others, the children should be touched first by one of the alleged witches and then by an innocent person. The children behaved in precisely the same way with both and, for too brief a while, 'This put the Court and all persons into a stand'. Presently, however, it was agreed that the children were so much afraid of the witch that the innocent person caused the same reaction, since they fancied she was their persecutor; the eyewitness comments: 'There appears no malice in it. For the prisoners themselves did scarse so much as object it.' After the children's examination, and after Sir Thomas Browne's testimony, four other witnesses were called: one had had his cart bewitched; it had touched Rose Cullender's gate and she had cursed it so that twice during the day it overturned; another had suffered similarly with his horses; four of them died in consequence; a third had lost her geese through the black magic of the witches; a fourth had been warned by one of the prisoners that her chimney needed mending, and sure enough, though it was new, it collapsed the same day. After all this the prisoners were asked what they had to say for themselves.

They replied, nothing material to anything that was proved against them. Whereupon, the judge in giving his direction to the Jury, told them, that he would not repeat the evidence to them, lest by so doing

[1] Cobbett, *op. cit.* col. 694.

he should wrong the evidence one way or other. Only this he acquainted them, that they had two things to enquire after. First, whether or no these children were bewitched? Secondly, whether the prisoners at the bar were guilty of it.

That there were such creatures as witches he made no doubt at all; for first the scriptures had affirmed so much. Secondly, the wisdom of all nations had provided laws against such persons.... And such hath been the judgment of this Kingdom.... And he desired them strictly to observe their evidence; and desired the great God of heaven to direct their hearts in this weighty thing they had in hand. For to condemn the innocent, and to let the guilty go free, were both an abomination to the Lord.[1]

The two women were much urged to confess. They were hanged a week later 'but they confessed nothing'. Given the prevailing beliefs in the Court and the beliefs of the deservedly respected judge, one can hardly suppose that, had Sir Thomas Browne disbelieved in witches, the prisoners would have been saved. None the less one regrets that his usually inquiring and open mind should have been so fully made up about the existence of witches and their powers as Satan's agents. Matthew Hale left on record some thoughts set down soon after the trial in which he says it is a great Mercy of Providence that the Devil cannot:

infect the Body, but by means of a Witch. And all this God hath most wisely ordered in this manner that tho' the impure spirit itself be out of the reach or regiment of Human Justice or Government; yet the Instrument, without which he cannot ordinarily work, is within the reach of Human Justice and Government: whereby the wise and good God hath consequently as it were, reduced him, *viz.* in his Instruments, without which he cannot act, under the very Power of Human Laws and Government.[2]

This is the voice of the man of law; similarly, Sir Thomas spoke as a physician when he laid stress on the Devil's use of the natural disposition of the body. Sir Thomas too has left some further

[1] *Ibid.* col. 700.

[2] *A Discourse Concerning The Great Mercy of God in preserving us from Witches* (included in *A Collection of modern relations of matter of fact concerning Witches...*, 1693), p. 8.

thoughts on witches which may have been occasioned in part by reflections after the trial. They are to be found among the *Notes from Commonplace Books*:

Wee are no way doubtfull that there are wiches, butt have not been alwayes satisfied in the application of their wichcrafts or whether the parties accused or suffering have been guiltie of that abomination, or persons under such affliction suffered from such hands. In ancient time wee reade of many possessed & probably there are many still, butt the common crye & generall opinion of wiches hath confounded that of possession, men salving such strange effects from veneficiall[1] agents & out of the partie suffering. Many strange things have been done beyond the salvo of human reason whch might proceed as well from possession as veneficacion. If the man in the gospell had now lived who would not have said hee had been bewiched wch few or none might then suspecte; Or who now sayeth that Saul was bewiched. Many examples may occurre of the like nature among us wherin whether possession bee not sometimes mistaken for venefication may well bee considered.[2]

Had he supposed at the time of the trial that the children might be devil-possessed he would have doubted the guilt of the accused, but at that time he was himself conditioned by the prevailing belief.

The early *Transactions of the Royal Society* provide an indication of the slow development of scientific scepticism in the seventeenth century. As late as 1678, in vol. XIII, edited by William Grew, there is no repudiation of belief in witchcraft. Grew reports on Ralph Cudworth's *The True Intellectual System of the Universe* (1678), and summarizes its contents; in the last chapter he has found 'Atheism confuted by Apparitions, Witches, Demoniacs. By Miracles. How they confirm a Prophet. By Oracles. Scripture triumphing over *Pagan* Oracles', and his closing comment on Cudworth's book is: 'The whole Work aboundeth with variety of good Reading and Judicious Discourse thereupon.' There is no question raised about the validity of proofs from witchcraft, etc.

[1] venefic: 'poisoning by the secret art of sorcery' (*O.E.D.*).

[2] Keynes, vol. V, p. 252.

Yet as one reads through the *Transactions* from the first volume, edited by Henry Oldenburg in 1665,[1] to vol. XVII, 1683 (the year after Sir Thomas Browne's death), two things are evident: first, a gradually developing demand for evidence concerning marvels reported to the Society, and secondly, a gradually diminishing need to apologize for the kind of inquiry to which the Royal Society is committed. At first, marvels reported by correspondents, whether ignorant or learned, seem to be accepted on the mere testimony of the alleged eyewitness. For example, Oldenburg reports on 6 November 1665 that a stone has been found in the head of a serpent that will 'draw out' the poison from that serpent's victim: 'Some citizens of London affirm that they have tested the stone.' Again on Monday, 12 February 1666, he records that:

> The learned Doctor John Beale...communicated by some letters that he could make proof of (1) curing a wen by application of a dead man's hand; (2) curing warts by the same means; (3) curing the gout by a dog's lick; (4) that he can assure of an honest blacksmith who by his healing hand converted Barrs of iron into Plates of silver.

These marvels are merely recorded; nothing is said of further testing or of requests for evidence. But by 1667 the Society is already resisting insufficiently attested marvels. Oldenburg writes in his preface to the second volume:

> I hope our Ingenuous Correspondents have examin'd all circumstances of their communicated Relations, with all the care and diligence necessary to be used in such Collections; not taking up old Fame, or Flying Reports, upon too easie trust; nor straining for other kinds of Wonders, than the most wise Author of Nature hath allowed, but attending closely to the strict measures of *Natural Truth*, and to the useful Contrivances of Art.

When, in this volume, he reports a correspondent's account of hailstones measuring eight and twelve inches, weighing nine or

[1] *Philosophical Transactions, giving some accompt of the present Undertakings Studies and Labours of the Ingenious in many Considerable parts of the World.*

twelve ounces and being 'white and smooth without, shining within', he adds a sceptical reflection about the difficulty of 'their pillar of air keeping them aloft'. Meanwhile, from the beginning such a man as Robert Boyle was duly sceptical of information that conflicted with his own knowledge. When it was reported to the Society in November 1665 that milk had been found in a man's veins instead of blood he insisted that further news be given 'very circumstantially from the physician himself'. In the *Pseudodoxia* Sir Thomas Browne shows himself similarly reluctant to accept hearsay as evidence, but, like his contemporary scientists, he has little certainty about the limits of the possible.

Experimental philosophy was advancing gradually and in the face of opposition. For the first ten years, between 1665 and 1675, Oldenburg's prefaces to the annual record of the *Transactions* are written in a fighting spirit; in 1667 he asserts that attacks have not affected the members' 'unchangeable Resolutions',

> as unconcerned in scoffing Discourses, and standing firm as Rocks against the dashes of foaming Disputants. And truly they do much oblige us, in that they are pleased by their frets, and by their fruitless and obstreperous Verbosity, to make themselves a foil, to set off the Serene Lustre of the real and obliging performances of the Experimental Philosophers.

In 1671 he refutes the charge that the Royal Society are offering a 'New Philosophy':

> 'Tis so old as to have been the discipline of Paradise; and from the First of Mankind (who from observing the kinds and differences of Animals gave them Names) to have been countenanced by the Best of Men; Patriarchs and Prophets; offtimes with Divine Assistances and Inspirations; giving them that were successful therein, very eminent attributes of Glory, as in Noah, Moses, Solomon, Daniel and others.

In the following year, however, the preface is a shade less combative and more confident. Earlier attacks on Galileo, on Sir Walter Raleigh and on Gilbert are cited, and Oldenburg notes that Harvey was:

a long time esteemed extravagant for his diligent researches in pursuance of the Circulation of the Blood. But [he goes on], when our renowned Lord Bacon had demonstrated the Methods for a perfect Restauration of all parts of Reall knowledge...the success became on a sudden stupendious, and effective philosophy began to sparkle, and even to flow into beams of bright shining light, all over the World.

In 1675, the eleventh year of the *Transactions*, the preface is at last free from the combative note. It mentions no contemporary enemies and after a brief reference to the emptiness of the Peripatetick Philosophy it points to the positive gains already contributed to useful knowledge, and to the future that lies ahead.

Sir Thomas Browne was never combative; while his younger contemporary Joseph Glanvill wrote one book doing battle for belief in witchcraft, and another in pugnacious defence of the Royal Society, Browne quietly pursued his own researches. He thereby earned Robert Boyle's commendation as 'a naturalist so faithful and candid that he could not be mistrusted',[1] and also the recognition of the distinguished modern scientist Dr Joseph Needham. Dr Needham, in *A History of Chemical Embryology*, quotes both from *Pseudodoxia Epidemica* and from the *Commonplace Books* and comments:

The only conclusion that can be drawn from these remarkable observations is that it was in the 'elaboratory' in Sir Thomas' house at Norwich that the first experiments in chemical embryology were undertaken. His significance in this connection has so far been quite overlooked, and it is time to recognize that his originality and genius in this field shows itself to be hardly less remarkable than in so many others.[2]

In a footnote Dr Needham adds that though *Pseudodoxia* was published in 1646 and Harvey's *De Generatione Animalium* not until 1651, yet in his Third Book, chapter 28, Browne refers to

[1] Robert Boyle, *Second Essay upon Unsucceeding Experiments* (1661). Boyle recounts that he checked an experiment of Sir Thomas Browne's four times, 'being still concerned for the reputation of a person that so well deserves a good one'. At the fourth attempt, the reaction described by Browne took place.

[2] J. Needham, *A History of Chemical Embryology* (1931), vol. I, p. 137.

'Dr Harvey's excellent discourse of generation'. 'Did Browne see manuscript or proof-sheets?' Dr Needham asks. The truth is that chapter 28 is not to be found in the first edition, but only in the third edition, of 1658. The reference does not prove that Browne was in close touch with Harvey in 1646, but it does prove that, as well as reading widely in ancient authors, he kept himself abreast of contemporary research and revised his book accordingly.

Yet, despite his contributions to knowledge and the recognition of so eminent a contemporary as Robert Boyle, Sir Thomas Browne was never a Fellow of the Royal Society. Some literary historians have thought this might have been on account of his prose style, which never conformed to the ideal propounded in Sprat's *History of the Royal Society* (1665) that men should 'return back to the primitive purity, and shortness, when men delivered so many things almost in an equal number of words'. There is, however, a much simpler and more likely reason why Sir Thomas was not elected to a Fellowship of the Royal Society. He was a practising doctor living in Norwich, which was at this time a three days' journey from London.[1] Abraham Cowley, who had attended the first meetings of the Society before its establishment, was elected a member on 6 March 1661. 'But his residence in the country preventing him from attending the meetings of the society, he was not rechosen into it after the passing of the second charter of April 22nd 1663.'[2] In 1662 meetings were held weekly and all members undertook 'that we will be present at Meetings of the Society, as often as conveniently we can'. The members must for some years have been predominantly Londoners (not exclusively, since Joseph Glanvill was elected in December 1664 while he still held a living in Somersetshire). It was not until 1728 that the statutes made provision to exempt members

[1] Keynes, vol. VI, p. 191. Sir Thomas Browne, writing to his son Edward, says that the journey from London to Norwich now generally takes three days (22 October 1680). A Journal kept by Edward in 1664 shows that he did the journey in two days.

[2] *The History of the Royal Society for improving Natural Knowledge*, by Thomas Birch (1756–7), vol. II, p. 222.

whose 'usual place of residence is more than forty miles distance from London'[1] from the rule requiring them to be present within four weeks of their election. From all this we may conclude that a busy doctor in Norwich would have been unlikely to be made a Fellow and that there is no need to seek any other explanation why Sir Thomas Browne's name was not proposed.

Although he was not a Fellow of the Royal Society his relations with it were close, partly through the medium of his doctor son, Edward, who was elected and admitted 2 January 1668. In the same year, 27 February, 'Dr Brown of Norwich presented to the Society a great petrified bone, a double goose egg, the one included in the other, and a stone bottle, which had been filled seven years before with Malaga sack, and was well-stopped, but now found almost empty, and the outside covered all over with a mossy coat'.[2] In the following February Edward sent a letter with information (unspecified) from Vienna. 'It was ordered that he should be thanked and encouraged.' His father had written to him in March to 'take as good account and as particular as you can. Whether you should give an account now or rather hereafter to the R.S. I make some doubt, for in your return you may observe many things perhaps considerable in these poynts, butt however you may signifie them & write of them in your letters to mee.' On 3 March 'Dr Thomas Brown' forwarded to the Society a letter from his son 'containing an account of two parhelia lately seen in Hungary'. In October of the same year Mr Oldenburg read a letter written to him by Sir Thomas 'inclosing a relation of his son Dr Edward Brown then travelling in Germany, concerning quicksilver mines...', and on 25 January 1670 the Society received an account of gold, silver and copper mines in Hungary from 'the ingenious and learned Dr Edward Brown (son to that deservedly famous Physician Dr Thomas Brown)'. The following spring a paper by Sir Thomas Browne

[1] *The Record of the Royal Society of London* (1901), p. 102.
[2] T. Birch, *op. cit.* vol. II, p. 253.

was read to the Society, 'concerning a Bulimia[1] in a woman one hundred and two years old'.

In 1671 Thomas Browne was knighted by Charles II, then visiting Norwich. Charles was, as Dr Johnson puts it, 'a prince, who with many frailties and vices, had yet skill to discover excellence, and virtue to reward it, with such honorary distinctions at least as cost him nothing, yet, conferred by a King so judicious and so much beloved, had the power of giving merit new lustre and greater popularity'.[2] Simon Wilkin throws doubt upon Charles's discernment of merit and thinks it probable that 'though the literary celebrity of Browne must have been well-known, his loyalty was the crowning excellence in the eyes of Charles. In perilous times Dr Browne had steadily adhered to the Royal cause. He was one of the 432 principal citizens who, in 1643, refused to subscribe towards a fund for regaining the town of Newcastle.'[3] We know nothing, however, of any honours conferred on the other 431 principal citizens, and it seems reasonable to suppose that Charles conferred the knighthood in recognition of Browne's contributions to the increase of knowledge and his particular services to the Society of which the King was patron.

In the remaining eleven years of Sir Thomas Browne's life there are no recorded events except for domestic joys and sorrows. His son Edward married in 1672 and settled in London. In 1675 his daughter Mary died at the age of twenty-four. He had sustained what was, I think, an even more overwhelming loss in the death of his charming and brilliant sailor son Thomas, in 1667, at the age of twenty-one.[4] In 1680 his daughter Elizabeth married George Lyttleton, her father's close and much valued companion, and the letters show that she was much missed. In

[1] Bulimia (*O.E.D.*) 'a morbid hunger'. (The paper is extant in the *Transactions* and goes into considerable detail.)

[2] Dr Johnson's *Life of Sir Thomas Browne*: preface to the second edition of *Christian Morals* (1756).

[3] Wilkin, vol. I, p. xci.

[4] See p. 35.

The Commonplace Book of Elizabeth Lyttleton there is a list of the books she read to her father, copied from his own note, and headed: 'The books which my daughter Elizabeth hath read unto me at nights till she read them all out.'[1] Sir Thomas Browne's correspondence allows us to imagine what these family events meant to him, and it also throws considerable light on his principal activities in these years, those of a practising doctor.

On his birthday, at the close of his seventy-seventh year, he died of a severe attack of colic, after a few days' illness, leaving to

> my deare wife, Dame Dorothie Browne, all my Lands, Leases, and Tenements, all my bonds, bills, moveables, money, plate, jewells, and all my goods whatsoever, thereby to have provision for herself, and make liberall maintenance and portions for my deare daughters Elizabeth Browne and Frances Browne, excepting such lands and tenements as were assigned and made over unto my sonne Edward Browne upon marriage, and to bee entered upon a yeare after my decease.[2]

This will was drawn up in 1679, at which time Elizabeth and Frances were both unmarried. Dame Dorothy was made the sole executrix of the will; she survived her husband by two years. In the same year in which the will was drawn up she had asked their friend, the Reverend John Whitefoot, Rector of Heigham in Norfolk, to prepare some 'Minutes for the Life of Sir Thomas Browne'. These include a sketch of his appearance and of his bearing and character. His hair was brown, his height medium, his dress sober: 'In his Habit of Cloathing, he had an Aversion to all Finery, and affected Plainness, both in the Fashion and Ornaments.'[3] His interest in human beings is confirmed by the statement that he 'knew not only all Persons again that he had ever seen at any distance of Time, but remembered the Circumstances of their Bodies, and their particular Discourses and Speeches'.

[1] Keynes, vol. v, p. 295.
[2] *Ibid.* p. 427.
[3] Whitefoot, p. xxviii.

As one might expect from the width and variety of his interests, and from his aversion to controversy, 'He was Excellent Company when he was at leisure, and expresd more Light than Heat in the Temper of his Brain'. His published writings bear witness to a quiet, ironical sense of humour, as well as to his peace of mind and religious confidence. Whitefoot affirms that 'He was never seen to be transported with Mirth, or dejected with Sadness: always Chearful, but rarely Merry, at any sensible Rate, seldom heard to break a Jest; and when he did, he would be apt to blush at the Levity of it: his Gravity was Natural without Affectation'. He was reluctant to talk, but when he did so was 'never Trite or Vulgar'.[1]

[1] The above quotations from Whitefoot are to be found on pp. xxix–xxxi.

CHAPTER II

DOMESTIC CORRESPONDENCE

THE letters between Sir Thomas Browne and his family allow us an intimate knowledge of his domestic relationships; they also throw light by contrast upon the conscious art of his published prose. He did not write these letters for posterity and most of them are singularly artless; only rarely is there anything in their style to recall the master of English prose who wrote *Religio Medici*, *Urne-Buriall* and *The Garden of Cyrus*. He may admonish his sons about spelling and punctuation, telling Edward, 'Write not sceleton with a K' [Letter 150], and Tom, 'Remember to make Commas as , and full points at the end of the sentance thus . ' [Letter 9]. Nevertheless, his own punctuation is, by modern standards, as erratic as his own spelling. The advice just quoted follows, without full-stop, immediately after:

> ...; you may goe from Orleance to Paris by Coach, and from Paris to Rouen by Coach; you must intrust yr trunk with Mr Bendish at Rochell or with Mr Dade at Bourdeaux to be sent by the Vintage Ships to Yarmouth, and must travail only with a Portmanteaux or Valis and one sute of Cloths, for it will be hard to carry more; be directed herein by some English friend; have a Care of yr Draughts and observations, remember...,

etc., and the only full-stop is the exemplary one, quoted above. Not only is Browne here using the semi-colon, not the full-stop, to separate his sentences, but he is paying no attention to balance or harmony of phrasing. Furthermore, topics follow one another just as they happen to arise in his mind. In another letter to Tom political news is followed, without full-stop, by: 'Good boy do not trouble thyself to send us anything, either wine or Bacon.' Then the boy's offer of presents calling to mind his probable shortage of money, his father goes straight on with: 'I would have sent money by Exchange, but Charles Mileham would not have me send any Certain Sum, but what you spend shall be made good by him.' The ensuing sentence expresses a wish that Tom would find someone to teach him to write and to pronounce French, and this may also be linked with possible expense but, with no heavier stop than the semi-colon, he adds other advice, which can be followed without money-cost: 'be Patient Civil and debonair unto all, be Temperate and stir litle in this hot season'; and then he comes back again to the account of current affairs at home. These include the hanging and burning in effigy of Cromwell, Ireton and Bradshaw; the date is 22 April 1661. The letter closes commending the boy to God, but with a final sentence, an afterthought clearly: 'If you meet with any Pretty insects of any Kind Keep them in a box, if you can send *Les Antiquités de Bourdeaux* by any ship, it may come safe' [Letter 6]. This informality in the letters, though it does not make Sir Thomas Browne in any literary sense a good letter writer, does add to their value as documents; by reading these family letters we grow familiar with the natural habits of his mind.

The earliest letters preserved are those to young Thomas, beginning in December 1660 when the boy was fourteen and was travelling on the continent for his education. They are the letters of an anxious, devoted father, filled with good advice about the care of his health and the wise laying out of money, or about making good use of his educational opportunities and remaining constant to the Protestant faith. Letters enclosed from his mother bid him take care of himself, write oftener and: 'Learn what you can though it be something Extraordinary, now you are where you may improve yourself; if you like to sing or dance, learn, or anything else you like' [Letter 4], and she tells him that his father was much pleased with his account of his voyage, 'and it will please him very much if you Continue informing him still what you observe there'. In the second year of his travels, 1661, Tom was presumably showing signs of homesickness; Sir Thomas writes: 'now beare up thy spirits and be not Malancholy sad or dejected, for the hot weather will soon be at an end and haveing made good entrance into the language I would have you remove out of those Parts and to approach neerer England' [Letter 8]. This letter contains detailed instructions about the prospective journey, the direction he is to take, the cities he is to see on the way and the amount of luggage he can take with him: 'yu must not carry much lugadge about for that is Chargeable and apt to be stollen'. In this and several letters he shows some anxiety that the boy should remain a good Protestant. It would be well, he writes, to have some Protestant with him on the journey 'altho' you may boldly acknowledge yourself a Protestant in any Part of France'. A week later Sir Thomas writes again; he seems to have had another unhappy letter from Tom, 'but I hope by this time you are not so Mallencholy as you seem to be; hold out a little, diffuse thy spirits and trust in God's Protection, and aply thy heart unto him'. After this there is no further mention of melancholy and presumably Tom settled down, for he remained in France for another six months. The last letter to France is dated 4 January 1662.

In September 1662 Tom travelled in Derbyshire with his elder brother Edward and wrote an account of their adventures. Tom writes in a fluent and spirited style. He can describe vividly 'a lamentable day both for weather and way'; the relief of arriving at an inn: 'having lifted our cramped legs off our horses, wee crawl'd upstairs to a fire, where in two houres time wee had so well dried ourselves without and liquor'd ourselves within, that wee began to bee so valiant as to thinke upon a second march'. There they met some 'Darbishire blades' and hoped for their guidance over the moor that lay ahead:

Wee...were desirous to ride in company with them so as wee might bee conducted in this strange mountainous, misty, moorish, rocky, wild, country; but they, having dranke freely of their ale, which inclined them something to their countrie's naturel rudeness, and the distaste they tooke at our swords and pistols with which wee rid, made them loth to bee troubled with our companies; till I, being more loth to loose this opportunity...went into the roome and perswaded them so well as they were willing, not onely to afford us their company, but staid for us till wee accoutred ourselves.[1]

Tom evidently had charm and had profited from his father's advice: 'be courteous and humble in yr Conversation, still shunning *Pudor Rusticus*, which undoes good natures' [Letter 11]. But the 'Darbishire blades' did not prove ideal travelling companions. The weather continued foul and the country was rugged; water came down the steep hills in floods. Tom writes of it all with gusto, enjoying, one feels, discomforts overcome almost as much as the beauty of the countryside when:

After four or five miles riding, wee came to have a prospect as delicious as almost England can afford....From this place wee could see the mountains in Wales, and have a fair view of most parts of the county Palatine of Chester, together with the southerne parts of Lancashire. Here the Valle Royall of England which seemed like paradise to us adorn'd with pleasant rivers, cristall springs, delighted [sic] buildings, high woods, which seem'd bending by sweet gales to becken us to come to them, afforded us so much delight as wee travailed without any discontentment over the back of these swelling mountains, till wee came to Maxfield where they end.[2]

Sir Thomas Browne noticed signs of promise in his younger son's style; in the following summer, when Edward and Thomas were both at Cambridge, he wrote: 'Honest Tom, be of good heart, and follow thy businesse. I doubt not butt thou wilt doe well. God hath given thee parts to enable thee. If you practise to write, you will have a good pen and style' [Letter 14]. Tom remained at Cambridge for one year only; in the autumn of 1664 he joined the navy. There is a letter sent to him in London by his father, 25 November 1664; it suggests that Tom was seeking the best way

[1] Wilkin, vol. I, p. 27.

[2] *Ibid.* p. 36.

into his chosen profession and that Sir Thomas was not sure how to advise him:

Do nothing rashly butt as you find just grounds for your advantage, wch will hardly bee at the best deservings without good and faythfull freinds; No sudden advantage for rawe though dangerous services. There is another & more safe way whereby Capt. Brookes & others come in credit, by going about 2 yeares before they were capable of places, where I am not well acquainted. God & our good freinds advise you [Letter 15].[1]

The letter is accompanied by a characteristic one from his Mother [Letter 15]:

Deare Tom,

I am glad to heare you will [judge] prudantly of things and if you dooe not find them according to expectation com home to us a gaine. I will send your weg by the choch and the Buf cotte if I can gett it. If you want more monyes then you thinke fit to take of my cossn Mr Scoltow will latt you have it, butt bee suer to spand as little as you can. Latt mee here from you: bee carfull and sivell to my cosens Mrs Cottrall and the Howalls and carry all our serves to them.

I besich god bles and dereckt you.

Your loving Mothar,

Dorothy Browne.

In fact Captain Brookes was able to help; three months later Tom made his first voyage under his command, in the *Foresight*. The next letters from both parents are sent to Tom at sea, 1 January 1665. Sir Thomas advises him about the care of his health and gives him a prescription against scurvy; he also regrets that the young man has not provided himself with enough books to read 'without which you cannot well spend time in those great shipps'. But he trusts that he will have Wagenar's *Speculum Nauticum*. He tells of his own recent observations of the stars and, as usual, urges his son to keep his eyes open and learn all he can. The brief enclosure from his mother expresses her anxiety for his health and

[1] Captain Brookes was 'Commander of the Foresight and brother of Sir Thomas Browne's friend Sir Robert Brookes, M.P. for Aldboro', Suffolk'.

also concerning expenses; she was clearly in her husband's confidence about money-matters and well aware that he was spending rather more than he could afford on his sons: 'Bee as god husband as you can posable, for you know what great charges wee ar now att.' Whitefoot tells us that Sir Thomas Browne's 'Indulgence and Liberality to his Children, especially in their Travels...spent him more than a little. He was liberal in his House Entertainments, and in his Charity; he left a comfortable, but no great Estate, both to his Lady and Children, gained by his own Industry, having spent the greatest Part of his Patrimony in his Travels.'[1]

Several of Dorothy Browne's letters indicate uneasiness about money and suggest that she was business-like and well aware of the outgoings. At this time the eldest son Edward, travelling on the continent after taking his B.A. at Cambridge, was still financially dependent on his father, as were Thomas and the five younger children at home.

By June 1665 Tom had joined the fleet under the command of Prince Rupert and the Earl of Sandwich; he took part as lieutenant in the naval battle against the Dutch on 3 June 1665, and in all the naval battles of 1666. There is a letter from him to his father dated 'From aboard the *Marie Rose*, at the Buoy of the Middle Grounds, July 16th, 1666'.[2] It reveals his enjoyment of his chosen profession: 'being now so neare the grand action, from which I would by no meanes bee absent; because it is generally thought it will bee the conclusion of the warre, and an utter confusion of one partie. I extremely long for that thundering day; wherein I hope you shall heare wee have behaved ourselves like men, and to the honour of our country.' But he is not merely the man of action; he still shares his father's intellectual energy: 'I receaved your last two letters, and give you many thanks for the discourse you sent me out of Vossius *De Motu Marium et Ventorum*. It seemed very hard to mee at first; butt I have now beaten it out, and wish I had the booke.'[3] In September of the same year he

[1] Wilkin, vol. I, p. xlvi. [2] *Ibid.* I, pp. 128–9. [3] *Ibid.* p. 130.

thanks his father for a violin and for a copy of Wagenar; this is the first reference to his musical talent, though there are several indications that he had a gift for drawing and painting. In this letter he expresses his grave concern about the long-standing failure to pay the wages of the seamen.

The discontent of the seamen, for want of pay, is no newes unto you. Yesterday divers of them, now bound outward, presented a petition to the Duke of York, for some of their pay, to provide for themselves and families, wch they are to leave at home. What the event will bee it is easie to judge, by what hath alreadie passed. Certaine it is that they are in a sad and pitifull condition; and no small trouble it is unto us, who are to command a company of mutinous unpayd men. For my part, while I have a penny, I cannot but relieve them, of whose fidelity and valour I can give so good testimonie; nor do I find them so untractible, who all this while, though the captaine were ashoare, have kept them aboard and unto their duties better then I might have feared I should have done. I cannot butt wonder at this unreasonable and unpolitick course, to disoblige the seamen, who have behaved themselves so stoutly, and discontent the whole land, who have so largely disbursed for their paye. The consequence must be bad, and at least no honourable peace.[1]

Tom is evidently confident of his father's sympathetic interest when he speaks of the seamen. He goes on to express his relief that he has at any rate obtained a life-pension for 'my boy Will Blanchot' who had his thigh broken 'by a splinter in the last fight butt one: it will be hard to meet with a boy so boald and useful in a fight, though I have another that doeth well....His father was chief gunner of our shipps at Bergen, where hee was slayne, and his sonne left to the wide world till I took him into my care.' Lastly he tells of a Moor who has leave to go to London, but whom he hopes to have with him on the next voyage since he is 'a right honest and stout man' and an accomplished linguist. Tom practises his French and Latin with him and hopes, with his help, to acquire Italian: 'Hee is much affected to my brother

[1] *Ibid.* p. 132.

Edward since he was with us at Southwould bay; whether if we come agayn I intend that he should wayt upon you at Norwich. I intend to draw his picture in little, as I have done the masters and some others.'[1]

There are no extant letters to Tom from his father in 1666. It may well have been difficult for Tom to preserve them. The correspondence begins again in February 1667; Tom writes from Plymouth Sound; he has been reading Lucan with immense admiration; he has been particularly struck by the speech of Vulteius, which he says is 'very remarkable, and handsomely expressed; and I was much affected with it. I believe the translation by May will come short of it...' and Tom goes on to recount the story:

Hee was one of Caesar's commanders, who, finding his shippe entangled by ropes layd purposely in the sea, and surrounded with a great body of Pompey's forces, fought it out an whole day with them; and seeing no way to avoid taking, rather than to bee slaves and prisoners, exhorted his souldiers in the shippe to kill one another, which was effected the next morning, himself being first slayne, and afterward all the rest.[2]

Sir Thomas answers at once; it is clear to him that Tom is not only, nor primarily, admiring Lucan's style; he is alarmed at the influence the Stoical Roman ideal may exert:

I receaved yours & would not deferre to send unto you before you sayled, wch I hope will come unto you; for in this wind, nether can Reare Admirall Kempthorne come to you, nor you beginne your voyage. I am glad you like Lucan so well; I wish more military men could read him. In this passage you mention there are noble straynes & such as may well affect generous minds. Butt I hope you are more taken with the verses then the subject, and rather embrace the expression then the example. And this I the rather hint unto you, because the like, though in another waye, is sometimes practised in the King's shipps; when in desperate cases they blowe up the same. For though I know you are sober & considerative, yet knowing you also to bee of great resolution; & having also heard from ocular testimonies with what

[1] Wilkin, vol. I, pp. 131–4. [2] *Ibid.* p. 143.

undaunted & persevering courage you have demeaned yourself in great difficulties, & knowing your Captaine to bee a stout and resolute man, & withall the cordiall freindshippe that is between you, I cannot omitt my earnest prayers unto god to deliver you from such a temptation. Hee that goes to warre, must patiently submitt unto the various accidents thereof. To bee made prisoner by an unequall and overruling power, after a due resistance, is no disparagement; butt upon a carelesse surprizall or faynt opposition. And you have so good a memorie that you cannot forgett many examples thereof, even of the worthiest commanders, in your beloved Plutark. God hath given you a stout, butt a generous and mercifull heart withall, & in all your life you could never behold any person in miserie butt with compassion & releif; wch hath been notable in you from a child. So have you layd up a good foundation for gods mercy, & if such disaster should happen hee will without doubt mercifully remember you. However let god that brought you in the world in his owne good time, lead you thorough it, & in his owne season bring you out of it, & without such wayes as are displeasing unto him [Letter 17].

It is a noble piece of pleading, eloquent in a way the letters rarely are. It is clear that Sir Thomas had been gravely disturbed by Tom's letter and, writing under the stress of that disturbance, his especial love for Tom is fully evident. If Tom was his favourite child, as I suspect, it is not hard to understand why. He had, as we can see from his success with the 'Darbishire blades' and with the seamen, the indefinable quality of personal charm. He had a keen intelligence, an inquiring mind, and, as this letter states and his feeling for his men confirms, he was sensitive to other people's pain. All these were qualities his father shared; and Tom's chosen career had put him to the proof and shown him to have, in addition, great courage and presence of mind in danger. Sir Thomas's letter is not, obviously, prompted merely by the fear of losing such a son; he is genuinely afraid lest the Christian teaching about suicide should be replaced in Tom's mind by the Stoical ideal.

The next extant letter from Tom is assigned by Wilkin to May 1667; it makes no reference to the question of self-destruction and there may have been intervening letters. A second letter assigned to the same month announces that he is 'newlie come into Portsmouth'.[1] This is Tom's last letter to his father. Sir Thomas Browne's last letter to him was sent to Portsmouth in May or June 1667; he writes:

Dear Sonne,

I am very glad that you are returned from the strayghts mouth once more in health and safetie. God continue his mercifull providence over you. I hope you maintaine a thankfull heart and daylie blesse him for your great deliverances in so many fights, and dangers of the sea, whereto you have been exposed upon severall seas and in all seasons of the yeare [Letter 18].

Sir Thomas reminds him how, before he entered the service, he had given him Plutarch's *Lives* to read and had given him Aristotle's description of fortitude:

That which I then proposed for your example, I now send you for your commendation. For to give you your due, in the whole cours of this warre, both in fights and other sea affayres, hazards and perills, you have very well fulfilled this character in yourself. And allthough you bee not forward in commending yourself, yett others have not been backward to do it for you, and have so earnestly expressed your courage, valour, and resolution; your sober and studious and observing cours of life; your generous and obliging disposition, and the notable knowledge you have obtayned in military and all kind of sea affayres, that it affoordeth no small comfort unto mee. And I would by no meanes omitt to declare the same unto yourself, that you may not want that encouragement which you so well deserve.

And then he tells him specifically what has been said about him:

Mr Scudamore, your sober and learned chaplaine, in your voyage with Sir Jeremie Smith, gives you no small commendations for a sober, studious, courageous, and diligent person; that hee had not met with any of the fleet like you, so civill, observing, and diligent to your charge, with the reputation and love of all the shippe....Captain Fenne, a meere rough seaman, sayd, that if hee were to choose, hee would have your company before any hee knewe....

[1] Wilkin, vol. I, p. 147.

Three more, Mr W. B. of Lynn, 'another who was with you at Schellinck' and Sir Thomas Allen, are quoted as praising Tom in similar terms. Sir Thomas Allen is anxious to encourage him by the hope of preferment, in case he should leave the sea, 'which otherwise probably he might do, having parts to make himself considerable by divers other wayes'. A 'Mr I' told Sir Thomas that his son was 'compleately constituted to do your country service, honour, and reputation, as being exceeding faythfull, valiant, diligent, generous, vigilant, observing, very knowing, and a scollar'. After his service on the *Foresight*, in 1665, someone reported to Sir Thomas that the Earl of Sandwich was heard saying to young Thomas Browne:

Sir, you are a person whom I am glad to see, and must bee better acquainted with you, upon the account which Captain Brooke gave mee of you. I must encourage such persons and give them their due, which will stand so firmely and courageously unto it upon extremities, wherein true valour is best discovered.

Sir Thomas says that he himself is even more delighted that Tom has kept up his scholarship than that he is such a brave naval officer:

You are like to prove not only a noble navigator butt a great schollar, which will bee much more to your honour and my satisfaction and content. I am much pleased to find that you take the draughts of remarkable things were ere you goe; for that may bee very usefull, and will fasten themselves the better in your memorie. You are mightily improved in your violin, butt I would by no means have you practise upon the trumpet for many reasons. Your fencing in the shippe may bee good against scurvie, butt that knowledge is of little advantage in actions of the sea.

Without knowing it, Sir Thomas was writing the obituary of this admirable and delightful son. The fatherly pride and the accumulated praises from others are all the more moving and convincing because Sir Thomas did not know the end had come. Young Thomas Browne died, aged twenty-one, early in 1667; neither the cause of death nor the exact date is known.

By far the largest number of Sir Thomas Browne's extant letters are those to his first-born child, his eldest son, Edward. The first of these was written in 1665, when Edward was twenty-one, the last in the year of Sir Thomas Browne's death, 1682. Edward followed with distinction his father's profession, shared his father's taste for the accumulation of knowledge and his father's reputation for accurate reporting of what he saw. He was educated at Norwich Grammar School and Trinity College, Cambridge, where he took his B.A. in 1661 (his mother wrote the news to Tom, then travelling in France), and his M.B. in 1663. In that year Tom was with him at Trinity for a short while; perhaps Sir Thomas sent the boys to Cambridge at this time, rather than to his own University, because it was nearer to Norwich. After graduating M.B. Edward went home and worked at his profession under his father's direction; he was in Norwich from 1 January to 22 February 1664 and then in London for a few weeks, attending the lectures of Dr Terne, physician at St Bartholomew's Hospital, whose daughter he later married. He returned to Norwich in March but only for three weeks. By the beginning of April he was on his way to France. A diary Edward kept during these months at home with his father throws enough indirect light on Sir Thomas to be worth quoting from. Eighteen years after the first edition of *Pseudodoxia* we find the son both as ready to believe and as ready to put a belief to the test as was his father. Edward records his dissection of a hare, a pike, a monkey, a dog, a calf, a badger.[1] He also records:

Feb. 5 I went to see a serpente that a woman living in St Gregories church yard in Norwich vomited up, but she had burnt it before I came.

He evinces no more doubt whether it was a serpent than whether jaundice can be cured by magic:

Jan 30th. A magical cure for the jaundise; Burne wood under a leaden vessel fill'd with water, take the ashes of that wood, and boyle it with

[1] Wilkin, vol. I, pp. 46, 47, 48.

the patient's urine, then lay nine long heaps of the boyld ashes upon a board in a ranke, and upon every heap lay nine spears of crocus, it hath greater effects then is credible to any one that shall barely read this receipt without experiencing.

Edward was a serious and up-to-date student of medicine; but the date was 1664. In his father's *Miscellaneous Writings* we find a similar readiness to give fair trial to strange remedies, at any rate when all the orthodox ones have been tried in vain; an extract from a letter reads: 'Since you are so much unsatisfied with the many rationall medicines which you say you have for the gout, when you have leisure enough consider or make triall of some empiricall or odde medecines',[1] and he gives a number of examples, such as 'To weare shoes of leather made of lyon's skinne;...Use the decoction of a fox for a fomentation & swallow's blood to appease the payne, commended by Trallianus'. More likely to be effectual is the advice: 'To begett an abstemiousnesse from wine which promotes the gout, suffocate an eele and a frogge in wine and drinck it.'[2] These cures, since they require to be administered to the patient, externally or internally, are 'odd' but not magical. But at least one magical cure is set down in Sir Thomas Browne's *Commonplace Books*: 'Trie the magnified amulet of Muffetus of spiders leggs worn in a deers skinne or Tortoyses leggs cutt off from the living Tortoys & wrapped up in the skinne of a kid.'[3] It was not a squeamish age and it was still, despite the rapid advances being made, from our point of view, a credulous one. But Edward was, like his father, observant and inquiring; his diary records what he sees in the way of plants, shells or the fungus growing in a damp cellar. It also registers his gaieties: 'I was at Mr Howard's brother to the Duke of Norfolk, who kept his Christmas this year at the duke's palace in Norwich, so magnificently as the like hath scarce been seen.' He gives a detailed account, but rather dryly. Edward did not share his brother Tom's gift for lively writing; he is satisfied with

[1] Keynes, vol. v, p. 226. [2] *Ibid.* [3] *Op. cit.* p. 261.

mere statements such as: 'I went to Mr Howard's dancing at night; our greatest beautys were Mdm Elizabeth Cradock, Eliz. Houghton, Ms Philpot, Ms Yallop; afterwards to the banquet and so home.—*sic transit gloria mundi*!'[1]

But, though Edward was not made eloquent by the beauty of women, he could be by their ugliness. In this diary the only entry in which his fact-recording style becomes lively is when he describes the horror with which he first viewed the women of France:

> April 6....I was not sick at all in coming over from Dover to Calais, upon the sea, but yet could hardly forbear spuing at the first sight of the French women: they are most of them of such a tawny, sapy, base complection and have such ugly faces, which they here set out with a dresse would fright the divel.[2]

This apparent insularity is very unlike Sir Thomas, and perhaps Edward overcame it during his travels; however that may be, no such animadversions on foreigners occur in his letters to his father. While in Norwich he had seen his first patient and collected his first fee, which was 10*s*. He was not in any doubt about his profession when he went abroad; he travelled, as his father had done before him, to improve his mind and further his education. On his first journey he went from Paris to Italy, where he was at Rome, Naples, Bologna, Venice and Padua. He returned in 1666 and entered Merton College, Oxford, where he took his doctor's degree in 1667. In the same year he was made a Fellow of the Royal Society. He renewed his travels, with instructions from the Society to send to them any interesting information. This journey took him to Holland, Belgium, Poland, Austria, Hungary and finally, despite his father's strong dissuasions, to Turkey. He was home again in December 1669. In 1672 he married Henrietta Susan Terne, daughter of the physician under whom he had studied in London. From this time, except for one short spell abroad, Edward was settled in London. In 1675 he

[1] Wilkin, vol. 1, p. 45.

[2] *Ibid.* p. 58.

became a Fellow of the Royal Society of Physicians. It was a distinguished career and one in which he was helped by his father's prestige, his father's generous prolongation of his education, and his father's advice and co-operation while he lived in whatever work the son undertook.

The letters exchanged between Sir Thomas and Edward when the son was on his travels between 1667 and 1669 reveal the strong mutual tie of affection and also the surprising degree in which the son (now Doctor of Medicine and Fellow of the Royal Society, twenty-three years old) was dependent on the father. He was dependent financially; but he was also directed by his father intellectually and morally. He received constant advice about what he should study, what he should observe, what countries were worth visiting and how he should take care of his health. The father's control was not, however, tyrannous and when Edward ultimately went to Turkey in defiance of his father's wishes the bond of love between them took the strain. We first hear of Edward's strong desire to extend his travels, 29 November 1668: 'butt I have trespassed too farre alreadie upon your goodnesse, and intend to look no farther'.[1] Before receiving this, Sir Thomas had written on 2 December that he had made money available for his son 'Whereof I hope you will make use butt upon good occasion and moderately'. He was anxious for Edward's return home: 'Consider how neerely it concerneth you to bee in your country, improving your time to what you intend, and what most concerneth you' [Letter 23]. A fortnight later he is particularly insistent that Edward should not go further east:

> I should bee glad if you could escape a journey to Venice, butt rather thither then any farther eastward, ether to Poland, Hungarie or Turkie, which both myself and all your freinds do heartily wish you would not so much as thinck of....From Constantinople or Turkey I am most averse for many reasons. Wee all wish you in England or neerer it [Letter 24].

[1] Wilkin, vol. I, p. 159.

This letter was sent to Vienna and accompanied by a brief note from his sister Elizabeth, wishing he were at home and sending messages from the two younger sisters 'Molls and Frank' (Mary and Frances). By 23 December Sir Thomas had received Edward's letter of 29 November with its strong note of *wanderlust*; he was fully sympathetic with regard to further travel in Germany and gave detailed advice about the itinerary and what to observe, with the usual caution about caring for his health and not doing too much. On 28 April 1669 Edward reports that he has 'taken up three hundred florins in preparation to goe into Turkey this next weeke'.[1] He did not, however, go there and his father expresses relief in a letter of 25 June. However, by 25 August the temptation had proved too strong; Edward writes from Vienna and does not specifically mention Turkey, but the next letter shows that that is where he was bound for; all he says on 25 August 1669 is: 'If I go somewhat out of my way, I hope, sir, you will pardon it, and continue your goodnesse and blessing to me, which maketh me happy, and able to go through many difficulties.'[2] He left Vienna for nearly three months and wrote to his father after his return there:

Vienna. Oct 17, 1669

Most Honoured Father.

I am just now arrived again at Vienna after a hard journey. God's holy name be praised for ever! His mercy hath been infinite to me, in preserving me; and I hope, sir, that you will forgive this excursion. I will make haste homeward, soe that I beg of you to write to me into Hollande soone after the receipt of this.[3]

There is no extant letter from Sir Thomas about this escapade. Edward continued to feel uneasy about it. In the next letter from Vienna, written only a week later, he again drew attention to the way God had protected him:

I would willingly set downe something more of my Turkish journey; but the consideration of my rashnesse and obstinate folly in under-

[1] Wilkin, vol. I, p. 180. [2] *Ibid.* p. 192. [3] *Ibid.* p. 193.

taking it, renders my thoughts of it unpleasing. Howsoever, God's infinite goodnesse and mercy protecting me and preserving me, etc.[1]

Edward was making good use, perhaps unfair use, of his knowledge of his father in order to win his forgiveness. He played both upon his curiosity and upon his faith. Sir Thomas will want to know all there is to be known about Turkey and he will perhaps feel that God's protection of his son implies approval, or at any rate that an earthly father should not be sterner than a heavenly. There are several more letters from Edward between the end of October and mid-December. He was travelling towards home and perhaps no reply from his father caught up with him. By 15 December he was at 'Relzbütell or Cookes-haven' waiting for a favourable wind. He was not, one feels, when he reached Norwich in any doubt of the welcome he would receive. His well-justified confidence is expressed in his last letter to his mother, November 1669.

I have not done, I think, advisedly to stay so long from my most dear parents; but I hope you will forgive it, and that your goodness will meet your prodigal son now that he returneth. I should be sorry to have travelled beyond your goodness. If it be so, I should be much out of my way. I hope the best; having had all my life-time experience of your goodness.[2]

The bond between father and son was strengthened by the many interests they had in common. They shared an avid curiosity about everything that is to be seen and known in the world. Edward was less imaginative and less speculative than his father, but he had the same impulse to notice and record the facts, and the same excitement, shared with many men of the time, about the gradual accumulation of curious information. Sir Thomas is proud of his son's membership of the Royal Society and eager that he should prove himself worthy by sending information; but his ambition for his son is tempered by the fear that he may overstrain himself, or that omnivorous curiosity may distract

[1] Wilkin, vol. I, p. 194. [2] *Ibid.* p. 198.

him from the study of medicine. 'For satisfaction of the queries of the R.S. putt yourself to no hazard or adventure, butt learne and make the best enquiries you can of things in Hungarie and at distance by others, and what is neere Vienna or in it, you may observe yourself' [Letter 27]. Or again:

Bee never without some institution or the like of physick where, you may daylie or often read, and so continue in mind the method and doctrine of physick, wch intention upon varietie of objects or other subjects may make you forget: wearie not nor wast your spirits to much in pursuing after varietie of objects, which I knowe you cannot butt do with earnestnesse, for thereby you shall by Gods blessing conserve your health; whereof I am very sollicitous [Letter 23].

He knows Edward cannot do otherwise than earnestly pursue every kind of inquiry because his own curiosity is similarly omnivorous. Yet, in spite of anxiety for his health and for his professional studies, he cannot resist urging him on. 'Enquire also after the polycie and government of places.'

Take notice of the various Animals, of places, beasts, fowles, & fishes; what the Danow affordeth, what depth, if conveniency offers, of mines, minerall workes etc.... You are to be commended for observing so well alreadie. I wish you could take notice of something for the information of the Soc. Reg. to learne speciall medecines & preparations, butt, as I still say, trye not thy spirits too farre, butt give due rest unto them [Letter 25].

For both father and son many things are credible which no longer seem so to us; Edward writes on 14 February 1669, 'I have herin enclosed the figure of a magicall glasse, whereby the Emperor Rudolphus saw many strange sights, and the manner of conversing with spirits; perhaps the same or like that of Dee and Kelly'.[1] His father asks, on 1 March, with only a hint of scepticism, 'How came you to see Rudolphus his glasse & what credit doth it beare?' Transmutation of metals seems probable to both father and son; Sir Thomas writes to Edward in Vienna: 'I have

[1] Wilkin, vol. 1, p. 175.

heard that among the emperours Rarities, several conversions there are of basser metall into gold' [Letter 26]. But in the same letter he tells Edward of Boyle's recent experiments 'concerning the spring and weight of the Ayre', and adds that he is keeping the monthly sheets of the transactions of the Royal Society. It seems the very moment of transition between alchemical belief and experimental chemistry and there is no gap between father and son; they speak the same language, and each is equally likely to accept or doubt the marvellous. Sir Thomas inquires of his son: 'What kind of stone is that wch stoned St Stephen, pebble, flint or freestone?' [Letter 27], and is answered by Edward with the same quiet certainty with which he described, in the previous sentence, the wood used in Salzburg to make violins: 'The stone with which St Stephen was stoned is a kinde of pebble. I will send you, sir, a piece just like it; but it looketh like marble, and is polished and worne a little hollow in the middle by the continual touching of it by everyone that goeth in or out of that door of the church wherein it is fixed.'[1] Yet, although alchemy, crystal gazing and the validity of the relic go unquestioned, the credulity of the son is no more unbounded than that of the father. Edward writes from Prague, 9 November 1669:

In the mines at Brunswick is reported to be a spirit; and another at the tin mines at Slackenwald, in this Kingdome, in the shape of a monke, which strikes the miners, singeth, playeth on the bagpipes, and many such tricks. But I doubt, if I should go thither, I should find them as vain as Montparion's [sic] drumme; but the winter, and my great desire to return home speedily, will not permit me to goe so far out of the way.[2]

Although Sir Thomas was 64 and Edward only 25 when this part of their correspondence was written, there seems to be no difference in outlook or in basic assumptions, and this is a little

[1] Wilkin, vol. I, p. 185.

[2] *Ibid.* p. 196. This drummer, and his alleged haunting of Mr Mompesson's house, were investigated by Joseph Glanvill, who gives an account of his experience in Part II of *Sadducismus Triumphatus*. (Fourth edition 1668.) The drummer was acquitted by the Petty Jury after having first been found guilty of Black Magic by the Grand Jury.

surprising at a time when knowledge was advancing so rapidly. It is an additional evidence that Sir Thomas kept himself abreast with the advancement of learning.

During the years when Edward lived in London and practised his profession there was constant co-operation between him and his father. Sir Thomas sometimes sent patients to consult his son; when he did so he introduced them with a letter giving an account not only of their medical history but of their personal characteristics and behaviour. Whatever modern medical science may think of the prescriptions that he sometimes includes in these letters, he was clearly an adept in those human relationships which must always be an important part of the physician's art. He writes to Edward in 1682 'purposely on behalf' of the hypochondriacal Mr Payne:

I pray have the best care you can of him; hee is not acquainted with physitians in London, butt is willing to bee directed by my good freind Dr Witherley and yourself....You must have good patience, for he abounds in questions & doubts, & is soone discouraged and apt to laye hold of any words & to argue agaynst himself or any remedies....A great part of the last winter it was playnly observed that hee became melancholicall, full of perverted imaginations attended with feare of everything which concerned himself or hee could apply unto it, & to have butt litle & temporary satisfaction from anything that could bee done or sayd toward his comfort, & so grew sollicitous & querimonious and wearying of all his freinds. I prescribed divers medecins & constant drincks & he made use of every thing hee could heare of or was commended by any one. Butt so it was that hee eat & dranck & slept indifferently, butt of late runne much about complayning & his thoughts busied perpetually & solely of himself, feareing that hee should never recover or bee the same man hee had been; though he bled not much, yet hee had disquieting thoughts after it. All his freinds & many who had been under the like symptomes recommended Tunbridge waters & the waters about London, wch have runne much in his mind, And I promised to write a letter unto you concerning him. Hee is in his temper an active, stirring man & full of words, & now I think weakens himself by to much speaking ever of things wch are not comfortable unto him. You may conferre with him & go with him to

Dr Witherley & to consider & determine some way for him, both concerning waters and otherwise, if hee will admitt thereof, as I hope hee will. Hee will be unsatisfied if hee make not some triall of the waters; hee liketh whay & soft drincks. Hee must bee often visited, & if hee drincketh Tunbridge waters you must take some care to have him directed by some physitian on the place. In this condition hee may be apt to bee cheated by empericks, & give him good words & what satisfaction you can [Letter 160].

The last letter to Edward also concerns a hypochondriacal patient, 'my loving freind and long acquaintance', Mr John Repps, who has been 'since I knew him subject to hypochond' [Letter 166]. But with other patients too, in whom he recognizes the physical symptoms and is able to prescribe hopeful remedies, he takes account of character and describes to his son not only a patient but a person; for instance, Mrs Suckling whose symptoms are such that special tact is necessary: 'Pray have speciall care of her for she is a very good person', he tells Edward, after a full account of her symptoms and situation [Letter 159]. In Edward's last letter to his father, written two months before Sir Thomas' death, he is asking him to prescribe inexpensive medicines for St Bartholomew's Hospital, to which he had been elected physician a month previously: 'Pray, sir, thinke of some good effectual cheape medecines for the hospitall, it will be a piece of charity, which will be beneficiall to the poore, hundreds of years after we are all dead and gone.'[1]

It was not only in his profession that Edward enjoyed his father's co-operation. If he prepared a lecture his father advised him how to revise it, to see that all is 'cleare and full enough expressed' [Letter 40]. If Sir Thomas dissects a carp he sends a dried specimen of its bladder to Edward (the carp was dressed for the table by Mrs Browne), or Sir Thomas sends him very detailed notes for a lecture he is to give on skin [Letter 46]. There is continuous interchange of information about natural history. In

[1] Wilkin, vol. I, p. 349.

the spring of 1682 Edward is keeping a live ostrich, preparatory to giving a lecture on the bird's behaviour and anatomy. Sir Thomas writes: 'I believe you must bee carefull of your Ostridge this return of cold wether, least it perish by it being bredd in so hot a country...' [Letter 148], and he advises how it is to be protected and also what Edward is to observe. Is it watchful and quick of hearing like a goose, 'for it seems to bee like a goose in many circumstances.' He tells him what food to give and how to find it and prepare it; advising cabbages, bran, and grain of any kind, mixed with water: 'To geese they give oates etc., moystnd with beere, butt sometimes they are inebriated with it'. The ostrich, however, is threatened with sterner diet so that the old question about its digestive powers may be resolved. 'If you give any Iron, it may be wrapped up in dowe or past: perhaps it will not take it up alone.' And the letter closes with a shrewd point about what will and will not interest the king and the gentlemen for whose entertainment the ostrich is being investigated. 'The king or gentlemen will bee litle taken with the Anatomie of it, though that must also bee, butt are like to take more notice of some other things wch may bee sayd upon the animal and which they understand.' Edward reports a week later that he has given the ostrich a piece of iron weighing two and a half ounces 'which we found in the first stomack again not at all altered'. This is very much what Sir Thomas had expected might happen when he wrote of the ostrich in *Pseudodoxia* in 1646.[1]

When Dr Edward Browne becomes interested and personally involved in a new translation of Plutarch's *Lives* his father is just as ready with help and advice as he is in medical matters or nature study. On 9 February 1681 Edward writes to his father, now seventy years old, in the same letter in which he tells of giving iron to the ostrich:

> There is a designe of translating Plutarch's lives into English again, the English of the former being not so pure as what is now spoken;

[1] Keynes, vol. II, Bk III, c. xxii.

divers are to be employed in it, and I am desired to translate the life of Themistocles for my share. I shall have the Greeke and the French sent me; if I doe it, it must be in the evenings, and I may take my owne time.[1]

Sir Thomas takes the keenest interest in the project. He reminds his son of former translations in French and in English. It was North's translation 'that you and your brother Thomas used to read at my house'. He advises him: 'If you have the Greek Plutarke, have also the Latin adjoyned unto it, so you may consult ether upon occasion, though you apply yourself to translate out of French, & the English translation may bee sometimes helpfull' [Letter 151]. In May of the following year, Edward is sending sheets for his father's perusal and correction. Sir Thomas makes detailed suggestions about the precise meaning of the Greek [Letter 161]. In June of the same year, he has read over four sheets and inquires whether Edward intends to put marginal notes 'wch denotes some particulars how the storie proceeds in the subject thereof according as it is in our English translation, wch is somewhat more gratefull to the Reader then a bare margin, and affords some direction when a man would find out any particular' [Letter 163]. On 16 June he writes that he is returning another four sheets and 'I am glad you have putt an end to that labour, though I am not sorry you undertooke it' [Letter 165].[2]

As well as adding to our knowledge of Sir Thomas Browne as doctor and virtuoso, the correspondence with Edward gives many insights into the domestic life of the Brownes. Family affection was strong and relations close. Whether on his travels or settled in London, Edward is always kept in touch with his mother and sisters. He writes letters from abroad to his sister Elizabeth at home, and to his two younger sisters Mary, known as Moll, aged eleven, and Frances, known as Frank, aged six,

[1] Wilkin, vol. I, p. 329.

[2] '*Plutarch's Lives, Translated from the Greek by Several Hands,* London 1685, 5 vols 8°, contains two lives translated by E. B., Themistocles and Quintus Sertorius.' [Keynes, footnote to Letter 151.]

adapting his style to their respective ages.[1] In December 1665 Frances is sickly. Sir Thomas writes to Edward:

Your mother prayes for you and sends her blessing, and would bee happy to see you. Shee is in health, as your sister B. and Moll. Franc lively and cheerily, butt leane, and another sharp fever might soon take her away. Beside limning, Bet. practiseth washing in black and colours and doth very well [Letter 23].

To modern ears the reference to Frances' possible death sounds casual; early death from natural causes was more probable and more expected than it is today, nor had Sir Thomas any doubt of the soul's survival. As a matter of fact, Frances survived her father. Three of Browne's children died in infancy in the 1650's and in the same decade he lost one boy at the age of twelve. Mary was to die, aged twenty-four, in 1676. Save for these, and Tom's tragic death in 1667, the children survived their father. The messages to Edward on his travels are all cheerful, affectionate and expressive of a strong wish for his speedy return.

It is chiefly from these letters to and from Edward that we can form a picture of the life and character of Dorothy Browne. We know, for instance, that she did her own cooking although she was not without servants (for they all sent their love to young Thomas when he was a boy of fourteen, travelling in France) [Letter 4]. Sir Thomas mentions the good dish she made out of the dolphin whose anatomy he describes to Edward on 14 June 1676. 'Your mother hath an art to dresse & cooke the flesh so as to make an excellent savory dish of it' [Letter 40]; and Dorothy herself writes to her son on 29 August 1678 about preparing some venison for him. His wife was at this time expecting a baby.

Dear Sonne,

I had this last weeke som venoson, and I putt a platt in to a pott for you, for fare I should not gett any more; but if I had thought of my Daughters time I would have seasoned it more. I intend to send it the next Friday in a baskett direc seled to you. I pray latt mee know as nere

[1] Wilkin, vol. 1, pp. 180 and 190.

as you can for your Cacke [cake?], and if I have any more venoson I will make you another pott. I bless god your Tomey is very well: goos to scolle and is a very good Boy and delights his grandfather when hee coms home [Letter 56].

'Tomey' is Edward's eldest child. The first mention of him in the letters is 13 June 1678 when Tommy was five years old. His grandmother writes that his cough is better. It may have been on account of the cough that he first came to Norwich, or on account of the coming baby; but, whatever caused him to be sent to his grandparents, he stayed with them for at least four years. The last mention of him is in a letter from Dorothy to her daughter-in-law, 29 May 1682; a visit from his mother with his little sister 'prity Sucky' is expected [Letter 162]. Perhaps after that visit he went home with his mother and baby sister. In the four years intervening, Dorothy never writes to Edward without mentioning Tommy, and he figures at least once in his grandfather's letters. Sir Thomas, writing to Edward three weeks after his grandson's arrival, says: 'Tom holds well, though he toyles and moyles at all sorts of play and after schoole. We take all care we can to make him sitt still and spare himself and to bee a little more composed and attentive to instructions and learne, and do all wee can to have sober stayd litle girles for his playfellowes that he maie imitate them' [Letter 55].

Many of Tommy's needs have to be supplied from London; for instance, his grandmother writes the following 9 June 1679: 'I hope you thinke of Tomey[s] Briches against the Asesise, for wee shall be out of all manar of lyning by that time, that is to be worne with cotts [coats]. He growes a brave tall boy and will be much a Man if wee have but Briches' [Letter 77]. Tommy is six and a half; but the breeches do not come at once. Three weeks later 'Wee dayly wish for the new cloths all our linen being worne out but shefts and Tomey would give all his stock to see his Briches' [Letter 80]. A week later he is still 'much longing' for them, but the very next day they arrive: 'Tomey have received his Cloues and is much delighted and sends you [Edward] and his Mo. and Grandmother dutty and thanks and promis to war them carfully' [Letter 82]. In November 1679 Tommy seems to have paid a visit to his parents and his other grandmother in London. Dorothy Browne is eagerly expecting him back.

Deare Daughter,

I thanke God for your letter and shall be so joyd to see my Tomey returne in helth; though ever so durty, hee knows fullars earth will cleane all [Letter 93].

It seems that Tommy did not behave well on this visit to London; Dorothy writes to Edward three weeks after his return thanking him for some service rendered to his sisters and adds a line about Tommy's penitence and how good he is now:

I give you and my good Daughter [Tommy's mother] many thankes for your great kindnes to your sisters. Thay are very sensable of it, and Tomey very much ashamed that hee behaved himselfe no better, but hops hee shall the next time. Hee is now as sivell as I can wish him, and spends much of his time with his grandfather [Letter 95].

By September 1680, aged seven and three-quarters, Tommy is reported to be reading to his grandfather and in the following February 'is beging books and reading of them' [Letter 130]. The next spring, 13 February 1682, when Sir Thomas is writing concerning the ostrich, Dame Dorothy encloses a letter to her daughter-in-law asking for playthings for Tommy. She is also much concerned about her daughter Anne, married to Henry Fairfax. Anne is expecting a baby and is in great distress because her little daughter is suffering from fits; it seems that Edward has been giving medical advice.

Deare Daughter,

I am glad to heare you ar all well. I bless god wee are so att present, and I hope your sister Fairfax little on [one] may have no more fitts; she is very thankfull to my sonne for his care of her and wee hope all so thanke him. I find by her writing she is so much consarned as I feere [fear] it may doe that which she is with all much hurt. I have writ to her what I can to perswad her to patiance; your Tomy grows a stout fellow. I hope you will com and see him this summer; hee is in great expechtion of a Tumbler you must send him for his popet show, a punch hee has and his wife and a straw King and Quen, and ladis of Honor, and all things but a Tumbler which this Town cannot aford, it is a woodin fellow that turns his heles over his head.

Your sister Frank presents her serves to my Daughter and begs that she would send sombody to Mr Browns att the Blew belkcaney [Bell and Key] in Little Queens Street and by her a set of croians [crayons] which will cost a crown she is told; perhaps cheaper [Letter 151].

Tommy grew up to be a Doctor of Medicine and a Fellow of the Royal Society like his father. He died in 1710 as a result of a fall from his horse.

Dorothy Browne's activities, her cooking and preserving, her care of expenditure, her requests for purchases in London (sometimes for neighbours and friends as well as for the family) may remind us of the housewife's cares in the *Paston Letters*. But family relations are singularly different. Sir Thomas and Dame Dorothy are the centre of a family, close-knit by ties of affection. Their considerate care for their children continues into adult life, and when a daughter marries, Dame Dorothy Browne, unlike Margaret Paston, attaches more importance to her husband's character than to his means. On the eve of Elizabeth's wedding, she writes to Edward concerning the bridegroom, George Lyttleton: 'Hee is of a very good Humor and Temprat as can be and sartainly as a greable as ever cuple war' [Letter 123].

To this much-loved daughter Sir Thomas Browne wrote one of the very few letters in which, at least for one long paragraph, the style resembles that of his published prose. The subject is death and it can fitly close these extracts from his domestic correspondence. The letter itself makes clear the circumstances that called it forth.

Sir Thomas Browne to his daughter
Mrs Lyttleton in Guernsey.

Dear Betty,

Tho it were noe wonder this very Tempestious and stormy winter, yet I am sorry you had such an uncomfortable sight, as to behold a ship cast away, so neer you; this is noe strang [strange] tho unwelcom sight at Yarmouth, Cromer, Winterton and sea Towns; tho you Could not save them I hope they were the better for yr Prayers, both those that Perishd and those that scapd. Some wear away in Calmes, some are Caried away in storms: wee Come into the World one way, there are many gates to goe out of it. God give us grace to fit and prepare our selves for that Necessity, and to be ready to leave all when and how so ever he shall call; the Prayers of health are most like to be acceptable; sickness may Choak our devotions, and we are accepted rather by our life then our death; we have a rule how to lead the one, the other is uncertain and may Come in a Moment. God I hope will spare you to serve him long, who didst begin early to serve him.

In the closing sentences of this paragraph Sir Thomas tells of the many recent deaths from smallpox in Norwich, and in the next he speaks of his sailor son Thomas; the letter closes with a definition of melancholy and counsel to avoid it [Letter 143]:

Yr Brother Thomas went once from Yarmouth in the evening and arrived at the Isle of White the next day at one a Clock in the afternoon, but it was with such a wind, that he was never so sick at sea as at that time. I came once from Dublin to Chester at Michaelmas and was so tossed, that nothing but milk and Possets would goe down with me 2 or 3 days after; yr self is not impatient, you will have noe Cause to be sad, give noe way unto Malencholy, wch is purely sadness without a reasonable cause. You shall never want our dayly Prayers and also our frequent Letters. God Bless you both. I rest,

Yr Loving father,
Tho. Browne

CHAPTER III

'RELIGIO MEDICI' (PART I)[1]

'THE Iniquity of Oblivion blindly scattereth her poppy', and the distinction of mind and charm of character revealed in Sir Thomas Browne's life and correspondence would not have caused him to be remembered for nearly three hundred years. Many are totally forgotten, others are remembered only in the history of science, who shared Sir Thomas Browne's patience in collecting facts and his wide-ranging curiosity. His memory is green because he was a master of English prose. He enjoyed the art of writing; we perceive this when we notice the contrast between the merely workmanlike or useful style of the letters and the subtle and elaborate use of language in the published works. He enjoyed discovering and expressing precisely what he thought and felt. He always chose subjects which allowed him to explore his own mind, not confining him too closely to particular facts, nor requiring him to keep within too narrow a framework. As he says in the Epistle Dedicatory to the *Garden of Cyrus*, he liked subjects which 'allow excursions and venially admit of collateral truths, though at some distance from their principals'. In his first published work, *Religio Medici*, the subject is his own religious faith and its relation to his profession. This allows him scope to glance at some odd varieties of human temperament and belief as well as at his own doubts and vagaries of thought, which are restrained by his serenely confident acceptance of basic Christian doctrine and his willing submission to Anglican orthodoxy. In the preface to the authorized edition in 1643 he writes:

This I confesse about seven yeares past, with some others of affinitie thereto, for my private exercise and satisfaction, I had at leisurable

[1] The numbers after the quotations indicate the Part and Section of *Religio Medici*. The text is that of Denonain (1953).

houres composed; which being communicated unto one, it became common unto many, and was by transcription successively corrupted untill it arrived in a most depraved copy at the presse.

Yet one can hardly doubt that Browne hoped to commune not only with himself but with others. The *Religio Medici* is beautifully composed and expressed; it is a work of art. He prepared manuscripts for private circulation, eight copies of which still survive. But to publish any work about religion in the seventeenth century was to invite controversy and this he certainly wished to avoid. He knew that 'a man may be in as just possession of Truth as of a City, and yet bee forced to surrender; 'tis therefore farre better to enjoy her with peace, then to hazzard her on a battel' [I, 6]. Browne was the reverse of pugnacious and this may well be why, for seven years, he refrained from publishing; as soon as the pirated edition appeared in 1642 the heresy hunt began. Sir Kenelm Digby wrote his *Observations upon Religio Medici* between 19 December, when he received a copy sent to him by the Earl of Dorset, and 23 December, when he returned the copy with his commentary. Alexander Ross printed his attack on the authorized edition in 1645; it was entitled: *Medicus Medicatus: or the Physician cured by a Lenitive or Gentle Potion: with some Animadversions upon Sir Kenelm Digbie's Observations on Religio Medici.* But when we read the *Religio* we know that the hunters were on a false trail. It is not a work of controversy; the heresies Browne describes are recorded as part of his endeavour to explore the relations between his faith, his temperament and his profession.

Browne begins by defining his own position; he declares that he is a Christian, not merely by the accident of his birthplace or of his education: 'But that having, in my riper yeares, and confirmed judgement, seene and examined all, I finde my selfe obliged by the principles of Grace, and the law of mine owne reason, to embrace no other name but this.' This sentence is characteristically followed by an expression of charitable feelings towards those outside that heterogeneous community: he does not hate but 'pity Turkes,

Infidels, and (what is worse) the Jewes, rather contenting my selfe to enjoy that happy stile, then maligning those who refuse so glorious a title' [I, I]. If any modern readers mistake Sir Thomas Browne's frequent harping on his own tolerant sympathies for mere self-praise they should read Alexander Ross and other religious controversialists of those times. It was by no means assumed in the seventeenth century that religious tolerance and wide sympathies were virtues. Gradually, Browne confines himself within a narrower circle; he is not only a Christian but, 'I am of that reformed new-cast Religion, wherein I dislike nothing but the name'. The name, he means, of Protestant; it is not his habit to protest against those who differ from him. As to the Roman Catholics

> we have reformed from them, not against them; for omitting those improperations and termes of scurrility betwixt us, which onely difference our affections, and not our cause, there is between us one common name and appellation, one faith, and necessary body of principles common to us both; and therefore I am not scrupulous to converse and live with them, to enter their Churches in defect of ours, and either pray with them, or for them [I. 3].

And yet he goes on to say that he is not only a child of the Reformation but a willing servant of one particular reformed Church, 'the Church of England, to whose faith I am a sworne subject, and therefore in a double obligation, subscribe unto her Articles, and endeavour to observe her Constitutions' [I, 5]. In the MSS he added, 'No man shall reach my faith unto another Article, or command my obedience to a Canon more'. This challenging phrase he deleted in the authorized edition, but retained the rest of the sentence to which it was prelude:

> whatsoever is beyond, as points indifferent, I observe according to the rules of my private reason, or the humour and fashion of my devotion, neither believing this, because *Luther* affirmed it, or disapproving that, because *Calvin* hath disavouched it. I condemne not all things in the Councell of *Trent* nor approve all in the Synod of *Dort*. In briefe, where

Scripture is silent, the Church is my Text; where that speakes, 'tis but my Comment; where there is a joynt silence of both, I borrow not the rules of my Religion from *Rome* or *Geneva*, but the dictates of my owne reason [I, 5].

Thus Browne secured for himself as much freedom of thought as he felt he needed; he was tethered to the Church most willingly, for he was well aware of the fallibility of human reason, but he claimed a long rope to browse at large in the fields of speculation.

He recalls some former speculations from which his loyalty to the Church of England now restrains him, in particular, three heresies to which he found himself temperamentally inclined [I, 7]. First the heresy of the Arabians 'That the soules of men perished with their bodies, but should yet bee raised again at the last day'. He was not a convinced mortalist, but speculated on the possibility that the soul 'entered the grave' with the body and both would rise together; such a belief, he says, did not disturb him, 'so I might enjoy my Saviour at last I could with patience be nothing almost unto eternity'. The second heresy that appealed to him was Origen's belief that at last all souls would be saved: 'Which error I fell into upon a serious contemplation of the great attribute of God, his mercy; and did a little cherish it in my selfe, because I found therein no malice, and a ready weight to sway me from that other extream of despaire, where unto melancholy and contemplative natures are too easily disposed.' Thirdly, although he says he neither argued for it nor practised it, he would have liked to believe in prayer for the dead:

whereunto I was inclined from some charitable inducements, whereby I could scarce containe my prayers for a friend at the ringing out of a Bell, or behold his corpse without an oraison for his soule: 'Twas a good way me thought to be remembered by Posterity, and farre more noble then an History [I, 7].

They are three gracious heresies springing, as he points out, from humility and charity. None the less, he was sternly reproved for the first two by Sir Kenelm Digby and, much more roughly, for all three by Alexander Ross. Neither controversialist was mollified by Browne's assurance that he never attempted to propagate these heretical beliefs.

Browne did not want to propagate his unorthodox beliefs, partly because he was temperamentally sceptical and therefore willing to suppose he might be mistaken, partly also because he saw that heresies could lead to an ever-increasing fragmentation of the Church:

> for heads that are disposed unto Schisme and complexionally propense to innovation, are naturally indisposed for a community, nor will ever be confined unto the order or oeconomy of one body...they knit but loosely among themselves; nor contented with a generall breach or dichotomie with their Church, do subdivide and mince themselves almost into Atomes [I, 8].

He found room enough for his own intellectual vagaries in areas bounded by no Church doctrines:

> for there is yet, after all the decrees of counsells and the niceties of the Schooles, many things untouch'd, unimagin'd, wherein the libertie of an honest reason may play and expatiate with security, and farre without the circle of an heresie [*ibid.*].

But though he loved to reason, he would have agreed with Dryden that:

> Dim, as the borrow'd beams of Moon and Stars
> To lonely, weary, wandring Travellers
> Is reason to the Soul [*Religio Laici*].

Consequently, like Dryden in that poem, he welcomed revelation. Revealed truths are beyond reason; moreover he enjoys the perplexity in which they involve him.

> 'Tis my solitary recreation to pose my apprehension with those involved aenigma's and riddles of the Trinity, with Incarnation, and Resurrection. I can answer all the objections of Satan, and my rebellious reason with that odde resolution I learned of *Tertullian*, *Certum est, quia impossibile est* [I, 9].

These mysteries, inaccessible to reason, have been revealed. They cannot be apprehended by sense nor deduced from what is known, they can only be accepted by faith. Browne values such faith above knowledge and therefore he goes on to say:

I blesse my selfe and am thankfule that I lived not in the dayes of miracles, that I never saw Christ nor his Disciples; I would not have beene one of the Israelites that passed the Red Sea, nor one of Christs Patients on whom he wrought his wonders; then had my faith beene thrust upon me, nor should I enjoy that greater blessing pronounced to all that believe and saw not [I, 9].

Alexander Ross comments: '*You blesse yourselfe, and are thankfull, that you never saw Christ nor his Disciples.* Was it because he or they, by curing all diseases freely, would have hindered your practice?'[1] The cheap jibe betrays the dishonest controversialist; no Christian reader of the seventeenth century could have genuinely misunderstood what Browne meant. Towards the close of *Religio Medici* he returns to Christ's injunction 'have faith'.

Meanwhile, for a later generation the section that follows is enlightening; we may be chary of erecting blind faith into a virtue, but we are accustomed to think of reason and knowledge as limited and we recognize that what cannot be proved can sometimes nevertheless be expressed and apprehended. Browne begins sect. 10 by saying that, though the metaphor of a sword can express what faith is for some people, he himself 'in these obscurities' prefers to think of faith 'in the adjunct the Apostle gives it, a buckler'. He can protect himself by faith from total scepticism:

Since I was of understanding to know we know nothing, my reason hath beene more pliable to the will of faith; I am now content to understand a mystery without a rigid definition, in an easie and Platonick description...where there is an obscurity too deepe for our reason, 'tis good to sit downe with a description, periphrasis, or adumbration; for by acquainting our reason how unable it is to display the visible and

[1] Alexander Ross, *Medicus Medicatus* (1645), p. 16.

obvious effects of nature, it becomes more humble and submissive unto the subtilties of faith: and thus I teach my haggard and unreclaimed reason to stoope unto the lure of faith [I, 10].

Shielded by the traditional fourfold interpretation of Scripture (literal, allegorical, anagogical, tropical), Browne feels free to notice, and to amuse himself with, the contradictions that might dismay mere literalists. He gaily plays with self-contradictions in Genesis which were to disturb some inquiring minds some two hundred years later. Like Keats's 'man of achievement, especially in literature' Browne is sometimes 'willing to be in uncertainties without irritably seeking after fact and reason' [Keats's Letters, 21 December 1817].

In his 'solitary and retired imagination' he contemplates the attributes of God, 'especially those two mighty ones, his wisdome and eternitie'. The first is, he says, his recreation; all his observation and experiments with creatures were his way of contemplating God's wisdom. But the second confounds his understanding:

Time we may comprehend; 'tis but five dayes elder then our selves, and hath the same Horoscope with the world; but to retire so farre backe as to apprehend a beginning, to give such an infinite start forward as to conceive an end in an essence that wee affirme hath neither the one nor the other; it puts my Reason to Saint *Paul's* Sanctuary [*O! Altitudo!*]; my philosophy dares not say the Angells can doe it [I, 11].

Such play with the idea of the Timeless can 'tease us out of thought', and this Sir Thomas Browne enjoys; Sir Kenelm Digby, however, took him to task over this piece of intellectual frivolity; eternity is not (he reminded the Earl of Dorset) 'an infinite extension of time'. But, if he read to the end of the section, he knew that Browne was aware of this—'in eternity there is no distinction of Tenses' he wrote, and thereby he hoped to by-pass the fearful doctrine of '*Predestination*, which hath troubled so many weake heads to conceive, and the wisest to explaine', but which

is in respect of God no previous determination of our estates to come, but a definitive blast of his will already fulfilled, and at the instant that he first decreed it; for to his eternitie which is indivisible and altogether, the last Trumpe is already sounded, the reprobates in the flame, and the blessed in *Abrahams* bosome [I, 11].

If, for any one, this made predestination more intelligible, it can hardly have made it more acceptable to the moral sense. But then neither can the words that Milton was to put into the mouth of the Almighty:

If I foreknew,
Foreknowledge had no influence on their fault,
Which had no less proved certain unforeknown.

Milton was one of those 'wisest heads' that troubled to explain; as for Sir Thomas Browne, he will later admit that he has no literal belief in that flame [I, 51].

However we look at it, eternity or timelessness adds to the mystery of the Trinity, and Browne dwells for a moment, in sect. 12, on the problem of priority between Father and Son. But his mind is attracted to Philosophy (by which he means the study of nature) rather than to metaphysics, and the study of nature, he says, is also a way which leads to the knowledge of God.

The severe Schooles shall never laugh me out of the Philosophy of *Hermes*, that this visible World is but a picture of the invisible, wherein, as in a pourtract, things are not truely, but in equivocall shapes, and as they counterfeit some more reall substance in that invisible fabrick [I, 12].

Sir Kenelm Digby accepted this as neither eccentric nor unorthodox, and indeed many thinkers and poets in the seventeenth century shared this opinion, which derived as much from Plato as from writings ascribed to the Egyptian sage, *Hermes Trismegistus*. It informs the poetry of Vaughan and the prose of the Cambridge Platonists. Milton's Raphael was to sanction it in Book v of *Paradise Lost*:

what if Earth
Be but the shadow of Heaven, and things therein
Each to other like more than on Earth is thought?

and in Book VIII, before he bids Adam

> Solicit not thy thoughts with matters hid:

Raphael approves his astronomical questions and rewards them with a long discourse expounding the conjectures both of Ptolemy and of Copernicus:

> To ask or search I blame thee not; for Heaven
> Is as the Book of God before thee set,
> Wherein to read his wondrous works, and learn
> His seasons, hours, or days, or months, or years.

In sect. 13 Browne returns to the first of God's two 'mighty attributes' introduced in sect. 11—his 'Wisdome'; throughout Part I of *Religio Medici* the thread of thought is unbroken, although the weave is intricate. Eternity, the Trinity, the Being of God himself, are all beyond our comprehension. God alone is wise, 'because he knows all things; and he knoweth all things, because he made them all; but his greatest knowledg is in comprehending that he made not, that is himselfe'. If God's greatest knowledge is self-knowledge then, by persuasive analogy, self-knowledge is also what man ought chiefly to seek; none do this more obviously than physicians and so Browne congratulates himself on his profession:

> For this do I honour my own profession, and embrace the counsell even of the Devill himself: had he read such a Lecture in Paradise as hee did at *Delphos*, we had better knowne our selves, nor had we stood in feare to know him [I, 13].

In the margin he reminds us of the Delphic Oracle Γνῶθι σεαυτόν (know thyself), for he accepts here and elsewhere the current assumption that the Delphic Oracle was Satan's mouthpiece. The joke depends upon our being aware of this as well as of what happened in Paradise. After further arabesques on the theme of the impossibility of comprehending God, Browne turns to browse in his chosen field:

> These are Contemplations Metaphysicall; my humble speculations have another Method, and are content to trace and discover those

impressions hee hath left on his creatures, and the obvious effects of nature; there is no danger to propound these mysteries, no *Sanctum sanctorum* in Philosophy: The world was made to be inhabited by beasts, but studied and contemplated by man: 'tis the debt of our reason wee owe unto God, and the homage we pay for not being beasts; without this, the world is still as though it had not been, or as it was before the sixth day when as yet there was not a creature that could conceive or say there was a world [*ibid.*].

In the next three sections Browne explores and embroiders upon the revelation of God in the created world. He reminds us of Aristotle's Four Causes, the prime mover or first cause and the three second causes discernible in all phenomena: (efficient, material, formal and final). God alone is without efficient cause, since nothing preceded him; the angels are without material cause; the first matter (or chaos) was without formal cause:

but every Essence, created or uncreated, hath its finall cause, and some positive end both of its Essence and operation. This is the cause I grope after in the workes of nature, on this hangs the providence of God; to raise so beauteous a structure as the world and the creatures thereof, was but his Art, but their sundry and divided operations, with their predestinated ends, are from the treasury of his wisedome [I, 14].

Browne never ceased to assume that the intention of God (the final cause) was discernible in every detail of the phenomenal world. He was to follow Bacon's lead and to experiment with creatures to find out how they lived; but he ignored Bacon's advice in *The Advancement of Learning* not to confuse the question *how* with the question *why*. Bacon wrote:

For the handling of final causes, mixed with the rest in physical inquiries, hath intercepted the severe and diligent inquiry of all real and physical causes, and given men the occasion to stay upon these satisfactory and specious causes, to the great arrest and prejudice of further discovery. For this I find done not only by Plato, who ever anchoreth upon that shore, but by Aristotle, Galen, and others which do usually likewise fall upon these flats of discoursing causes. For to say that *the hairs of the eye-lids are for a quick-set and fence about the sight*; or that *the firmness of the skins and hides of living creatures is to defend them from the extremities of heat or cold*...and the like, is well inquired and collected in metaphysic, but in physic they are impertinent [II, 7].

Sir Thomas Browne never accepted this distinction; in *Vulgar Errors* he often relies on the axiom with which he opens sect. 15 of *Religio Medici*: '*Natura nihil agit frustra.*'

The opening of sect. 15 is a well-known and characteristic example of Browne's prose, but to a modern reader the rhythm and feeling may be more obvious than the precise meaning. The thought is firmly rooted in contemporary beliefs about the created world:

Natura nihil agit frustra, is the only indisputable axiome in Philosophy; there are no *Grotesques* in nature; nor anything framed to fill up empty cantons, and unnecessary spaces; in the most imperfect creatures, and such as were not preserved in the Arke, but having their seeds and principles in the wombe of nature, are everywhere, where the power of the Sun is; in these is the wisedom of his hand discovered: Out of this ranke *Solomon* chose the object of his admiration, indeed what reason may not goe to Schoole to the wisedome of Bees, Aunts, and Spiders? What wise hand teacheth them to doe what reason cannot teach us? ruder heads stand amazed at those prodigious pieces of nature, Whales, Elephants, Dromidaries and Camels; these I confesse, are the Collossus and Majestick pieces of her hand; but in these narrow Engines there is more curious Mathematicks, and the civilitie of these little Citizens more neatly sets forth the wisedome of their Maker; Who admires not *Regio-Montanus* his Fly beyond his Eagle, or wonders not more at the operation of two soules in those little bodies, than but one in the trunck of a Cedar? [I, 15].

The little insects who have their seeds 'in the womb of nature' and are generated by the sun are creatures of whom a modern entomologist would tell a different story. But in 1643 no one, I think, doubted their spontaneous generation. The subject was being investigated as late as 1663 when the *Transactions* of the Royal Society record that 'Mr Hoskyns related an experiment of the production of bees out of a dead bullock. This was directed to be tried.' The fly and the eagle of the fifteenth-century professor of medicine, Regio Montanus, is a more fanciful example because these creatures were alleged artifacts. The story is on record in Sylvester's translation of du Bartas:

> Why should I not that wooden Eagle mention?
> A learned German's late admir'd Invention,
> Which mounting from his Fist that fram'd her,
> Flew far to meet an Almain Emperor:...
> Once as this Artist more with Mirth than Meat,
> Feasted some friends that he esteemed great,
> From under's Hand an Iron Fly flew out,
> Which having flown a perfect round about,
> With weary Wings return'd unto her Master,
> And as judicious on his Arm he plac'd her.

Browne means that it was even more remarkable to construct the fly than the eagle; only the thoughtless are impressed by mere size. The great cedar tree with its one, vegetative soul is less wonderful than the insect who, in so small a compass, has two souls, vegetative and animal. (Man has of course a third, the reasonable soul.)

The main thread of the pattern of thought is taken up in sect. 16: 'Thus there are two bookes from whence I collect my Divinity; besides that written one of God, another of his servant Nature, that universall and publik Manuscript, that lies expans'd unto the eyes of all.' By the word Nature, Browne explains, he means 'that streight and regular line, that setled and constant course the wisedome of God hath ordained the actions of his creatures, according to their severall kinds'. Nature is merely the instrument and deserves praise no more than do our hammers for building our houses or our pens for writing our books; therefore he is not tempted to adore Nature. In a fashion reminiscent of the metaphysical poets Browne then pursues and teases his metaphor of the artificer. God does not often interfere with the course of nature,

> for God is like a skilful Geometrician, who when more easily and with one stroak of his Compasse, he might describe, or divide a right line, had yet rather doe this, though in a circle or longer way, according to the constituted and forelaid principles of his art.

He argues that nothing can be ugly since all is designed by God, and he concludes sect. 16:

To speak yet more narrowly, there was never anything ugly or unshapen but the Chaos; wherein notwithstanding to speake strictly, there was no deformity, because no forme, nor was it yet impregnate by the voyce of God: Now nature is not at variance with art, nor art with nature; they both being the servants of his providence: Art is the perfection of Nature: Were the world now as it was the sixth day, there were yet a Chaos: Nature hath made one world, and Art another. In briefe, all things are artificiall, for nature is the Art of God [I, 16].

Browne now turns from the complex but uniform laws of nature to the operations of God, within this pattern, affecting the lives of individuals and of nations. We speak of fortune, but

It was the ignorance of mans reason that begat this very name, and by a carelesse terme miscalled the providence of God: for there is no liberty for causes to operate in a loose and stragling way, nor any effect whatsoever, but hath its warrant for some universall and more superiour cause [I, 18].

God governs all; it may be true that 'men of singular gifts of mind' are commonly 'destitute of those of fortune', but this is consonant with a just and wise provision:

'tis not partiality, but equity in God, who deales with us but as our naturall parents: those that are able in body and mind, he leaves to their deserts; to those of weaker merits hee imparts a larger portion, and pieces out the defect of the one by the excesse of the other. Thus have wee no just quarrell with Nature, for leaving us naked, or to envie the hornes, hoofs, skins, and furs of other creatures, being provided with reason, that can supply them all [*ibid.*].

Jeremy Taylor, in *Holy Living* (1650), was to use the same argument for contentedness:

He were a strange fool, that should be angry because dogs and sheep need no shoes, and yet himself is full of care to get some. God hath supplied those needs to them by natural provisions, and to thee by an artificial:

for he hath given thee reason to learn a trade, or some means to make or buy them; so that it only differs in the manner of our provision: and which had you rather want, shoes or Reason? [Cap. II, vi, I.]

These thoughts about providence, erroneous opinions of which 'have perverted the devotions of many', lead to meditations concerning doubt which continue through the next four sections (19–22). In them we perceive the tension in Browne's mind between faith and scepticism. First he illustrates how his studies have led him to doubt whether some Old Testament miracles were in fact miraculous; they might have been effected by nature for instance: 'I know that Manna is now plentifully gathered in *Calabria*, and *Josephus* tells me, in his dayes 'twas as plentifull in *Arabia*; the Devill therefore made the *quere*, Where was then the miracle in the dayes of *Moses*?' [I, 19]. He leaves the question unresolved, and focuses his doubts in an image of the Devil playing at chess with him, 'taking advantage of my honest endeavours; and whilst I laboured to raise the structure of my reason, hee striv'd to undermine the edifice of my faith'. It is obvious from the tone that such doubts amused, but did not trouble him. Why should they since nature was the art of God? He expected that miracles would, at most, be very rare. For the moment he drops the subject of miracle, to return to it in sect. 27 after he has explored other doubts and themes to which these contemplations give rise.

Such doubts, he says, never tempted him towards atheism: indeed, he asserts, no one was ever an atheist. He invites us to consider some of the pagan philosophers: Epicurus denied the providence of God, but only because he thought God was too majestic 'to minde the triviall actions of...inferior creatures'. The Stoics believed in necessity, but this is only a name for 'the immutable law of his Will'. To deny the divinity of the Holy Ghost, as some have done, is heresy, but not atheism, nor is it atheism to deny the divinity of Christ, 'for though they deny two persons in the Trinity, they hold as we do, there is one God'.

Even 'that Villain and Secretary of Hell, that composed that miscreant piece of the three Impostors,[1] though . . . neither Jew, Turk nor Christian, was not yet a positive atheist'. But, though none are atheists, yet 'every Countrey hath its *Machiavell*, every Age its *Lucian*, whereof common heads must not heare, nor more advanced judgements too rashly venture on: 'tis the Rhetorick of Satan, and may pervert a loose or prejudicate beleefe' [I, 20].

Sir Thomas claims, however, in the following section to have read them all; he is confident of the strength of his own head. He recalls some of the doubters he met with on his travels; the Doctor of Physick in Italy who could not believe in immortality because Galen denied it; a divine in France who was 'gravelled' by three lines in Seneca; as for himself he does not expect to resolve all the problems raised by the stories in Scripture. This does not trouble him and he selects, with evident amusement, some of the puzzles that could perplex one who was prepared to vex himself with trifles:

I can read the story of the Pigeon that was sent out of the Ark, and returned no more, yet not question how shee found out her mate that was left behind: [For a literalist the non-return of the pigeon to her mate should have raised a problem about the continuance of the kind.] That *Lazarus* was raised from the dead, yet not demand where in the interim his soule awaited; or raise a Law-case, whether his heire might lawfully detaine his inheritance, bequeathed unto him by his death; and he, though restored to life, have no Plea or title unto his former possessions. Whether *Eve* was framed out of the left side of *Adam*, I dispute not; because I stand not yet assured which is the right side of a man, or whether there be any such distinction in Nature: that she was edified out of the ribbe of *Adam* I believe, yet raise no question who shall arise with that ribbe at the Resurrection.

With these and other examples Browne mocks the solemn disputation of learned doctors, closing the section with the comment: 'There are a bundle of curiosities, not onely in Philosophy but in Divinity, proposed and discussed by men of the most supposed

[1] The book referred to is *De Tribus Impostoribus*, of unknown authorship. The three alleged impostors are Christ, Moses and Mahomet.

abilities, which indeed are not worthy our vacant hours, much less our more serious studies; Pieces onely fit to be placed in *Pantagruels* Library, or bound up with *Tartaretus De Modo Cacandi*'[1] [I, 21]. In his *Medicus Medicatus* Alexander Ross supplies unconscious proof that the mockery is deserved. He solemnly resolves the question 'which is the right side of a man?': 'The right side is that where the liver lyeth, which is the fountaine of blood, wherein our life consisteth; therefore that side is stronger, and more active, and the limbs thereof bigger' [sect. 21].

In sect. 22 Browne discusses some possible reinterpretations of the Scriptures, but emphasizes that the matters concerned are not important; sect. 23 opens with: 'These are but the conclusions and fallible discourses of man upon the word of God, for such doe I beleeve the holy Scriptures: yet, were it of man, I could not choose but say, it were the singularest and superlative Piece that hath been extant since the Creation'; and, after comparing it with other writings, he concludes: 'This onely is a Worke too hard for the teeth of time, and cannot perish but in those generall flames, when all things shall confesse their ashes.'

This leads him to a relevant digression (sect. 24) on a theme raised by Milton in *Paradise Regained* when Christ says:

> However, many books,
> Wise men have said, are wearisome;... [IV, 321–2.]

Browne, who was as far as Milton himself from behaving as though he believed this, develops a similar argument against the multiplicity of books: 'Of those three great inventions of Germany, there are two which are not without their incommodities.' Simon Wilkin thinks clocks are the exempted third invention; gunpowder and printing are the denigrated. Browne claims that not only he, but 'better heads' as well, wish

> that there were a generall Synod; not to unite the incompatible difference of Religion, but for the benefit of learning, to reduce it as it lay at first

[1] Here Browne is adopting Rabelais's jibe at Tartaretus, who was a doctor of the Sorbonne notorious for his refinements on the subtleties of Duns Scotus.

in a few and solid Authours; and to condemne to the fire those swarms and millions of *Rhapsodies*, begotten onely to distract and abuse the weaker judgements of Scholars, and *to maintaine the Trade and Mystery of Typographers.*

In the two following sections, 25 and 26, Browne is mainly concerned with persecution and martyrdom. But here again there is no interruption of the train of thought. He has been thinking about canonical scripture, and then more generally about the written word. Now he thinks of other scriptures, Jewish and Mahomedan. From this to constancy, or obstinacy in belief, is a short step. He admires the Jews, both in the older sense of the word (is amazed by) and in the modern, for their obstinate adherence to their own beliefs: 'This is a vice in them but were a vertue in us; for obstinacy in a bad cause is but constancy in a good.' And fifteen hundred years have only confirmed the Jews in their error:

> they have already endured whatsoever may be inflicted, and have suffered, in a bad cause, even to the commendation of their enemies. Persecution is a bad and indirect way to plant Religion; it hath beene the unhappy method of angry devotions, not onely to confirme honest Religion, but wicked Heresies and extravagant opinions [I, 25].

Neither the conviction that causes men to inflict martyrdom, nor the courage that enables men to endure it, is any proof that their belief is true. But Browne has a deep admiration for the courage of martyrs (he will return to the Jews in *Pseudodoxia* and to the martyrs in *Urne-Buriall*). Here he says that 'these are the true and almost onely examples of fortitude'. Acts of audacity on the battlefield are not such pure examples of valour: 'If wee shall strictly examine the circumstances and requisites which *Aristotle* requires to true and perfect valour, we shall finde the name onely in his Master, *Alexander*, and as little in that Romane Worthy, *Julius Caesar*' [I, 25]. At any rate the 'active part' of courage is easy compared with 'the passive and more terrible piece'. But, he concludes, ''Tis not in the power of every honest faith to proceed thus farre or passe to Heaven through the flames'. He does not doubt that those who, unfit for martyrdom, yet 'Doe truly adore their Saviour', have also 'a faith acceptable in the eyes of God'.

But he has not yet had his say out about martyrs; moved by their courage, convinced that nothing is gained by persecution, he now asks in what circumstances should a man allow himself to be martyred?

There are questionlesse, many canonized on earth, that shall never be called Saints in Heaven; and have their names in Histories and Martyrologies, who in the eyes of God are not so perfect Martyrs as was that wise Heathen, *Socrates*, that suffered on a fundamentall point of Religion, the Unity of God [I, 26].

To expose oneself to die for any belief less fundamental is, he suggests, at best folly and at worst suicide. He says:

I have often pitied the miserable Bishop that suffered in the Cause of the *Antipodes*, yet cannot choose but accuse him of as much madnesse, for exposing his living on such a trifle, as those of ignorance and folly that condemned him [*ibid.*].

The bishop in question is Virgilius, bishop of Salzburg in 764; Browne is accurate in saying that he exposed his *living* not his life. He asserted that the earth was a globe, inhabited all round; his superiors thought this involved belief in two suns, two moons—a plurality of worlds. He was deprived of his bishopric and Sir Thomas Browne pitied his folly for incurring even so slight a martyrdom in such an unimportant cause. For his own part, he says:

I would not perish upon a Ceremony, Politick point, or indifferency.... The leaven, therefore, and ferment of all, not onely Civill, but Religious actions, is wisdome; without which, to commit ourselves to the flame is Homicide, and, (I feare) but to passe through one fire into another [*ibid.*].

The next section, 27, opens with: 'That Miracles are ceased I can neither prove, nor absolutely deny'; to the modern reader the transition from martyrs to miracles may seem abrupt; but not, I think, to his contemporary reader. He has been thinking of saints and martyrs. Canonization by the Roman Church, then as now, depended upon miracles. But Browne is not convinced that, in his own time, any miracles occur; yet he cannot be certain that they do not:

> that may have some truth in it that is reported of the Jesuites and their Miracles in the Indies; I could wish it were true, or had any other testimony then their owne Pennes: they may easily beleeve those Miracles abroad, who daily conceive a greater at home; the transmutation of those visible elements into the body and blood of our Saviour.

He does not, he says, doubt God's power to effect any miracle, because none would be more wonderful than what we know him to have done: 'For this also is a miracle, not onely to produce effects against or above Nature, but before Nature; and to create Nature as great a miracle as to contradict or transcend her.' Here he picks up a part of the pattern of his thought that he seemed to have abandoned in sect. 19, but that is in fact central to his conception of the universe. He does not doubt God's unlimited power: 'how he should work contradictions, I do not understand, yet dare not, therefore deny...'. But he is willing to affirm that, though he *can*, God rarely, if ever, *will* interrupt the course of nature:

> I will not say God cannot, but hee will not performe many things, which wee plainely affirme he cannot: this, I am sure, is the mannerliest proposition, wherein notwithstanding I hold no Paradox. For strictly his power is but the same with his will, and they both, with all the rest doe make but one God [I, 27].

Thus elaborately, with verbal dexterity suavely used, he safeguards for himself a law-abiding, intelligible, created world. 'Therefore that Miracles have beene, I doe beleeve, that they may yet bee wrought by the living I doe not deny: but have no confidence in those which are fathered on the dead' [I, 28]. This is how he opens the section: in it, as in the preceding section, he is defining his opposition to Roman Catholic teaching with more urbanity than was customary at the time, but with no less precision. He does not believe in the power of relics to effect miracles: 'I cannot conceive why the Crosse that *Helena* found and whereon Christ himself died should have power to restore others unto life'; and he enumerates other instances of alleged miracle-working relics which do not convince him. Attempts to explain such effects only confuse the issue: 'Those that hold the sanctitie of their soules [souls of saints] doth leave behind a tincture and sacred facultie on their bodies, speake naturally of Miracles and doe not salve the doubt.' They are offering what we would call a scientific explanation; Sir Thomas Browne feels that this merely denies the claim that the effects are miraculous without persuading him that they occur. Here he leaves his intellectual reasons for doubt and moves on to underlying habits of mind, closing the section with a characteristic paradox.

Now one reason I tender so little devotion unto reliques, is, I think, the slender and doubtfull respect I have alwayes held unto Antiquities: for that indeed which I admire is farre before antiquity, that is Eternity, and that is God himselfe; who though hee be stiled the Antient of dayes, cannot receive the adjunct of antiquity, who was before the world, and shall be after it, yet is not older then it; for in his yeares there is no Climacter; his duration is eternity, and farre more venerable than antiquitie [I, 28].[1]

Within the individual sections, as in the whole work, Browne's thought travels along a discernible path, although one is continually surprised by its twists and turns.

In the following sections Browne moves from miracles ascribed to God and his saints to wonders performed by the Devil and his agents. Surprising and intricate relationships emerge between

[1] Cf. Plato, *Timaeus*: '*Was* and *shall be* are generated forms of Time, although we apply them wrongly, without noticing, to Eternal Being...but it belongs not to that which is ever changeless in its uniformity to become either older or younger through time, nor ever to have become so, nor to be about to be so hereafter, nor in general to be subject to any of the conditions which Becoming has attached to the things which move in the world of Sense.'

Browne's scepticism and his faith. Section 29 begins by pointing to 'that great and indisputable miracle', the cessation of Oracles after the resurrection of Christ. His contemporary editor Thomas Keck, in a learned note, claims that they did not cease, for they never occurred; there was never anything but human trickery. It seems then that Browne, as with his beliefs in witches, was in this matter more credulous than some of his contemporaries. By 1646, in *Pseudodoxia*, Book VII, c. 12, he was much more cautious about cessation; he by then knew that Oracles had declined before Christ's death, and that they were 'not altogether dumb' afterwards. But he still assumed that Oracles were, literally, the Devil's mouthpieces; the Devil spoke through them just as he still speaks through 'Witches, Magicians, Diviners and such inferior seducers'. Browne advises us to mistrust oracles; he is as sceptical of their validity as a modern rationalist, but the reason for his scepticism is rooted in faith, it is 'the soverign degree of folly, and a crime not only against God but against our own reasons, to expect a favour from the Devil'. Oracles and similar prognostications are not to be believed, since we know from whom they come. Here we may say that one over-credulous belief defends Browne from another. In the same section he announces his scepticism about human testimony and, consequently, histories: this is partly based on his experience of chronicle plays (there are other indications in *Religio Medici* that Browne enjoyed the theatre).

And truely since I have understood the occurrences of the world, and know in what counterfeit shapes and deceitfull vizzards times present represent on the stage things past, I doe beleeve them little more than things to come. Some have beene of my opinion, and endevoured to write the history of their own lives; wherein *Moses* hath outgone them all, and left not onely the story of his life, but as some will have it of his death also [I, 29].[1]

[1] Thomas Keck comments on this: 'Those who are of opinion that *Moses* wrote the five Books, ought also to believe that he wrote the history of his death. I had rather believe that he did not write the fifth book; but some conclude from thence that he wrote none at all' (*Religio Medici*, 1656).

From this scepticism based on experience Browne draws, logically yet paradoxically, the conclusion that our faith in the Canonical Scriptures must be implicit: 'Certainly it is not a warrantable curiosity, to examine the verity of Scripture by the concordance of humane history, or seek to confirme the Chronicle of *Daniel*, or *Hesther*, by the authority of *Megasthenes* or *Heroditus*' [*ibid.*]. Thus, just as his belief in the Devil ensures his mistrust of all prognostics or devil-messages, so his mistrust of human records protects his belief in canonical scripture, the revealed word of God.

Browne's Christianity is linked with a total view of the universe based not solely on the Bible but on Christian tradition, including its heritage from Plato and Plotinus. The next section (sect. 30) begins:

It is a riddle to me, how this very story of Oracles hath not worm'd out of the world that doubtfull conceit of Spirits and Witches; how so many learned heads should so farre forget their Metaphysics, and destroy the Ladder and scale of creatures, as to question the existence of Spirits.

The theory was that a perfect God would necessarily create a perfect universe and that this meant a universe in which everything that could exist would exist. It would also be a perfectly continuous universe, a chain downwards from God, through angels to man, animals, vegetables, minerals—the amount of life or soul gradually decreasing with increasing distance from the Creator. Each link in the chain had something in common with the link immediately above it and the one immediately below. It is to this almost universally accepted metaphysic that Browne appeals to counter the materialism of 'many learned heads' who doubted the existence of spirits. He can up to this point be confident of the assent of his contemporary fellow-Christians;[1] since there is a full and ordered universe of creatures it must include

[1] Professor A. O. Lovejoy, the historian of the idea of the 'chain of being', says that this conception prevailed from the Middle Ages until the late eighteenth century and that 'many philosophers, most men of science, and indeed most educated men' accepted it without question. The idea derived from Plato's *Dialogues*; it was elaborated by Plotinus, Christianized by St Augustine, by the Pseudo-Dionysius and by St Thomas Aquinas.

angels. He himself, however, proposed to go beyond this: 'for mine owne part, I have ever beleeved, and doe now know, that there are Witches: they that doubt of these, doe not onely deny them, but Spirits; and are obliquely and upon consequence a sort not of Infidels, but Atheists.' He had already written, in sect. 20, that consistent atheism is unthinkable and unexampled. He is, then, accusing those who disbelieve in witches of unexampled perversity of thought; this rhetorical excess did not go unchallenged. Sir Kenelm Digby wrote:

> I acknowledge ingenuously our *Physicians* experience hath the advantage of my *Philosophy*, in knowing there are witches. Yet I am sure, I have no temptation to doubt of the *Deity*; nor have I any unsatisfaction in believing there are Spirits. I do not see such a necessary conjunction betweene them, as that supposition of the one, must needs inferre the other. Neither do I deny there are witches, I onely reserve my assente, till I meete with stronger motives to carry it.[1]

Certainly Browne's logic is here faulty. His parenthesis, 'and do now know', relies on experience, not logic; presumably he had already in 1635 (thirty years before he gave evidence at a witch-trial) been convinced that some peculiar symptoms in sick persons could have no other explanation than that they were bewitched. Many in various professions throughout the seventeenth century believed in witches. Simon Wilkin, in a note on this passage of *Religio Medici*, reminds us of some notable and intellectually distinguished men who believed in witchcraft; he names Francis Bacon (1561–1626), Bishop Joseph Hall (1574–1656), Richard Baxter (1615–91), Dr Henry More (1614–87), Joseph Glanvill (1636–80) and Sir Matthew Hale (1609–76). It was not, then, an eccentric or outmoded belief, although one cannot but wish that Sir Thomas Browne had rejected it. He is oddly dogmatic in sect. 30 about what particular devil-tricks he can and cannot believe in. He is 'puzzled' concerning Changelings; incredulous of the alleged metamorphoses of 'reasonable creatures into

[1] Sir Kenelm Digby, *Observations on Religio Medici*, p. 36.

beasts'; ready to believe that 'Spirits use with men the act of carnality', but not that any creature can be born from such unions. He knows that there are impostors, both those who deny that they are devil's agents and those that pretend that good angels act through them, yet he believes 'that the Devill doth really possesse some men'. In the next section he adds to all this his belief that the secrets of Nature have sometimes been revealed by the Devil: 'What invented by us is Philosophy, learned from him is Magicke.' But good Angels, he thinks, also have revealed such secrets: 'I doe thinke that many mysteries ascribed to our own inventions have beene the courteous revelations of Spirits.' To the modern reader most of the beliefs and all of the assertive confidence in these two sections will seem very odd. It would not all have seemed so odd to Dr Johnson more than a century later. Boswell records a conversation of 10 June 1784 in which 'he admitted the influence of evil spirits upon our minds, and said, "Nobody who believes the New Testament can deny it"', and another of 16 August 1773, specifically concerning witchcraft, in which Johnson reminded Mr Crosbie:

> You have all mankind, rude and civilized, agreeing in the belief of the agency of preternatural powers. You must take evidence: you must consider, that wise and great men have condemned witches to die.
>
> *Crosbie*. But an act of Parliament put an end to witchcraft.
>
> *Johnson*. No, sir; witchcraft had ceased; and therefore an act of Parliament was passed to prevent persecution for what was not witchcraft. Why it ceased, we cannot tell, as we cannot tell the reason of many other things.

It was not until 1736 that the act which made witchcraft a capital offence was repealed: more than a hundred years after Sir Thomas Browne wrote *Religio Medici*.

In sect. 32 Browne entertains the notion that there may be 'an universall and common Spirit to the whole world' as well as these 'divided spirits', the good Angels and the ministers of Satan, of which he has been writing. 'It was the opinion of Plato and it is yet of the *Hermeticall* Philosophers; if there be a common nature that unties and tyes scattered and divided individuals into one species, why may there not bee one that unites them all?'[1] But the question is only raised, one feels, as a prelude to the assertion that follows it:

Howsoever, I am sure there is a common spirit that playes within us, yet makes no part of us; and that is, the Spirit of God, and scintillation of that noble and mighty Essence, which is the life and radicall heat of spirits, and those essences that know not the virtue of the Sunne, a fire quite contrary to the fire of Hell: This is that gentle heate that brooded on the waters, and in six dayes hatched the world; this is that irradiation that dispells the mists of Hell, the clouds of horrour, feare, sorrow, despaire; and preserves the region of the mind in serenity: whosoever feels not the warme gale and gentle ventilation of this Spirit, (though I feele his pulse,) I dare not say he lives; for truely, to mee, without this, there is no heat under the Tropick; nor any light, though I dwelt in the body of the Sunne [I, 32].

Here Browne is no longer speculating about metaphysics; he is writing a prose poem in praise of God. His style has become lyrical and the effect of joyous serenity is conveyed as much by cadence, and by the metaphors of light and warmth and ventilation, as it is by the coherent paraphrasable sequence of thought. He closed the section with twenty-four lines of verse in which he prays to God to be always 'the Sunne to this poor Orbe of mine'. But in verse this master of ornate prose is seldom more skilled than any clumsy apprentice.

In the next three sections, 33, 34 and 35, Browne picks up again the idea of the scale of being which had led to the digression concerning evil spirits. Evil spirits are not logically necessary to the idea of the scale but angels are, and to them he returns:

for there is in this universe a Staire, or manifest Scale of creatures, rising not disorderly, or in confusion, but with a comely method and proportion: Betweene creatures of meere existence and things of life, there

[1] Plato in *Parmenides* and in *Timaeus*.

is a large disproportion of nature; betweene plants and animals or creatures of sense, a wider difference; between them and man, a farre greater: and if the proportion hold on, betweene man and Angels there should bee yet a greater [I, 33].

The Angels are what we only hope to be, they are spirits; man alone is both spiritual and corporeal:

we are onely that amphibious piece betweene a corporall and spirituall essence, that middle frame which linkes those two together, and makes good the method of God and nature, that jumps not from extreames, but unites the incompatible distances by some middle and participating natures [I, 34].

Here he is referring to a theory concomitant with that of the chain of being; St Thomas Aquinas saw man as the link in the chain which united spirit and matter. In this sense man was a Microcosm, reproducing in himself the dual nature of the Macrocosm, spiritual and corporeal. Browne says that he had once thought of this as 'a pleasant trope of rhetoric'; now, however, his study of embryology has given it substance:

for first wee are a rude masse, and in the ranke of creatures which only are, and have a dull kinde of being not yet priviledged with life, or preferred to sense or reason; next we live the life of plants, the life of animals, the life of men, and at last the life of spirits, running on in one mysterious nature those five kinds of existences, which comprehend the creatures not of the world onely, but of the Universe [I, 34].

How this mysterious universe came into being is, he says, only obscurely described in Genesis; divines have 'to the power of humane reason endeavoured to make all go in a literall meaning, yet those allegoricall interpretations are also probable'. He suggests that since Moses 'was bred up in the Hieroglyphicall schools of the *Egyptians*', he intended us to interpret in this way; but some twenty years later, in *The Garden of Cyrus*, Sir Thomas recognized that the method could lead to absurdities.

These speculations lead on to the elaborately metaphysical speculations of sect. 35. We rely upon Scripture for the knowledge that there is only one world, created by God for his own glory. Creation means production out of nothing; but what, Browne asks, is nothing? Nothing is the opposite of Something and, since God is all, nothing is his opposite. Well then, in Divinity, as in Philosophy (that is in theology as in natural history), life springs from the union of opposites: 'And generation not onely founded on contrarieties, but also creation; God, being all things, is contrary unto nothing, out of which were made all things, and so nothing becomes something, and *Omneity* informed *Nullity* into an essence.' Although Browne is talking of God, as he was in sect. 32, this is not in the least lyrical; it is wit-writing. He is enjoying the complex paradoxical ideas that arise out of a game with words. In this kind of writing we recognize his kinship with Shakespeare and, still more, with John Donne.

In Genesis ii we read that 'The Lord God formed man of the dust of the ground and breathed into his nostrils the breath of life; and man became a living soul'. This is the mystery upon which Browne expatiates in sects. 36 and 37. There were two principal theories current in the seventeenth century about the birth of an individual soul; the one, known as traducianism, supposed that in all generations after Adam the soul was transmitted, in the act of conception, from parents to children. This was the accepted Protestant doctrine; it is the simplest explanation of the heritage of original sin. The second main theory, known as creationism or infusionism, was that God created new souls and infused them into the body, either at conception or at birth. Browne says that neither opinion is inconsistent with religion; he would himself prefer the latter, 'did not one objection haunt mee, not wrung from speculations and subtilties, but from common sense, and observation, not pickt from the leaves of any author, but bred among the weeds and tares of my own braine'. His one objection is surprising and, though it could be said to derive from common sense, it certainly cannot rely on his own observation. It is that the fruit of 'copulation between man and beast' have 'a tincture of reason'; unless the soul is 'transmitted and transfused in the seed of the parents' such creatures would, he thinks, be 'merely beasts'. Browne would have read about such monsters in Plutarch and Pliny and perhaps heard about them in travellers' tales. His contemporary French translator writes in a footnote: 'Les ecrivains ou auteurs temoignent que cela arrive encore aux Indes en plusieurs endroits; et moi-même en ai vu un à Leyden.' Browne was ready to accept such 'facts' on testimony; 'observation' does not necessarily imply that he was the observer. At the end of the section, however, he is relying on his own anatomical knowledge and medical practice. He rejoices to know that there is no organ for the soul; this confirms its mysterious provenance and character, so that whether it be traduced or infused does not worry him:

In our study of Anatomy there is a masse of mysterious Philosophy, and such as reduced the very Heathens to Divinitie; yet amongst all those rare discoveries and curious pieces I finde in the fabricke of man, I doe not so much content my selfe as in that I finde not, that is, no Organe or proper instrument for the rationall soule; for in the braine, which wee tearme the seate of reason, there is not anything of moment more than I can discover in the cranie of a beast: and this is a sensible and no inconsiderable argument of the inorganity of the soule, at least in that sense wee usually so receive it. Thus are we men, and we know not how; there is something in us that can be without us, and will be after us; though it is strange that it hath no history, what it was before us, nor can tell how it entred in us [I, 36].

Anatomical considerations lead him, at the opening of sect. 37, to an exuberant play of fancy and dialectics. What is this flesh in which the soul is walled up? It is a composition of elements and therefore will fall to ashes; but he can go further; it is literally grass: '*All flesh is grasse*, is not onely metaphorically, but literally true, for all those creatures which we behold are but the hearbs of the field, digested into flesh in them, or more remotely carnified in ourselves' [I, 37]. But if the cattle are the grass they have eaten, and consequently when we digest our meat it is grass that nourishes us, by a similar reasoning (carried on with obvious relish) we are cannibals. If the cow is the grass she eats, so is man: but if creatures are what they eat, it follows that they eat what they are, and so:

> We are what wee all abhorre, *Anthropophagi* and Cannibals, devourers not onely of men, but of our selves; and that not in an allegory, but a positive truth; for all this masse of flesh that wee behold, came in at our mouths; this frame wee looke upon, hath beene upon our trenchers; In briefe, we have devoured our selves, and yet doe live and remayne our selves [I, 37].

This is a joke Hamlet would have enjoyed; nor is this the only passage of *Religio Medici* that brings that play to mind; Browne could have seen or read it; more certainly his mind worked on words and their consequences in a Jacobean way. Metamorphosis from grass into flesh leads him on to traditional stories of metamorphoses. Except for the scriptural translation of Lot's wife into a pillar of salt (and even concerning this he has reservations which, in *Pseudodoxia*, become more explicit) he thinks that none of these is literally true. Nor can he suppose that so wise an author as Pythagoras believed literally in metempsychosis. It is incredible, because man has an immortal soul, which cannot reside in an animal. The body is comic—mere perishable stuff: he writes of the soul in a different style, gravely stating his *credo* 'that the soules of men know neither contrary nor corruption; that they subsist beyond the body, and outlive death by the privilege of their proper natures, and without a miracle; that the soules of the faithfull, as they leave earth take possession of Heaven' [I, 37]. This goes a little beyond orthodox teaching, either Protestant or Catholic; only the souls of martyrs went immediately to Heaven; others waited until the Day of Judgment; the wicked more miserable and the good happier than while on earth, but not as yet in the presence of God.[1] But what Browne is most concerned to say is that Ghosts are not the souls of the dead. Here again he

[1] My authority is an article in the *Encyclopedia of Religious Knowledge* (1905), by C. A. Beckwith.

could have been prompted by memories of *Hamlet*. His creed goes on:

that those apparitions and ghosts of departed persons are not the wandring soules of men, but the unquiet walkes of Devils, prompting and suggesting us unto mischiefe, bloud and villany, instilling, and stealing into our hearts, that the blessed Spirits are not at rest in their graves, but wander solicitous of the affaires of the world; that these phantasmes appeare often, and doe frequent Cemiteries, charnall houses, and Churches, it is because these are the dormitories of the dead, where the Devill like an insolent Champion beholds with pride the spoyles and Trophies of his victory in *Adam* [I, 37].

This leads on into seven sections about death.

Browne says he is not so closely bound to the world as to 'dote on life or be convulsed and tremble at the name of death', not because, as a doctor, he has seen it so often at close quarters as to have 'become stupid, or have forgot the apprehension of mortality, but that marshalling all the horrours, and contemplating the extremities thereof, I finde not anything therein able to daunt the courage of a man, much lesse a well resolved Christian' [I, 38]. He is not angry with our first parents for bringing death into the world; on the contrary:

When I take a full view and circle of my selfe, without this reasonable moderator, and equall piece of justice, Death, I doe conceive my selfe the miserablest person extant; were there not another life that I hope for, all the vanities of this world should not intreat a moments breath from me [*ibid.*].

This is not, as we shall presently see, because he thinks of his own particular lot in life as unfortunate; but because he has

so abject a conceit of this common way of existence, this retaining to the Sunne and Elements, I cannot thinke this is to be a man, or to live according to the dignitie of humanity; in expectation of a better, I can with patience embrace this life, yet in my best meditations doe often desire death.

After demonstrating, in sect. 37, the absurdity of the flesh, here, in 38, he welcomes death as the release from it. 'For a Pagan there may bee motives to bee in love with life; but for a Christian that is amazed at death, I see not how hee can escape this Dilemma, that he is too sensible of this life, or hopelesse of the life to come.'

In sect. 39 Browne elaborates his interpretation of man as the microcosm which he adumbrated in sect. 33; here it completes what he wants to say about death as our fulfilment. In the womb we live without access to the objects of sense and reason: 'entering afterwards upon the scene of the world, wee arise up and become another creature', but we are still incomplete: 'till we have once more cast our secondine, that is, this slough of flesh, and are delivered into the last world, that ineffable place of *Paul*, that proper *ubi* of spirits'. He likens this to 'Those strange and mysticall transmigrations that I have observed in Silkewormes'.

But, although he is prepared to welcome his own transmigration to the world of spirit he confesses to what is, he thinks, an idiosyncratic reluctance concerning the circumstances of death: 'I am not so much afraid of death, as ashamed thereof' [I, 40]. These circumstances (of which Jeremy Taylor writes so vividly in the famous passage in *Holy Dying* 'For so I have seen a rose...' [cap I, ii]) make wife, children, friends afraid to be in the room with us, and birds and animals become bold enough to prey on us. He has sometimes therefore been 'willing to be swallowed in the abysse of waters, wherein I had perished, unseene, unpityed, without wondring eyes, teares of pity, Lectures of mortality, and none had said, *quantum mutatus ab illo!*' And then, with pardonable pride, he guards himself against unjust surmises. He is not ashamed to be seen dead because of any special deformity, either congenital or brought upon himself, 'whereby I might not call my selfe as wholesome a morsell for the wormes as any' [I, 40].

Section 41 introduces a theme to which he will return in *Urne-Buriall*, the futility of hoping to survive on this earth, either in our descendants or by virtue of tombs and monuments. He tells us his present age: 'as yet I have not seene one revolution of *Saturne*, nor hath my pulse beate thirty yeares'—yet he has been contemporary with three Emperors, four Grand Signiors, and as many

Popes—'me thinkes I have outlived my selfe, and begin to bee weary of the sunne'. Macbeth used the same words with considerably more reason; the section closes in a similar vein, with words that suggest a Jacobean tragic hero: 'I perceive I doe Anticipate the vices of age, the world to mee is but a dreame or mockshow, and wee all therein but Pantalones and Antickes to my severer contemplations.' Sir Kenelm Digby took exception to such autobiographical revelations: 'What should I say of his making so particular narration of personal things, and private thoughts of his own; the knowledge whereof cannot conduce to any man's betterment (which I make account is the chief end of his writing this discourse).' But that is an improbable conjecture. Sir Thomas wrote as an artist, not as a preacher, to discover his own thought, not to instruct others, and he wrote because he enjoyed the play of mind and the power of language to reveal it.

In the next section, 42, he develops his reasons for not desiring long life. Sins increase with age, and even if they do not increase in number or gravity, they grow ever less excusable: 'the maturity of our judgement cuts off pretence unto excuse or pardon'.

In section 43, still contemplating the span of life, he emphasizes how precarious life is: 'And truely there goes a great deale of providence to produce a mans life unto threescore.' Opening thus, the section closes:

> Our ends are as obscure as our beginnings; the line of our dayes is drawne by night, and the various effects therein by a pencill that is invisible; wherein though wee confesse our ignorance, I am sure wee doe not erre, if wee say, it is the hand of God.

For six sections his thought has circled around the fear of death; he has repudiated such fear and suggested rather that death is to be wished for. Now sect. 44 begins with:

> I am much taken with two verses of *Lucan*, since I have beene able not onely, as we doe at Schoole, to construe, but understand them:
>
> *Victurosque Dei celant, ut vivere durent,*
> *Felix esse mori.*

and he paraphrases:

> We're all deluded, vainely searching wayes
> To make us happy by the length of dayes;
> For cunningly to make's protract this breath,
> The Gods conceale the happines of Death.

It may be remembered how Browne was to write to his son Tom in February 1667 warning him against the doctrine of this Stoic who has 'noble straynes and such as may well affect generous minds' [Letter 17]. His own had been affected thirty years before: he tried then to counteract the Stoic philosophy, just as he does in the letter to Tom. It is a mistake 'so highly to extoll the end and suicide of Cato'[1] [I, 44]. It is, he says, sometimes braver to live than to die; Job was more courageous than 'Curtius, Scevola or Codrus',

> and sure there is no torture to the racke of a disease, nor any Poynyards in death it selfe like those in the way and prologue unto it.... Were I of *Caesar*'s Religion, I should be of his desires, and wish rather to goe off at one blow, then to be sawed in peeces by the grating torture of a disease.

From his knowledge as a physician he knows in how many ways our health is threatened: 'and considering the thousand dores that lead to death doe thanke my God that we can die but once'. It is a near-echo of the cry of Webster's Duchess of Malfi 'I know that death hath ten thousand severall doores for men to take their exits'. Did Browne, one wonders, read or see the plays of the last age? Whether or no, he certainly shared Webster's admiration for Stoic courage; as a Christian he condemns suicide; but he reminds his Christian reader that:

> though it be in the power of the weakest arme to take away life, it is not in the strongest to deprive us of death: God would not exempt himselfe from that, the misery of immortality in the flesh, he undertooke not that was in it immortall.

[1] The words 'and suicide' were added in 1643—they are not in the manuscripts or the pirated editions.

The close of the section barely evades the doctrine of Lucan's verse with which it opened: 'in his own sense, the Stoick is in the right. Hee forgets that hee can die who complaines of misery; wee are in the power of no calamitie while death is in our owne' [I, 44]. But in the next section his theme is the Judgment to come, with which he is occupied one way or another until the close of Part I.

One current of thought that has run through all his meditations upon death in the foregoing sections is the unimportance of the body. Consistent with this is his declaration:

Nor can I thinke I have the true Theory of death, when I contemplate a skull, or behold a Skeleton with those vulgar imaginations it casts upon us; I have therefore enlarged that common *Memento Mori*, into a more Christian memorandum, *Memento quatuor novissima*, those foure inevitable points of us all, Death, Judgement, Heaven and Hell [I, 45].

But what does he think about the end of the world and the expected Day of Judgment? First, he does not think the world is perishing by natural decay, although he believes its end is approaching. 'As the creation was a worke above nature, so is its adversary, annihilation; without which the world hath not its end, but its mutation.' In his own time God will annihilate the world he created. Nor does Browne believe that, literally, judicial proceedings will follow:

I cannot dreame there should be at the last day any such Judiciall proceeding, or calling to the Barre, as indeed the Scripture seemes to imply, and the literall commentators doe conceive: for unspeakable mysteries in the Scriptures are often delivered in a vulgar and illustrative way, and being written unto man, are delivered, not as they truely are, but as they may bee understood; wherein, notwithstanding, the different interpretations according to different capacities may stand firme with our devotion, nor bee any way prejudiciall to each single edification [I, 45].

It will have been noticed how often Browne emphasizes the allegorical element in the Scriptures.

Section 46 is eloquently and wittily occupied with making manifest the absurdity of all attempts to predict 'the day and yeare of this inevitable time'. In 47 he turns to the important moral question: does good behaviour depend upon belief in the Last Judgment? His reflections here are complex and close-knit; to extract a sentence here or there might be misleading. It seems better to quote this section in full:

> This is the day that must make good that great attribute of God, his Justice, that must reconcile those unanswerable doubts which torment the wisest understandings, and reduce those seeming inequalities and respective distributions in this world, to an equality and recompensive Justice in the next. This is that one day, that shall include and comprehend all that went before it, wherein as in the last scene, all Actors must enter, to compleate and make up the catastrophe of this great peece. This is the day whose memory hath onely power to make us honest in the darke, and to bee virtuous without a witnesse. *Ipsa sui pretium virtus sibi*, that virtue is her owne reward, is but a cold principle, and not able to maintaine our variable resolutions in a constant and setled way of goodnesse. I have practised that honest artifice of *Seneca*, and in my retired and solitary imaginations to detaine me from the foulenesse of vice, have fancyed to my selfe the presence of my deare and worthiest friends, before whom I should lose my head, rather than be vitious; yet herein I found that there was nought but morall honesty, and this was not to be vertuous for his sake that must reward us at the last. I have tryed if I could reach that great resolution of his and be honest without a thought of Heaven or Hell; and indeed I found upon a naturall inclination, and inbred loyalty unto virtue, that I could serve her without a livery, yet not in that resolved and venerable way, but that the frailty of my nature, upon an easie temptation, might be induced to forget her. The life therefore and spirit of all our actions is the resurrection, and stable apprehension, that our ashes shall enjoy the fruits of our pious endeavours; without this, all Religion is a Fallacy, and those impieties of *Lucian*, *Euripides* and *Julian* are no blasphemies, but subtile verities, and Atheists have been the onely Philosophers.

Not only are these Atheists, who so properly round off the sentence, incompatible with his assurance [I, 19] that none such ever existed, but under strict logical examination the paragraph reveals contradictions, or at least ambivalence. Only the memory that we shall be judged can make us 'honest in the darke'. Yet Browne has sometimes 'detained' himself from vice by imagining his friends could see him—he does not suggest that this was ineffective, but that it was 'doing the right thing for the wrong reason'. He has found that, because of his 'naturall inclination and inbred loyalty unto virtue' (meant quite literally as a tribute to his parents),[1] he is able to serve virtue without thought of reward or punishment, except when occasionally betrayed by frailty of his nature. All this does not lead with inevitable logic to the conclusion that 'the spirit of all our actions is the resurrection, etc.'. But in sect. 52 what he means will become clearer.

Meanwhile, for four sections, he postpones the moral question while he considers the resurrection of the body, the whereabouts of heaven and hell and the meaning of everlasting fire. At the opening of sect. 48 he declares that belief in the resurrection of the body is a matter of faith and to 'believe only in possibilities is not faith, but mere Philosophy'. Nevertheless, the whole section is written in his character of philosopher, or natural scientist; the theme of the whole work is, after all, the religion of a doctor. The study of nature strengthens, for him, the foundations of belief; the senses (observation and experiment) discover facts which mere reasoning could not have arrived at. Similarly, there are some religious truths which neither man's reason nor his sense-experience can reach. Natural phenomena present us with 'types' of our resurrection; for instance: 'I have often beheld (like a miracle) that artificiall resurrection and revivification of *Mercury*, how being mortified into a thousand shapes, it assumes againe its owne, and returns into its numericall selfe' [I, 48]. His second

[1] Compare *Christian Morals*, Part I, sect. 35: 'Bless not thyself only that thou wert born in Athens; but among thy multiplied acknowledgements lift up one hand to Heaven, that thou wert born of Honest Parents, that Modesty, Humility, Patience and Veracity lay in the same Egg, and came into the World with thee. From such foundations thou mayst be Happy in a Virtuous precocity and make an early and long walk in Goodness; so mayst thou more naturally feel the contrarie of Vice unto Nature and resist some by the Antidote of thy Temper.'

example will be less familiar, perhaps less convincing, to a modern reader, but was thought true natural history at the time and for at least thirty years after *Religio Medici* was published.

> A plant or vegetable consumed to ashes, to a contemplative and schoole Philosopher seemes utterly destroyed, and the forme to have taken his leave for ever: But to a sensible Artist [i.e. one who relies on the evidence of his senses] the formes are not perished, but withdrawne into their incombustible parts, where they lie secure from the action of that devouring element. This is made good by experience, which can from the ashes of a plant revivifie the plant, and from its cinders recall it into its stalk and leaves againe [*ibid.*].

On 3 November 1674 a detailed account of such an experiment was sent to the Royal Society by a Dr Daniel Cox. (The record can be found in vol. 9, p. 174 of the *Transactions of the Royal Society*.) Dr Cox begins: 'Having procured a quantity of Fern Ashes, I extracted their salt', and concludes, after describing the experiment in detail:

> And there did arise out of the whole mass of Salt, at a small distance from each other, several, I believe 40, branches, which, abating the colour, did most exactly resemble that sort of *Ferne* which is single like *Polypody*, and not branched, sending out several leaves on each side.... I preserved these Artificial, regenerated or resuscitated Vegetables many weeks in the same position, not moving them, they being of so tender a fabrick, that the least motion of the Glas did hazard their disappearance.

Unfortunately, when he tried to bring them to London to exhibit to the Society, 'these pretty appearances were resolved into the confused Chaos out of which they were educed'.

Browne closes sect. 48, in homage to his own studies as well as to God:

> What the Art of man can doe in these inferiour pieces, what blasphemy is it to affirme the finger of God cannot doe in these more perfect and sensible structures? This is that mysticall Philosophy, from whence no true Scholler becomes an Atheist, but from the visible effects of nature growes up a reall Divine, and beholds not in a dreame, as *Ezekiel*, but in an ocular and visible object the types of his resurrection.

Perhaps Browne believed that the resurrected plants were more solid and enduring than the 'pretty appearances' described by Dr Cox.

In sections 49, 50 and 51 Browne contemplates and dismisses notions of Heaven as a material place and of Hell as material flames:

where the soule hath the full measure and complement of happinesse, where the boundlesse appetite of that spirit remains compleately satisfied, that it cannot desire either addition or alteration; that I thinke is truely Heaven: and this can onely be in the enjoyment of that essence, whose infinite goodnesse is able to terminate the desires of it selfe, and the insatiable wishes of ours; wherever God will thus manifest himselfe, there is Heaven, though within the circle of this sensible world [I, 49].

In the next section he discourses upon the nature of fire and what it can and cannot consume in this 'sensible' world, which leads him, in orderly sequence of thought, to the opening of sect. 51: 'Men commonly set forth the tortures of Hell by fire, and the extremity of corporall afflictions, and describe Hell in the same manner as *Mahomet* doth Heaven.' But Hell, like Heaven, is a state of the soul:

The heart of man is the place the devill dwels in; I feele somtimes a hell within my selfe, *Lucifer* keeps his court in my brest, *Legion* is revived in me....And thus a distracted conscience here is a shadow or introduction unto hell hereafter.

Section 52 returns to the relation between virtuous living and the prospect of Heaven. To a careless reader (as once I was myself) it seems to contradict some of the ideas in sect. 47. Again, it would be misleading and disfiguring to disturb the sequence by quoting parts of the section; it is brief and I will quote it entire:

I thanke God, and with joy I mention it, I was never afraid of Hell, nor never grew pale at the description of that place; I have so fixed my contemplations on Heaven, that I have almost forgot the Idea of Hell; I am afraid rather to lose the joyes of the one than endure the misery of the other; to be deprived of them is a perfect hell, and needs me thinkes no addition to compleate our afflictions; that terrible terme hath never detained me from sin, nor do I owe one good action to the name thereof: I feare God, yet am not afraid of him; his mercies make me ashamed of my sins, before his judgements afraid thereof: these are the forced and secondary method of his wisedome, which he useth not but as the last remedy, and upon provocation, a course rather to deterre the wicked, than incite the virtuous to his worship. I can hardly thinke there was ever any scared into Heaven; they go the surest way to Heaven who would serve God without a Hell; other Mercenaries, that crouch unto him in feare of Hell, though they terme themselves servants, are indeed but the slaves of the Almighty [I, 52].

This is more lucid, homogeneous and succinct than sect. 47, but it is nowhere inconsistent with it. When he writes in the earlier section that the Judgment Day makes us honest in the dark, it is the hope of remaining in the presence of God for ever that produces this effect. Nothing is said about fear, the emphasis is, as in sect. 52, on hope and 'the stable apprehension that our ashes shall enjoy the fruits of our pious endeavours' [I, 47].

In sect. 53 Browne states, in his characteristically intricate and elaborate way, the Christian view that our preservation in this life and salvation in the life to come are entirely due to the mercy of God; he reaches the conclusion that:

Our offences being mortall, and deserving not onely death, but damnation, if the goodnesse of God be content to traverse and passe them over with a losse, misfortune or disease, what frenzie were it to terme this a punishment, rather than an extremity of mercy, and to groane under the rod of his judgements, rather than admire the Scepter of his mercies?

He closes this section with what I cannot but think is a reversal of the idea informing sect. 47. Here it is neither the hope of Heaven nor the fear of Hell that motivates his devotion to God and therefore, presumably, his endeavour to conform to God's will:

That I obtaine Heaven, or the blisse thereof, is accidentall, and not the intended worke of my devotion, it being a felicitie I can neither thinke to deserve, nor scarse in modesty expect. For these two ends of us all, either as rewards or punishments, are mercifully ordained, and disproportionally disposed unto our actions; the one being so far beyond our deserts, the other so infinitely below our demerits.

Here he discovers that his devotion is motivated solely by the love of God and would continue even if he knew himself predestined either to be admitted into God's presence or to be excluded from it. But implicitly here, and explicitly in sect. 59, it is clear that Browne is confident of his own salvation.

He is puzzled, however, by what the Church teaches concerning those who are not believers:

> There is no salvation to those that beleeve not in Christ, that is, say some, since his Nativity, and as Divinity affirmeth, before also; which makes me much apprehend the end of those honest Worthies and Philosophers which dyed before his Incarnation. It is hard to place those soules in Hell whose worthy lives doe teach us vertue on earth; methinks, amongst those many subdivisions of hell, there might have bin one Limbo left for these [I, 54].

But though puzzled, and reluctant to accept the teaching of theology on this matter, Browne continues to do so, and even to support it with an argument. (He makes partial amends for this in *Urne-Buriall.*) What he has already said of Hell indicates that he does not think of it as a place, or as a punishment, but as a deprivation: the heathen, like the animals, will not live for ever in the presence of God:

> Men that live according to the right rule and law of reason, live but in their owne kinde, as beasts doe in theirs; who justly obey the prescript of their natures, and therefore cannot reasonably demand a reward of their actions, as onely obeying the natural dictates of their reason. It will therefore, and must at last appeare, that all salvation is through Christ; which verily, I feare, these great examples of vertue must confirme, and make it good, how the perfectest actions of earth have no title or claime unto Heaven [I, 54].

Sir Kenelm Digby and Alexander Ross are at opposite poles in their comments on this passage. Digby, though emphasizing that to follow reason is difficult and rare, is sure that those who do will reach Heaven: 'Truly (my Lord) I make no doubt at all, but if any followed in the whole *tenor* of their lives the dictamens of right reason, but that their Journey was more secure to *Heaven*.'[1] Ross, on the other hand, is gloatingly sure that none but believers can escape punishment:

> How specious soever their lives and actions were in the eyes of men, yet without *Christ* they were nothing else but *splendide peccata*, glorious enormities: onely in this can I solace them, that it will be easier for them, (as it will be for *Sodome* and *Gomorrha*, for *Tyre* and *Sidon*) in the last day, then for *Jews* and *Christians* who have known their Master's will, and have not done it: Fewer stripes remain for *Socrates*, a Heathen, then for *Julian*, a Christian.[2]

The tone of this is of course utterly unlike anything Browne wrote or could have written. Browne solaces himself with the obvious escape from the moral dilemma concerning the virtuous heathen; their practice can seldom have conformed to their precepts. Milton follows the same course in *Paradise Regained*, Book IV, 303–8.

In sect. 55 Browne begins:

> Nor truely doe I thinke the lives of these or any other were ever correspondent, or in all points conformable unto their doctrines; it is evident that *Aristotle* trangressed the rule of his owne *Ethicks*; the Stoicks that condemne all passion, and command a man to laugh in *Phalaris* his Bull, could not endure without a groane a fit of the stone or collick. The *Scepticks* that affirmed they knew nothing, even in that opinion confuted themselves, and thought they knew more than all the world beside. *Diogenes* I hold to bee the most vaineglorious man of his time, and more ambitious in refusing all Honours, than *Alexander* in rejecting none.

The theme of this section is the complexity and unattainableness of pure virtue; nothing is said in it about the Christian's exclusive access to divine grace:

> There is no road or ready way to vertue, it is not an easie point of art to untangle our selves from this riddle and web of sin.... And indeed wiser discretions that have the thred of reason to conduct them, offend without a pardon; whereas under heads may stumble without dishonour.

[1] *Observations*, p. 71.
[2] Ross, *Medicus Medicatus*, p. 62.

This justifies demanding much of the Greek philosophers, but Browne does not suggest that well-endowed Christians find virtue any more attainable.

In briefe, we are all monsters, that is, a composition of man and beast, wherein we must endeavour to be as the Poets faigne that wise man *Chiron*, that is, to have the Region of Man above that of Beast, and sense to sit but at the feete of reason. Lastly, I doe desire with God that all, but yet affirme with men that very few, shall know salvation; that the bridge is narrow, the passage straite unto life; yet those who doe confine the Church of God, either to particular Nations, Churches, or Families, have made it farre narrower than our Saviour ever meant it [I, 55].

The next section, 56, did not exist in any of the manuscripts nor in the editions of 1642; Browne added it when he revised for the authorized edition of 1643. It is wholly occupied with the folly of mutual intolerance among Christians and concludes:

'Tis true we all hold there is a number of Elect, and many to be saved, yet, take our opinions together, and from the confusion thereof there will be no such thing as salvation, nor shall any one be saved; for first the Church of *Rome* condemneth us, wee likewise them, the Sub-reformists and Sectaries sentence the Doctrine of our Church as damnable, the Atomist, or Familist reprobates all these, and all these them againe. Thus, while the mercies of God do promise us heaven, our conceits and opinions exclude us from that place. There must be therefore more than one Saint *Peter*; particular Churches and Sects usurpe the gates of heaven, and turne the key against each other, and thus we goe to heaven against each others wills, conceits and opinions, and with as much uncharity as ignorance, doe erre I feare in points not onely of our own, but one anothers salvation [I, 56].

This does not represent any change of mind since the composition of the work in 1635; the section formerly following upon 55 (now sect. 57) opens in the same sense: 'I believe many are saved who to man seeme reprobated, and many reprobated, who, in the opinion and sentence of man, stand elected.' But the new section, explicitly attacking mutual exclusiveness and sectarian arrogance, was probably prompted by the increased animosities of the Civil War.

No one knows who will be saved; to guess at this is beyond the power of men or even of devils: 'those acute and subtill spirits, in all their sagacity, can hardly divine who shall be saved; which if they could prognostick, their labour were at an end; nor need they compasse the earthe seeking whom they may devoure'. This is the substance of sect. 57. God will save whom he pleases: 'by the letter and written law of God, we are without exception in the state of death, but there is a prerogative of God, and an arbitrary pleasure above the letter of his owne law, by which wee can alone pretend unto salvation...'.

Browne discloses, in sect. 58, that he is amazed to find how many confidently expect to be saved; yet he does not disguise the fact that he is among them:

The number of those who pretend unto salvation, and those infinite swarmes who thinke to passe through the eye of this Needle, hath much amazed me. That name and compellation of *little Flocke*, doth not comfort but deject my devotion, especially when I reflect upon mine owne unworthinesse, wherein, according to my humble apprehensions, I am below them all. I beleeve there shall never be an Anarchy in Heaven; but as there are Hierarchies amongst the Angels, so shall there be degrees of priority amongst the Saints. Yet is it, (I protest) beyond my ambition to aspire unto the first rankes, my desires onely are, and I shall be happy therein, to be but the last man, and bring up the Rere in Heaven [I, 58].

This is a flight of fancy expressing both humility and, I think, serene confidence; in the next section he states explicitly his belief that he will be among the saved, not this time in his lyrical style, fancifully communicating what he feels or prefers, but by employing logic and wit.

Againe, I am confident and fully perswaded, yet dare not take my oath of my salvation; I am as it were sure, and do beleeve, without all doubt, that there is such a City as *Constantinople*, yet for me to take my Oath thereon it were a kinde of perjury, because I hold no infallible warrant from my owne sense to confirme me in the certainty thereof.

This is the same line of argument as Newman was to use in his *Grammar of Assent*; we are certain of much that we cannot prove.

This section closes in Browne's 'metaphysical' style, in a high-spirited flourish of imaginative wit:

That which is the cause of my election, I hold to be the cause of my salvation, which was the mercy and beneplacit of God, before I was, or the foundation of the world. *Before Abraham was, I am*, is the saying of Christ, yet is it true in some sense if I say it of my selfe, for I was not onely before my selfe, but *Adam*, that is, in the Idea of God, and the decree of that Synod held from all Eternity. And in this sense, I say, the world was before the Creation, and at an end before it had a beginning; and thus I was dead before I was alive; though my grave be *England*, my dying place was Paradise, and *Eve* miscarried of mee before she conceived of *Cain* [I, 59].

The last phrases of the last sentence, from 'and thus I was dead' to 'before she conceived of *Cain*', were added in 1643. It is a characteristic, exuberant paradox, but perfectly lucid and logical. Since Browne and his total destiny existed in the mind of God before time was, he existed in the womb of Eve; by punning on the word miscarry he reaches his surprise conclusion, Eve brought him into the world stained with Original Sin. In this sense he was misbegotten.

But Browne was not merely giving rein to imagination and wit in sect. 59; he not only knew what he was saying but also where that line of thought led to and how far along it he was prepared to follow. He will not go as far as the logic of Calvin or of Jansen might drive him. Therefore he begins sect. 60 with:

Insolent zeales, that doe decry good workes and rely onely upon faith, take not away merits: for depending upon the efficacy of their faith, they enforce the condition of God, and in a more sophisticall way doe seeme to challenge Heaven.

It is obvious that he is now riding his Pegasus on the curb. The prose is stiff and comparatively clumsy; he wants to make a precise distinction. If we are predestined to salvation (as he believes he is), 'insolent zeales' may say that good works are irrelevant, faith is enough. Browne does not suppose so. His way out is to question whether anyone's faith is in fact sufficient.

There are scriptural illustrations of the truth that salvation is not the result of good works but of God's will: 'It was decreed by God, that onely those who lapt in the water like dogges, should have the honour to destroy the Midianites, yet could none of these challenge, or imagine hee deserved that honour thereupon.' Similarly, none can imagine that they deserve salvation by their works; Browne does not stop to explain the analogy, he goes straight on: 'I doe not deny but that true faith, and such as God requires, is not onely a mark or token, but also a meanes of our Salvation, but where to finde this, is as obscure to me, as my last end.' If even the disciples had not that faith which 'to the quantity of a graine of Mustard seed, is able to remove mountaines; surely, that which wee boast of, is not any thing, or at the most, but a remove from nothing'. By doubting whether any man can rely on the adequacy of his own faith, Browne—I believe within the framework of orthodoxy—rescues 'good workes', not as the means, but as the evidence of salvation. He has completed what he wanted to say about his faith and he brings Part I to a close with: 'This is the Tenor of my beleefe, wherein, though there be many things singular, and to the humour of my irregular selfe, yet, if they square not with maturer Judgements, I disclaime them, and doe no further father them, than the learned and best Judgements shall authorise them' [I, 60].

Milton would have been shocked by the expressed willingness to retract. But then Milton did not recognize that 'a man may be in as just possession of Truth as of a City, and yet be forced to surrender'. He believed that men could be convinced, and truth established, by reasoning; Browne was more sceptical. Milton was eager to engage in controversy and ready to extend toleration so that all should have the right to argue their case. Browne had the same wish for toleration, but little faith in the effectiveness of argument; therefore, sure of his own beliefs, he evaded intellectual combat.

CHAPTER IV

'RELIGIO MEDICI' (PART II)

IN Part I of *Religio Medici* Browne's central theme is his religious belief. It is a work which could only have been written by this one man at this one time; highly individual and characteristic, it also reveals a conception of the world and of the cosmos impregnated with classical and medieval ideas, modified by notions coming to birth in the seventeenth century. A part of the attraction of all Browne's writings is this combination, a markedly individual mind and style vividly expressing the thought of a particular time. In Part II the central theme is Christian Charity; it begins: 'Now for that other Vertue of Charity, without which Faith is a meer notion, and of no existence, I have ever endeavoured to nourish the mercifull disposition, and humane inclination I borrowed from my Parents....' He expands what he has already said in Part I about his temperamental tolerance, applying it now not to beliefs and modes of worship, but to tastes and sympathies:

I have no antipathy, or rather Idiosyncrasie, in dyet, humour, ayre, any thing; I wonder not at the *French* for their dishes of frogges, snailes, and toadstooles, nor at the Jewes for Locusts and Grasse-hoppers, but being amongst them, make them my common viands; and I finde they agree with my stomach as well as theirs; I could digest a Sallad gathered in a Church-yard, as well as in a Garden. I cannot start at the presence of a Serpent, Scorpion, Lizard, or Salamander; at the sight of a Toad or Viper, I feele in me no desire to take up a stone to destroy them.

In short, he has a natural aversion to nothing except the Devil, and is contemptuous of nothing, except a crowd:

If there be any among those common objects of hatred which I can safely say I doe contemne and laugh at, it is that great enemy of reason, vertue and religion, the multitude; that numerous piece of monstrosity, which taken asunder seeme men, and the reasonable creatures of God; but confused together, make but one great beast, and a monstrosity

> more prodigious than Hydra; it is no breach of Charity to call these fooles, it is the stile all holy Writers have afforded them, set down by *Solomon* in canonicall Scripture, and a point of our faith to beleeve so.

Browne guards himself against being taken to mean by the multitude any particular class of men; he closes the section with a discourse as nearly political as any in his writings; the pith of it is contained in one sentence:

> Neither in the name of Multitude doe I onely include the base and minor sort of people; there is a rabble even amongst the Gentry, a sort of Plebeian heads, whose fancy moves with the same wheele as these; men in the same Levell with Mechanickes, though their fortunes doe somewhat guild their infirmities, and their purses compound for their follies [II, I].

He goes on to say that just as three or four men together are inferior to one man alone, so a troop of such grandees as he has described are of less value than 'many a forlorne person, whose condition doth place them below their feet'. In 'primitive Common-wealths' men were ranked only according to their deserts, but now men can become powerful by getting rich and, since acquisition of wealth is not the aim of the wise, place and power are likely to be enjoyed by those with 'ruder desires'.

In this first section Browne has wandered from his own native catholicity of tastei nto a *quasi*-political discourse. At the opening of the second section he returns to Christian charity and his own propensities and practices with regard to it. Midway in the section he divagates into philosophical speculation. The weave of his thought is less close-knit in the fifteen sections of Part II than in the sixty of Part I; it seems likely that the whole of Part II was an afterthought, a garnering of the many thoughts about his own Christianity which had not found their way into Part I. It is usually possible, even here, to perceive some continuity in his ideas, but it is even less possible than in Part I to foresee into what paths they will lead him. At the centre there is the theme of Christian charity in relation to his own temperament and to this he always returns; but from this centre his thoughts radiate to the circumference of a circle which embraces his conception of the world.

Section 2 begins, then, at the centre; he recognizes that this 'generall and indifferent temper of mine' predisposes him to charity and that in this he is fortunate: 'It is a happinesse to be borne and framed unto vertue, and to grow up from the seeds of nature, rather than the inoculation and forced grafts of education.' But to be charitable because one feels like it is not enough; it is mere self-pleasing:

Therefore this great worke of charity must have other motives, ends, and impulses: I give no almes[1] to satisfie the hunger of my Brother, but to fulfill and accomplish the Will and Command of my God; I draw not my purse for his sake that demands it, but his that enjoyned it; I relieve no man upon the Rhetorick of his miseries, nor to content mine own commiserating disposition, for this is still but morall charity, and an act that oweth more to passion than reason [II, 2].

If benevolence to satisfy a kindly impulse is not Christian charity, neither will it serve to be charitable because we may some day be in need: 'For this is a sinister and Politick kind of charitie.' Doubtless it is logical and orthodox to dismiss all other motives than the love of God; but it is hard to reconcile such a cool consideration before acting with the nature Browne has told us he inherits. There is a contradiction between the two of which perhaps Browne became conscious, for he breaks off here and changes direction, tacking back to his starting-point with:

and truely I have observed that these professed Eleemosynaries, though in a croud or multitude, doe yet direct and place their petitions on a few and selected persons; there is surely a Physiognomy, which these experienced and Master Mendicants observe, whereby they instantly discover a mercifull aspect, and will single out a face wherein they spy the signatures and markes of mercy: for there are mystically in our faces certaine characters which carry in them the motto of our Soules, wherein he that cannot read A.B.C. may read our natures.

[1] Not till 1678 did he intercalate the word 'only' between 'almes' and 'to satisfie'.

With this Browne escapes from a somewhat arid discussion of motives, recollects that some men are naturally—even visibly—benevolent, and opens up the kind of speculation that he always finds alluring:

The finger of God hath set an inscription upon all his workes, not graphicall or composed of Letters, but of their severall formes, constitutions, parts, and operations, which aptly joyned together make one word that doth expresse their natures. By these Letters God cals the Starres by their names, and by this Alphabet *Adam* assigned to every creature a name peculiar to its Nature.

He points here to species rather than to individuals, but returns at once to the human face and the imprint of character upon it; then he recalls that it is not only faces, but hands too that have such hall-marks:

Now there are, besides these Characters in our faces, certaine mysticall lines and figures in our hands, which I dare not call meere dashes or strokes *à la volée*, or at randome, because delineated by a pencill, that never workes in vaine....

Perhaps then, although Aristotle 'in his acute and singular booke of Physiognomy' makes no mention of chiromancy, the Egyptians who 'were neerer addicted to those abstruse and mysticall sciences' had some knowledge of fortune-telling by the hand 'to which those vagabond and counterfeit *Egyptians* did after pretend, and perhaps retained a few corrupted principles, which sometimes might verifie their prognostickes' [II, 2]. Thus, in a paragraph, Browne has travelled from the proper motives for almsgiving to the fortune-telling gypsies. In a second paragraph of the same section he returns to human faces, noting their infinite variety and concluding with an elaborated truism:

There is never any thing so like another, as in all points to concurre; there will ever some reserved difference slip in, to prevent the Identity, without which, two severall things would not be alike, but the same, which is impossible [II, 2].

Never in Part I did Browne come so near to losing the thread. He is aware that he has digressed, and sect. 3 opens with an explicit return to the centre: 'But to returne from Philosophy to Charity....' Almsgiving, he reminds us, is a minor part of charity and in this section he is occupied with another part, the generosity that is peculiarly appropriate to the learned: dissemination of knowledge:

I cannot contemn a man for ignorance, but behold him with as much pity as I doe *Lazarus*. It is no greater Charity to cloath his body, than apparell the nakednesse of his Soule. It is an honourable object to see the reasons of other men weare our Liveries, and their borrowed understandings doe homage to the bounty of ours. It is the cheapest way of beneficence, and, like the naturall charity of the Sunne, illuminates another without obscuring it selfe.

This line of thought eventually leads Browne to the topic that attracts him in both parts of *Religio Medici*: the folly of being angry over a difference of opinion:

I cannot fall out or contemne a man for an errour, or conceive why a difference in opinion should divide an affection: for controversies, disputes, and argumentations, both in Philosophy, and Divinity, if they meete with discreet and peaceable natures, doe not infringe the Lawes of Charity. In all disputes, so much as there is of passion, so much there is of nothing to the purpose; for then reason, like a bad hound, spends upon a false scent, and forsakes the question first started.

Such serene discussion as Browne advocates is rare at any time; when he published his work (though not when he first composed it) men were fighting a Civil War, spurred to it, in part at any rate, by differing opinions. There was to be religious persecution for many years to come. But he asserts, here as in Part I, that the disputed questions are not important:

The Foundations of Religion are already established, and the principles of Salvation subscribed unto by all, there remaine not many controversies worth a passion, and yet never any disputed without, not onely in Divinity, but inferiour Arts.

Jeremy Taylor's *Liberty of Prophesying* (1647), based a persuasive plea for religious toleration on the same assurance as Browne's, that the controversial points were unimportant: 'all that is necessary is plain' [sect. x, 4] was the pith of his argument. But though Browne was not alone in his opinion, the majority were against him and enraged controversy continued. We still meet it in the nineteenth century and although today public discussion of religious differences is, I believe, polite, anger often intrudes in discussion of 'inferior arts', although, as Browne says:

> Schollers are men of peace, they beare no armes, but their tongues are sharper than *Actius* his razor, their pens carry farther, and give a louder report than thunder; I had rather stand the shock of a *Basilisco*, than the fury of a mercilesse Pen.

Nothing dates this except the elegant euphuism of the style. It is in fear of such bitter power, Browne says, that 'Princes Patron the Arts, and carry an indulgent aspect unto Schollers'. Their posthumous reputation depends upon these men who will speak the epilogue 'when they have played their parts, and had their *exits*'. It is a part of a scholar's charity to speak justly of them. Browne doesn't suggest that he ought to be charitable at the expense of truth, but:

> there goes a great deale of conscience to the compiling of an History, there is no reproach to the scandall of a Story; it is such an Authenticke kinde of falsehood that with authority belies our good names to all Nations and Posteritie [II, 3].

Throughout sect. 3 Browne has been occupied with the aspects of charity most appropriate to scholars. One might not have guessed that from the duty to impart knowledge he would arrive at the duty to write true histories of dead princes; or that he would reach this point by way of condemning hot-tempered controversialists. Yet, in the context, the transitions flow smoothly. Section 4 is more complex but not less continuous; the whole is a sermon on the text 'Judge not'. He begins by attacking sweeping condemnations and caricatures of, for instance, whole professions, trades or nations. Equally absurd is it, he says, 'to miscall and rave against the times'. We should not expect virtue to be widespread at any time, ''tis the priviledge of a few to be vertuous'. And we should not attempt to destroy vice, because virtue cannot exist without it:

> They that endeavour to abolish vice destroy also vertue, for contraries, though they destroy one another, are yet the life of one another. Thus vertue (abolish vice) is an Idea; againe, the communitie of sinne doth not disparage goodnesse; for when vice gains upon the major part, vertue, in whom it remaines, becomes more excellent; and being lost in some, multiplies its goodnesse in others which remaine untouched, and persists intire in the generall inundation.

Here Browne's theme is similar to Milton's in the *Areopagitica* (published only a year after the authorized edition of *Religio Medici*). Set beside Milton's superb passage beginning 'Good and evill we know in the field of this World grow up together almost inseparably...' Browne's sentences seem congested and obscure. Both writers sometimes falter in their command of prose and often, as Browne does here, overload their sentences with abstract ideas: each avoids this danger again and again by translating the idea into a concrete image as Milton does, half-way through his sentence:

> and the knowledge of good is so involv'd and interwoven with the knowledge of evill, and in so many cunning resemblances hardly to be discern'd, that those confused seeds which were impos'd on *Psyche* as an incessant labour to cull out, and sort asunder, were not more intermixt.

Browne's idea is not precisely the same; Milton's relates to his argument for free publication and therefore concerns *knowledge* of good and evil. Browne's argument is that we should not rail at the times and condemn communities because vice is common or prevalent. He reaches towards an analogy with Noah and the flood but leaves it merely adumbrated in the last words of the sentence: 'and persists intire in the generall inundation'.

Another reason Browne gives for not railing at vice is that: 'Noble natures and such as are capable of goodnesse, are railed into vice, that might as easily bee admonished into vertue....' So far Browne has been attacking wholesale condemnations; now, at about the middle of the section, he reaches a deeper insight by means, as often, of reference to his own experience:

No man can justly censure or condemne another, because indeed no man truely knowes another. This I perceive in my selfe, for I am in the darke to all the world, and my nearest friends behold mee but in a cloud; those that know mee superficially, thinke lesse of me than I doe of my selfe; those of my neere acquaintance thinke more; God, who knowes mee truely, knowes that I am nothing, for hee onely beholds me, and all the world, who lookes not on us through a derived ray, or a trajection of sensible species, but beholds the substance without the helpe of accidents, and the forme of things as wee their operations.

We can neither know ourselves, nor be known by other people; God alone sees through the world of appearance to the underlying reality, 'the forme'. Our adverse judgments of others, Browne deduces, can only be the expressions of self-love:

We censure others but as they disagree from that humour which wee fancy laudable in our selves, and commend them but for that wherein they seeme to quadrate and consent with us. So that in conclusion, all is but what we all condemne, selfe-love.

It is a general complaint against the times, he says, 'that charitie growes cold; which I perceive most verified in those which most doe manifest the fires and flames of zeale; for it is a vertue that best agrees with coldest natures'; the paradox points to a recognizable truth and need not, he suggests, surprise us, for 'how shall we expect charity towards others, when we are all uncharitable to ourselves?' Up to this point he has held to the theme of the section 'thou shalt not judge'; but our lack of charity to ourselves includes other things besides self-immolation. It is the physician rather than the moralist who invents the closing paradoxes:

Charity begins at home, is the voyce of the world, yet is every man his greatest enemy, and, as it were, his owne executioner. *Non occides*, is the

Commandment of God, yet scarse observed by any man; for I perceive everyman is his owne *Atropos*, and lends a hand to cut the thred of his own dayes.

From this it is but a step to declare that Adam, not Cain, was the first murderer:

Cain was not therefore the first murtherer, but *Adam*, who brought in death; whereof hee beheld the practise onely and example in his owne sonne *Abel*, and saw that verified in the experience of another, which faith could not perswade him in the Theory of himselfe [II, 4].

If Adam had not sinned we should not all be furthering our own deaths: there would have been neither vice nor death in the world; but then, as Browne has already said, neither would there have been any virtue.

Section 5 begins: 'There is I thinke no man that apprehends his owne miseries lesse than my selfe, and no man that so neerely apprehends anothers.' It is not at first obvious how this and what follows arise out of the closing idea of sect. 4. Nevertheless, there is a discernible continuity of thought. He has been rejecting the generalization that, nowadays, charity is cold; he found it only true among zealots. Now he tests the generalization by his personal experience; his own impulse to charity is overwhelming because the suffering of others disturbs him more than his own; this he states in an hyperbole:

I could lose an arme without a teare, and with a few groans, mee thinkes, be quartered into pieces; yet I can weepe most seriously at a Play, and receive with a true passion, the counterfeit griefes of those knowne and professed impostours.

(He was thus properly constituted to enjoy the theatre, and that he did so is confirmed by his echoes of Jacobean dramatists and by his use of stage metaphors.) The theme of this section is love between friends, which he illustrates from his own experience and finally relates to the love of God. His own experience of friendship, he tells us, has made him accept such heroic exemplars of it as '*Damon and Pythias, Achilles and Patroclus*' which once he thought were 'not so truely Histories of what had beene, as fictions of what should be'. But now they seem to him perfectly possible:

That a man should lay down his life for his friend, seemes strange to vulgar affections, and such as confine themselves within that worldly principle, Charity beginnes at home. For mine owne part I could never remember the relations I hold unto my selfe, nor the respect I owe unto mine owne nature, in the cause of God, my Country, and my Friends. Next to these three, I doe embrace my selfe; I confesse I doe not observe that order that the Schooles ordaine our affections, to love our Parents, Wives, Children and then our friends; for excepting the injunctions of Religion, I doe not finde in my selfe such a necessary and indissoluble Sympathy to all those of my bloud.

Browne was married a year before he prepared *Religio Medici* for the press, but when he composed the work in 1635 he had experienced impassioned love for his friends only. This he states, altering nothing of the substance of his work in revision; the text reads straight on:

I hope I doe not breake the fifth Commandment, if I conceive I may love my friend before the nearest of my bloud, even those to whom I owe the principles of life; I never yet cast a true affection upon a Woman, but I have loved my Friend as I do vertue, and as I do my soule, my God. From hence me thinkes I do conceive how God loves man, what happinesse there is in the love of God.

Professor Endicott, in the article previously referred to (p. 4), deduces from all this that Browne's relations with his mother and his stepfather were not good; he writes: 'It seems safe to say that he would never have phrased two of these sentences as he did, had he enjoyed an intimate or affectionate relationship with his mother or the friendship of his stepfather.' But I doubt whether it is safe. It must be unusual for friendship between mother and son, or son and stepfather, to be as close as this implies. Normally the friends of a man's own age and choice would be much closer, especially in times when manners between parents and children were more formal than they are today. In any case, before we assume anything about Browne's valuation of his mother, we need to take account of what he said earlier concerning his good fortune in being 'born and framed to vertue'. We know from *Pseudodoxia*, I, 11, that Browne did not hold the Aristotelian belief that 'the feminine sex have no generative emission' (he thought it a belief that Satan would always foster). He knew, then, that the virtuous propensities he inherited derived from his mother as well as from his father, who died when he was eight years old.

In the last two sentences of this section, friendship is seen as a type of the union between soul and body and of the union between the three Persons of the Trinity:

Omitting all other, there are three most mysticall unions: two natures in one person; three persons in one nature; one soule in two bodies. For though indeed they bee really divided, yet are they so united, as they seeme but one, and make rather a duality then two distinct soules [II, 5].

To a modern Christian reader, if unaccustomed to seventeenth-century 'metaphysical wit', this might seem blasphemous, but for Browne such analogies illustrate the nature of the universe.

Although Browne is thinking of love between men, his account of it recalls Donne's celebrations of love between man and woman. 'There are wonders in true affection, it is a body of *Ænigmaes*, mysteries, and riddles, wherein two so become one, as they both become two;', Browne writes at the opening of sect. 6; or as Donne has it in *The Extasie:*

A single violet transplant,
    The strength, the colour, and the size,
(All which before was poore, and scant,)
    Redoubles still, and multiplies.
When love, with one another so
    Interinanimates two soules,
That abler soule, which thence doth flow,
    Defects of lonelinesse controules.

Donne died in 1631, three years before Browne wrote *Religio Medici*; the *Songs and Sonets* were published two years later;

Browne may not have read them, but his mind was informed by the same ideas as was Donne's; he thought in similar terms. The next sentence reminds us of another poem *Loves Growth*; Browne writes: 'I love my friend before my selfe, and yet me thinkes I do not love him enough; some few months hence my multiplyed affection will make me beleeve I have not loved him at all'; and Donne:

> Me thinkes I lyed all winter, when I swore,
> My love was infinite, if spring make it more.

They are of course formulating experiences common to lovers in any age, but their way of apprehending the experiences is similar because, in spite of the thirty years between the dates of their birth, they have a common heritage of thought. Browne's prose continues:

> when I am from him, I am dead till I bee with him; when I am with him, I am not satisfied, but would still be nearer him; united soules are not satisfied with embraces, but desire each to be truely the other, which being impossible, their desires are infinite, and must proceed without a possibility of satisfaction.

And the reason, he says, for 'another misery', that we cannot recall the appearance of our dearest friends, is that 'they are our selves, and our affection makes their lookes our owne'. At this point he remembers that his theme is Christian charity. If, as seems possible, he had partly forgotten it, he easily captures it again with the assurance that those who know such love as he describes:

> are mark'd for virtue; he that can love his friend with this noble ardour, will in a competent degree affect all. Now, if wee can bring our affections to looke beyond the body, and cast an eye upon the soule, wee have found out the true object, not onely of friendship but charity....

Here he introduces a favourite theme. Such charity will wish to bestow salvation upon all men, since this is 'the greatest happinesse that wee can bequeath the soule'. And so he closes the section with a passage that once again reminds us of John Donne, not, this time, of a love poem but of the well-known Devotion XVII. Browne writes:

I never heare the Toll of a passing Bell, though in my mirth without my prayers and best wishes for the departing spirit; I cannot goe to cure the body of my Patient, but I forget my profession, and call unto God for his soule....

He writes as a physician, Donne as a dying patient, but their charity expresses itself in the same impulse, because, as Donne writes:

No man is an *Iland*, intire of it selfe; every man is a peece of the *Continent*, a part of the *maine*; if a *Clod* bee washed away by the *Sea*, *Europe* is the lesse, as well as if a *Promontorie* were, as well as if a *Mannor* of thy *friends* or of *thine owne* were; any mans *death* diminishes *me*, because I am involved in *Mankinde*; And therefore never send to know for whom the *bell* tolls; it tolls for *thee*.

Donne, however, goes on to think about his own salvation and the shared affliction that prepares him for it; Browne of his often reiterated wish that all men could be saved. St Thomas Aquinas had supposed that the torments of the damned would be witnessed with joy by the blessed; but Browne closes sect. 6: 'our bad wishes and malevolous desires proceed no further than this life; it is the Devill, and uncharitable votes of Hell, that desire our misery in the world to come', and we shall find him saying the same at the close of his latest work.

The next section is intricate and closely woven, beginning with a series of witty, but serious and penetrating paradoxes, which lead up to the idea of ourselves as small worlds. Within ourselves, as in the world, there are contraries, including the antitheses good and evil; we must hate evil in the larger world or in ourselves, and with similar charity:

To doe no injury, nor take none, was a principle, which to my former yeares, and impatient affections, seemed to containe enough of morality, but my more setled yeares and Christian constitution have fallen upon severer resolutions. I can hold there is no such thing as injury; that if there be, there is no such injury as revenge, and no such revenge as the contempt of an injury; that to hate another, is to maligne himselfe; that the truest way to love another, is to despise our selves [II, 7].

The first three paradoxes in the second sentence express familiar, but none the less cogent, moral ideas. It is good if we recognize that we have no injuries to avenge; it is certain that vengeance is a worse injury than any other (it is directly contrary to the command of God); moreover, there is no more effective vengeance than to ignore an injury. The closing clauses lead on to the image which is to govern this section, the image of man as a microcosm, so often used by Browne and summed up in the first couplet of Donne's *Holy Sonnet* V:

I am a little world made cunningly
Of Elements, and an Angelike spright.

The whole moral world is contained in each of us; self-contempt leads us to charity, because we recognize all faults as potentially our own. We are not more 'pure and unmixed' than is the world:

I finde there are many pieces in this one fabricke of man; and that this frame is raised upon a masse of Antipathies: I am one mee thinkes, but as the world; wherein notwithstanding there is a swarme of distinct essences, and in them another world of contrarieties;... The Devill, that did but buffet Saint *Paul*, playes mee thinkes at sharpes with me: Let mee be nothing, if within the compasse of my selfe, I doe not find the battell of *Lepanto*, passion against reason, reason against faith, faith against the Devill, and my Conscience against all. There is another man within mee that's angry with mee, rebukes, commands, and dastards mee.

Browne (and in this too he is like Donne)[1] repudiates the self-tormenting conscience that courts desperation by exaggerating small offences:

I have no conscience of Marble to resist the hammer of more heavie offences, nor yet so soft and waxen, as to take the impression of each single peccadillo and scape of infirmity. I am of a strange beliefe, that it is as easie to be forgiven some sinnes, as to commit others.

[1] See, for example, the close of Sermon XXXVII, epitomized in the sentence: 'thou canst not be so absolutely, so intirely, so essentially sinfull, as God is absolutely, and intirely, and essentially mercifull.' There are many other examples in which Donne protects his congregation against an overscrupulous, self-tormenting conscience.

The next sentence can be compared with Donne's reiterated 'Wilt thou forgive' in the *Hymn to God the Father*; Browne is asserting his confidence that the sin which he inherited from Adam, or which he committed in youth, or even yesterday, can be absolved:

For my originall sinne, I hold it to be washed away in my Baptisme; for my actuall transgressions, I compute and reckon with God, but from my last repentence, Sacrament or generall absolution; And therefore am not terrified with the sinnes and madnesse of my youth. I thanke the goodnesse of God, I have no sinnes that want a name; I am not singular in offences; my transgressions are Epidemicall, and from the common breath of our corruption.

He is not, he says, driven to strange perversities like 'that Lecher who carnald with a Statua', or like Nero in his 'Spintrian recreations', because 'the dullnesse of my reason, and the vulgarity of my disposition, never prompted my invention, nor solicited my affection unto any of these'. His ordinary, commonplace sins have sufficiently dejected him, so that whereas:

Divines prescribe a fit of sorrow to repentance; there goes indignation, anger, contempt and hatred, into mine, passions of a contrary nature, which neither seeme to sute with this action, nor my proper constitution.

This leads in to the complex and compressed close of this section, reconsidering the place of charity in this context by again reminding us of the parallel between the small world within each man and the large world without:

It is no breach of charity to our selves to be at variance with our vices, nor to abhorre that part of us which is an enemy to the ground of charity, our God; wherein wee doe but imitate our great selves, the world, whose divided Antipathies and contrary faces doe yet carry a charitable regard unto the whole, by their particular discords preserving the common harmony, and keeping in fetters those powers, whose rebellions, once Masters, might bee the ruine of all.

The moral content of sect. 7 can be summarized as an injunction to hate evil, but not to hate either ourselves or our fellows. The idea that binds all together is readily understood if we remember its use by the poets, not only by Donne but by Christopher Marlowe, writing some forty years earlier in *Faustus* of

> Nature that fram'd us of four elements,
> Warring within our breasts for regiment,

or Pope, summarizing the doctrine, almost a hundred years after Browne wrote *Religio Medici*, in his *Essay on Man*:

> Cease then, nor Order Imperfection name:
> Our proper bliss depends on what we blame.

Both in the Macrocosm and in the Microcosm, good and evil are interdependent.

In sect. 8 Browne begins by claiming to be free from one sin, the father of all others:

> I thanke God, amongst those millions of vices I doe inherit, and hold from *Adam*, I have escaped one, and that a mortall enemy to Charity, the first and father sin, not onely of man, but of the devil, Pride, a vice whose name is comprehended in a Monosyllable, but in its nature not circumscribed with a world.

This is not, of course, merely a paradoxically proud boast; it is the lead into a section concerning the form of uncharitableness to which scholars, like himself, are likely to be prone. He has escaped pride 'in a condition that can hardly avoid it'; some scholars are more proud of construing one Ode of Horace than the poet was of composing the whole book. But Browne himself is not puffed up because he knows six languages, the 'Chorography' of the provinces of many countries, the 'Topography' of their cities, laws, customs, policies; nor because he also can name the constellations, or the plants of his native country and their medicinal virtues. All knowledge such as this is 'for heads of capacitie' enough only to confirm Socrates' opinion that 'they know not any thing'....'Wee doe but learne to-day what our better advanced judgements will unteach us to-morrow: and *Aristotle* doth but instruct us, as *Plato* did him; that is, to confute himselfe', which is the cue for Browne's most explicit declaration of his own scepticism:

I have runne through all sects, yet finde no rest in any: though our first studies and junior endeavors may stile us Peripateticks, Stoicks, or Academicks, yet I perceive the wisest heads prove, at last, almost all Scepticks, and stand like *Janus* in the field of knowledge. I have therefore one common and authentick Philosophy I learned in the Schooles, whereby I discourse and satisfie the reason of other men, another more reserved, and drawne from experience, whereby I content mine owne. *Solomon*, that complained of ignorance in the height of knowledge, hath not onely humbled my conceits, but discouraged my endeavours.

Eleven years after writing this he published that odd compendium of knowledge *Pseudodoxia*; he never abandoned his pursuit of truth; but, in that work as in this, he preserved his 'negative capability and willingness to be in uncertainties'. Scepticism is the clue to Browne's characteristic humour, his amused and serene detachment. It is a limited scepticism, for he is confident of the divine purpose and of his own immortality. The point of this section is to insist that we never, in this world, achieve enough knowledge to be proud of, and he concludes with the thought that it would be more sensible to wait passively for what the next world will reveal:

it is but attending a little longer, and wee shall enjoy that by instinct and infusion which we endeavour at here by labour and inquisition. It is better to sit downe in a modest ignorance, and rest contented with the naturall blessing of our owne reasons, then buy the uncertaine Knowledge of this life with sweat and vexation, which death gives every foole gratis, and is an accessory of our glorification.

I have already sketched the pattern of sect. 9 in chapter 1 (pp. 8, 9) because of its odd relation to Browne's biography. It begins 'I was never yet once, and commend their resolutions who never marry twice', and Browne let this stand (in spite of his marriage in 1641) when he revised the text in 1643. It was not his purpose to recount the events of his life; the opening was an effective introduction to an essay on the idea of love as the expression of the soul's thirst for harmony. The idea is given, as are all ideas in *Religio Medici*, in the form of autobiography. To understand human nature Browne looks inward:

> It is my temper, and I like it the better, to affect all harmony, and sure there is a musicke even in the beauty, and the silent note which *Cupid* strikes, farre sweeter than the sound of an instrument.

Gradually he moves on from the love of beauty, rhythm, music and all harmonies to the endeavours of his own and other professions to restore harmony in their own province of the physical or moral world:

> those three Noble Professions which all civil Common wealths doe honour, are raised upon the fall of *Adam*, and are not any way exempt from their infirmities; there are not onely diseases incurable in Physicke, but cases indissoluble in Lawes, Vices incorrigible in Divinity.

His own success, he says, in curing diseases of the body sometimes exceeds the success of law courts in establishing just laws or of Divines in curing vices. So he reaches the conclusion of sect. 9:

> I boast nothing, but plainely say, we all labour against our owne cure, for death is the cure of all diseases. There is no Catholicon or universall remedy I know but this; which, though nauseous to queasier stomachs, yet to prepared appetites is Nectar, and a pleasant potion of immortality.

It is not until we reach the close that we perceive the link between sect. 8 and sect. 9. By diverse routes each comes to the same conclusion that death and immortality is our goal; the first exposes the vain pursuit of knowledge in this world and the second the vain pursuit of harmony. Each begins with a statement about himself. In these closing sections of *Religio Medici*, as though reluctant to stop (for clearly he has enjoyed the elaborate articulation of his self-discovery), Browne adds piece to piece lest something may have been omitted.

Now he does not always trouble to relate each section to its predecessor; sect. 10 begins: 'For my conversation, it is like the Sunne's with all men, and with a friendly aspect to good and bad.'

He is picking up the thread dropped at the close of sect. 7, carrying further and with other illustrations the knowledge that life is too complex for us to form moral judgments about our fellows. Virtue and vice consort together within a man, as they do within a community, and in some aspect the worst man may be the best:

Me thinkes there is no man bad, and the worst, best; that is, while they are kept within the circle of those qualities wherein they are good: there is no man's minde of such discordant and jarring a temper, to which a tuneable disposition may not strike a harmony.

Those parts of a man's nature which remain uncorrupted by his particular vice may be peculiarly excellent:

and persist entire beyond the generall corruption. For it is also thus in nature. The greatest Balsames doe lie enveloped in the bodies of most powerfull Corrosives; I say, moreover, and I ground upon experience, that poysons containe within themselves their owne Antidote, and that which preserves them from the venom of themselves.

Whether or not the asserted facts would be confirmed by a modern naturalist, the analogy expresses true insight into human nature. Because of it, Browne says, he has no fear of being corrupted by other men; those who seem worst may be in some respects greatly his superiors; what he fears is his own company:

it is the corruption that I feare within me; not the contagion of commerce without me. 'Tis that unruly regiment within me, that will destroy me, 'tis I that doe infect my selfe, the man without a Navell yet lives in me; I feele that original canker corrode and devoure me.

In the manuscripts he added a marginal gloss 'Adam, whom I conceive to want a Navill, because he was not borne of a woman'. He fears his own company; but no man is ever alone, not only because he is 'a Microcosm, and carries the whole world about him', as we have already been shown in sect. 7, but because 'the Devill ever consorts with our solitude, and is that unruly rebell that musters up those disordered motions, which accompany our sequestred imaginations'. Up to this point the argument of the section is, though in the manner characteristic of Browne, continuous. We have followed a consecutive train of thought and can easily retrace the steps by which we have come from 'for my conversation, it is...with all men' to the peculiar dangers of solitude. But now, near the end of the section, Browne is carried away from his base; he forgets about his 'conversation' with other men and about his belief that his own company is more likely than any other to corrupt him and he follows a new trail suggested by the word 'solitude'. There is 'to speake more narrowly' no such thing; none but God is solitary, 'who is his owne circle, and can subsist by himselfe'; all others, in addition to their own heterogeneous parts, 'which in a manner multiply their natures, cannot subsist without the concourse of God, and the society of that hand which doth uphold their natures'. So the section, which began with moral experience, ends with metaphysics: 'In briefe, there can be nothing truely alone, and by its self, which is not truely one, and such is onely God: All others doe transcend an unity, and so by consequence are many' [II, 10].

The next section is almost a separate essay; it belongs to the whole work in tone, style and thought, but it does not belong necessarily in this place. It begins, as does sect. 10, with the abruptness of an afterthought: 'Now for my life, it is....' This does not mean that he is about to recount the incidents of his life. What it does mean can only be understood if we keep the words in their context by quoting a long passage. While the larger form (the sequence of sections) is relaxed towards the end of Part II, the internal form within the section is sometimes even more closely woven. It is difficult to isolate any fragment without falsifying the meaning. Section 11 begins:

> Now for my life, it is a miracle of thirty yeares, which to relate, were it not an History, but a peece of Poetry, and would sound to common eares like a fable; for the world, I count it not an Inne, but an Hospitall, and a place, not to live, but to die in. That world which I regard is my selfe; it is the Microcosme of mine owne frame that I cast mine eye on; for

the other, I use it but like my Globe, and turne it round sometimes for my recreation. Men that look upon my outside, perusing onely my condition, and fortunes, do erre in my altitude; for I am above *Atlas* his shoulders.

It is not the events of his life which have been miraculous or to which he wants to call attention, but the thirty years of the life of a mind or spirit. In revising the work in 1642 he brought out more fully the relevance of his thought to the nature of man. In all the manuscripts he goes from '*Atlas* his shoulders' to 'Let me not injure the felicity of others, if I say I am as happy as any', thus directing the reader's attention to his individual experience: but in revising he inserted a passage that makes the wider, more metaphysical intention clear.

The earth is a point not onely in respect of the heavens above us, but of that heavenly and celestiall part within us; that masse of flesh that circumscribes me, limits not my mind: that surface that tells the heavens it hath an end, cannot persuade me I have any; I take my circle to be above three hundred and sixty; though the number of the Arke do measure my body, it comprehendeth not my minde: whilst I study to finde how I am a Microcosme, or little world, I finde my selfe something more than great. There is surely a peece of Divinity in us, something that was before the Elements, and owes no homage unto the Sun. Nature tels me I am the image of God as well as Scripture; he that understands not thus much, hath not his first lesson, and is yet to begin the Alphabet of man.

This gives a more significant context to the sentence ending 'I am happy as any'. The happiness he claims is attainable to all, as he goes on to explain:

Ruat coelum, Fiat voluntas tua, saveth all; so that whatever happens, it is but what our daily prayers desire. In briefe, I am content, and what should providence adde more? Surely this is it wee call Happinesse, and this doe I enjoy; with this I am happy in a dreame, and as content to enjoy happinesse in a fancie, as others in a more apparent truth and reality.

Life itself is perhaps only a dream, and Browne goes on in this same complex and elaborate section to tell of two kinds of dream in which he experiences a more acute joy than his waking life affords: 'my awaked judgement discontents me, ever whispering unto me, that I am from my friend; but my friendly dreames in the night requite me, and make me thinke I am within his armes.' So he thanks God for his dreams and thinks that 'the slumber of the body seemes to bee the waking of the soule'. Certainly Browne's dreams must have been especially delightful, for he goes on to say that, although he was 'borne in the Planetary hour of *Saturne*', and thinks he has 'a peece of that Leaden Planet in me':

> yet in one dreame I can compose a whole comedy, behold the action, apprehend the jests, and laugh my selfe awake at the conceits thereof; were my memory as faithfull as my reason is then fruitfull, I would never study but in my dreames; and this time also would I chuse for my devotions, but our grosser memories have then so little hold of our abstracted understandings, that they forget the story, and can only relate to our awaked soules, a confused and broken tale of what hath passed.

Neither Aristotle, who wrote a tract on sleep, nor Galen, who corrected it, has, he says, got to the bottom of the mystery. Night-walkers appear to sleep and, at the same time, have the use of their senses: 'wee must therefore say that there is something in us that is not in the jurisdiction of Morpheus.' And so Browne comes back to the mystery with which the section started, the miracle of the 'peece of Divinity in us'; he closes the section:

> Thus it is observed that men sometimes, upon the houre of their departure, doe speake and reason above themselves; For then the soule, beginning to bee freed from the ligaments of the body, begins to reason like her selfe, and to discourse in a straine above mortality [II, 11].

Our true life is the life of the soul, and this is why Browne thinks of the world as 'not an Inne, but an Hospitall, and a place, not to live, but to die in'. He has brought this section full circle.

But sleep is an emblem of death as well as of immortality. The soul lives while the body sleeps; on the other hand our earthly nature and human faculties are then inert. Therefore sleep is 'indeed the part of life that best expresseth death, for every man truely lives as long as he acts his nature, or some way makes good the faculties of himselfe'. Thus in sect. 12 Browne thinks of sleep as a constant reminder of our mortality; 'It is that death by which we may be literally said to die daily.' It is so like death that 'I dare not trust it without my prayers, and a half adiew unto the world'. He brings the brief section to an end with a verse prayer so much superior to the other remnants of his verse that it could be mistaken for a lost poem from Herrick's *Noble Numbers.*

In the last three sections Browne's thought has strayed away from the theme of Part II; he comes back to it abruptly, with no attempt at linking, at the opening of sect. 13:

> The method I should use in distributive justice, I often observe in commutative, and keepe a Geometricall proportion in both, whereby becomming equable to others, I become unjust to my selfe, and supererogate in that common principle, Doe unto others as thou wouldst be done unto thy selfe.

It is a cryptic saying and the whole section is an elaborate expansion of it. Bacon in the *Advancement of Learning* [II ,v, 3], speaking of relations between different branches of knowledge, had written: 'Is there not a true coincidence between commutative and distributive justice, and arithmetical and geometrical proportion?' Browne adopts the idea, but prefers to use a geometrical proportion in both kinds of justice; that is to say that, whether in exchanges between men or in giving out to each his deserts, Browne prefers a two-to-one rather than a one-to-one proportion; he will give twice as much as he gets, or twice as much as is deserved. Thus he goes beyond 'that common principle'. He was not, he tells us, born rich, nor is he probably destined to become so. Even if he were, 'the freedome of my minde, and franknesse of my disposition, were able to contradict and crosse my fates'. Indeed avarice (the wish to hoard gold) seems to him 'not so much a vice, as a deplorable piece of madnesse'. The insane believe in many curious things: 'some have held that Snow is blacke, that the earth moves, that the soule is fire, ayre, water; but all this is Philosophy...' (the inclusion of the Copernican theory among aberrations of the mind was not singular even by the mid-seventeenth century); Browne's point is that no speculative folly is as absurd as 'the folly and indisputable dotage of avarice'. For his part he is no gold-worshipper, gold may or may not be a cordial in physic, but:

Whatsoever virtue its prepared substance may have within my body, it hath no influence nor operation without; I would not entertaine a base designe, or an action that should call mee villaine, for the Indies; and for this onely doe I love and honour my owne soule, and have, mee thinkes, two armes too few to embrace my selfe.

Aristotle (in the *Nicomachean Ethics*, II, 3) taught that only the man of large means can be munificent; Browne insists that this is 'too severe'. He has a way round the obstacle; a man of moderate means cannot build hospitals or cathedrals, but:

I borrow occasion of Charity from mine owne necessities, and supply the wants of others, when I am most in neede my selfe; for it is an honest stratagem to take advantage of our selves, and so to husband the acts of vertue, that, where they are defective in one circumstance, they may repay their want and multiply their goodnesse in another.

Throughout this long section Browne sticks closely to the one aspect of charity, giving away money; *more suo*, he first lets his wit play over it and then he raises it to noble heights. The climax is reached in the long penultimate sentence; he has epitomized the motive by quoting from the Book of Proverbs '*Hee that giveth to the poore lendeth to the Lord*'; and he adds:

Upon this motive onely I cannot behold a Begger without relieving his Necessities with my purse, or his soule with my prayers; these scenicall and accidentall differences betweene us, cannot make mee forget that common and untoucht part of us both: there is under these *Centoes* and miserable outsides, these mutilate and semi-bodies, a soule of the same alloy with our owne, whose Genealogy is God as well as ours, and in as faire a way unto salvation as our selves.

The next and final sentence may seem an anti-climax: 'Statists that labour to contrive a Common-wealth without poverty, take away the object of charity, not understanding only the Common-wealth of a Christian, but forgetting the prophecy of Christ.'[1] This sounds too much like the thought presented with fierce irony in Blake's *Human Abstract*:

Pity would be no more
If we did not make somebody Poor;
And Mercy no more could be
If all were happy as we.

—the thought which grows only in the 'Human Brain'. But within Browne's conception, in which this world is literally a 'vale of soul-making', he can excusably accept, unperturbed, the perpetual opportunity that poverty offers to the charitable, relying upon God to make it also fruitful for the sufferer.

The next section [II, 14], brief and closely linked with the foregoing, explains how the love of God comprehends all charity:

Now, there is another part of charity, which is the Basis and Pillar of this, and that is the love of God, for whom wee love our neighbour: for this I thinke is charity, to love God for himselfe, and our neighbour for God.

In sect. 2 his insistence that the love of God is the only admissible motive for charity seemed cold and out of keeping with the inherited impulse to generosity he there described. But now, in sect. 14, the motive is given a new and more compelling meaning. We love our neighbour 'for God', not in the sense of for God's pleasure, or to obey his command, but because what we love in our neighbour is God:

All that is truely amiable is God, or as it were a divided piece of him, that retaines a reflex or shadow of himselfe. Nor is it strange that wee should place affection on that which is invisible; all that wee truely love is thus; what wee adore under affection of our senses, deserves not

[1] Browne supplies the reference, 'The poor ye shall have alwaies with you'.

the honour of so pure a title. Thus wee adore vertue, though to the eyes of sense shee bee invisible. Thus that part of our noble friends that wee love, is not the part we embrace, but that insensible part that our armes cannot embrace.[1]

Similarly, God 'loves us for that part [of us] which is as it were himselfe, and the traduction of his holy Spirit'—that is to say the soul. Browne suggests that we should measure the love between man and God thus defined against the transitory love between ourselves and our parents, whom we will leave for a wife, or between us and a wife, which we will transfer to our children:

They growing up in yeares, either desire our ends, or applying themselves to a woman, take a lawfull way to love another better than our selves. Thus I perceive a man may bee buried alive, and behold his grave in his owne issue.

The conceit leads him straight into his conclusion of the whole work in sect. 15:

I conclude therefore, and say, there is no happinesse under (or, as *Copernicus* will have it, above) the Sunne, nor any Crambe in that repeated veritie and burthen of all the wisedom of *Solomon*, *All is vanitie and vexation of spirit*; there is no felicity in what the world adores.

Happiness is 'that wherein God himselfe is happy, the holy Angels are happy, in whose defect the Devils are unhappy'. Browne is not here commiserating with himself nor contradicting the assertion he made in sect. 8: 'In briefe I am content.' He is repeating and expatiating on it.

Blesse mee in this life with but the peace of my conscience, command of my affections, the love of thy selfe and my dearest friends, and I shall be happy enough to pity *Caesar*. These are, O Lord, the humble desires of my most reasonable ambition, and all I dare call happinesse on earth: wherein I set no rule or limit to thy hand or providence; dispose of me according to the wisedome of thy pleasure. Thy will bee done, though in my owne undoing.

FINIS

[1] A modern reader is likely to miss the word-play. Embrace or imbrace could then mean buckle on (as a shield is buckled on to the arm).

The *Religio Medici* portrays a mind of singular charm. It is not a confessional autobiography, in the manner of Jean-Jacques Rousseau or the many subsequent attempts to portray the whole man. Browne is exploring the religion of a doctor—that is his own—he writes only of those aspects of himself which relate to his Christian faith and his Christian charity. The 'battle of Lepanto' within is never defined, we do not know his temptations nor his vices. Yet the result is no mere portrait of an ideal man. The character revealed is markedly individual: whimsical, witty, tireless in the pursuit of knowledge, sceptically inclined, widely compassionate and a passionate lover. Yet, despite the roving mind and the impassioned heart, it is the portrait of a serene man, detached and amused by the spectacle of himself and of the world about him. He is securely anchored in his belief that the God he worships is all-wise, all-loving, and all-powerful.

CHAPTER V

'PSEUDODOXIA' (BOOK I)

IN 1646, three years after the authorized edition of *Religio Medici*, Sir Thomas Browne published *Pseudodoxia Epidemica: or Enquiries into very many received Tenets, and commonly presumed Truths*: the work usually known, in his own day and in ours, as *Vulgar Errors*. He had found an admirable subject for the deployment of his gifts and one which offers the modern reader an insight into his mind and into contemporary currents of thought. As he displays for the reader's enlightenment examples of the vast range of human error he is often amused and ironical, but he is also basically serious and wise. He was convinced that the world was created by God and that the better we know and understand it the more we shall honour the Creator. Consequently, it is with a sense of high purpose that he indulges that indefatigable curiosity which he shared with his contemporaries, the members of Gresham's College. By 1645, the year in which Browne finished writing his book, they were meeting weekly to discuss all fields of knowledge, excepting only theology and affairs of State. In 1660 they were to be incorporated as the Royal Society of London. But whereas they met together and co-operated in their endeavours to discover facts and dispel erroneous beliefs, Browne undertook his self-imposed task alone. This was inevitable because his professional duties tied him to Norwich.

In his *Address to the Reader* he admits his temerity in undertaking so large a work by himself: 'a work of such concernment unto truth and difficulty in itself, did well deserve the conjunction of many heads'. For the modern reader, however, his 'single and unsupported endeavours' are of far greater value than could have been the work of any team. We no longer read *Vulgar Errors* to find out the facts about phenomena, but to enjoy the company of the author and the 'climate of opinion' in which he wrote. For forty years, it would seem, the book made its contribution to knowledge; six editions were published during his lifetime, each revised by the author. To the last of these, in 1672, he added a note to the effect that no further additions or alterations were to be expected. The work was printed again four years after his death, in 1686. After this there was no further edition before its inclusion in the complete works edited by Simon Wilkin and published (after twelve years' labour) in 1835. By that time Sir Thomas Browne's works were an accepted part of English literature. They belonged, in de Quincey's phrase, not to the literature of knowledge, but to the literature of power. I do not think Sir Thomas himself would have understood the distinction; he wrote this book in order to combat errors, because they impede the progress of knowledge. But, although some of the errors he exposes and many of the causes of error he describes are still active, we would not seek information from an author of the seventeenth century. *Pseudodoxia* survives because of Browne's involvement in his quest, because of his enjoyment of his insights and discoveries, because we can catch the tone of his voice in the cadence of his prose, because we delight in his faith and in his scepticism, in his humour and in his gravity. To gauge these aright, however, we need to follow his arguments closely and to recognize as clearly as we can the relation between his thinking and that of his contemporary readers.

In its final form *Pseudodoxia* consists of seven books. Book I describes how error originates and upon what grounds we can distinguish it from truth. In each of the remaining six books Browne examines errors that occur in different fields of knowledge; Book II concerns errors about minerals and vegetables; Book III about animals; Book IV about man. It was natural for Browne to ascend the scale of being; it is an order that would have occurred to any man of his time. In the remaining three books he shows how error is propagated in various fields; Book V shows how it is propagated by pictorial description; Book VI by geographical and historical writings and Book VII by other historical writings and by unwarranted conclusions from Holy Scripture.

It is obvious from his address to the reader that Browne anticipated that his book would be attacked and that he was not willing to be drawn into controversy. He endeavours to placate the theologians, the 'Philologers and Critical Discoursers', his 'Brothers in Physick' and: 'those honoured Worthies, who endeavour the Advancement of Learning'. These, he believes, will welcome his book: 'as being likely to find a clearer progression, when so many rubs are levelled, and many untruths taken off, which passing as principles with common beliefs, disturb the tranquility of Axioms, which otherwise might be raised', and wise men in general will know that arts and learning require such an eradication of errors as he proposes to offer. Moreover, he does not mean to dictate what should be believed.

Lastly, we are not Magisterial in opinions, nor have we Dictator-like obtruded our conceptions; but in the humility of Enquiries or disquisitions, have only proposed them unto more ocular discerners. And therefore opinions are free, and open it is for any to think or declare the contrary. And we shall so far encourage contradiction, as to promise no disturbance, or re-oppose any Pen, that shall Fallaciously or captiously refute us; that shall only lay hold of our lapses, single out Digressions, Corollaries, or Ornamental conceptions, to evidence his own in as indifferent truths. And shall only take notice of such, whose experimental and judicious knowledge shall solemnly look upon it; not only to destroy of ours, but to establish of his own; not to traduce or extenuate, but to explain and dilucidate, to add and ampliate, according to the laudable custom of the Ancients in their sober promotions of Learning.

Browne is remembering the attacks on his first book and reaffirming his dislike of angry argument; *Pseudodoxia* was in fact attacked, five years after the publication of the first edition, by that doughty defender of Aristotle and of orthodoxy, Alexander Ross, who had hunted for heresies in *Religio Medici*. Ross had constituted himself the defender of the Ancients against the

Moderns and he could not fail to detect in Sir Thomas Browne a dangerous enemy to the conservatism he championed. In June 1651 he published *Arcana Microcosmi: or the hid Secrets of Man's Body disclosed... With a refutation of Dr Browns Vulgar Errors; And the Ancient Opinions vindicated.* A second and enlarged edition was published a year later, including a refutation of *The Lord Bacon's Natural History, and Dr Harvey's Book De Generatione.* If Sir Thomas Browne read this work he did not think it worth while to answer it, nor indeed was it, for Ross had neither 'experimental' nor 'judicious' knowledge. But for the modern reader he is both entertaining and enlightening. His work illustrates an attitude of mind still prevalent in mid-seventeenth century, with which Browne and the other Baconians were confronted. If Sir Thomas Browne sometimes seems to the modern reader quaintly archaic, Ross's replies remind us how much the reverse of this he could seem to a contemporary. By keeping in mind on the one hand Ross's *Arcana* and on the other the early *Transactions of the Royal Society* we shall have some means of judging how far, in mid-seventeenth century, Browne deserved to rank among the Moderns.

In his prose style certainly he was not in the vanguard, nor did he ever conform to the new fashion for a plain style which became dominant about fourteen years after the publication of *Pseudodoxia.* His style was formed in the 1630's and it is a style of conscious art. Rhetoric was a principal subject in schools and universities during the time of his education and it would not have occurred to Browne to write his books in the casual style in which he wrote his private letters. Moreover, in *Pseudodoxia* he was deliberately aiming above the heads of the vulgar; he wanted to combat vulgar errors, but to do so he thought he must first gain the attention of the learned. He had considered writing this work in Latin so that it might be accessible to learned men throughout Europe:

Our first intentions considering the common interest of Truth, resolved to propose it unto the Latine republique and equal Judges of

> Europe, but owing in the first place this service unto our Country, and therein especially unto its ingenuous Gentry, we have declared our self in a language best conceived. Although I confess the quality of the Subject will sometimes carry us into expressions beyond meer English apprehensions. And indeed, if elegancy still proceedeth, and English Pens maintain that stream we have of late observed to flow from many, we shall within few years be fain to learn Latine to understand English, and a work will prove of equal facility in either.

He is mocking the pedants and clearly does not mean to emulate Holofernes; when he seems to do so we shall be wise to suspect a humorous intention. But, on the other hand, he expects learned readers: 'Nor have we addressed our Pen or Stile unto the people (whom Books do not redress, and are this way incapable of reduction), but unto the knowing and leading part of Learning.' It is they who must help his endeavours to bear fruit, for without their co-operation 'these weeds must lose their alimental sap and wither of themselves'.

In the eleven chapters that compose his Book I, Browne describes the general causes of error. If we hope fully to enjoy the work we need, I believe, to give him a patient and thorough hearing in this 'First Book or General Part'. Afterwards we can select the errors that appeal to us, or that evoke characteristic discussions from the author. But if we skip and choose in Book I we throw away the key to his mind; this discussion of the causes of error reveals Browne's thought as intimately as does *Religio Medici*; we discover both what in it is strange or dated and what is persuasive and perennial. Therefore I shall follow him chapter by chapter, trying to interpret and sometimes using contemporary witnesses who help us to imagine the audience for which he wrote.

Browne begins and closes Book I with the Devil. For many modern readers the combination in his mind of faith with scepticism cannot be clearly understood without an effort of historical imagination. He never abrogates the use of reason, it is active in his interpretation of scripture and he had employed it, as we have seen in *Religio Medici*, in what he felt to be his personal choice of the Christian faith and of the Anglican Church. There is no evidence that he ever doubted the basic Christian account of the origin of evil and it is not surprising that he believes that human proneness to error is a result of the Fall. This, therefore, is the subject of Book I, ch. I. Even so his sceptical intelligence, playing over the given story, raises a doubt whether angels and men were not prone to err even before Eve ate the apple, else how comes it that angels fell? Perhaps God alone is incapable of error: he is so by definition:

> In brief, there is nothing infallible but GOD, who cannot possibly Erre. For things are really true as they correspond unto His conception; and have so much verity as they hold of conformity unto that Intellect, in whose Idea they had their first determinations. And therefore being the Rule, he cannot be Irregular; nor, being Truth it self, conceaveably admit the impossible society of Error [I, I].

In his second chapter, however, Browne illustrates from the Bible how amazingly prevalent error was immediately after the Fall. There may have been before a liability to err; immediately after it appears as though it is almost impossible not to. He prides himself on being the first to notice that 'in the relations of Scripture before the Flood, there is but one speech delivered by Man, wherein there is not an erroneous conception; and, strictly examined, most heinously injurious unto truth'. For the remainder of ch. 2, happily a very short one, he discusses the examples that prove his point: it is a pedantic chapter into which he is betrayed by his pride in being the first to discover this, to his mind, pertinent fact. After this, in chs. 3–9, Browne discusses general causes of error which a modern reader, whatever his religious beliefs, will recognize as always prevalent. Vulgar errors may change, but not the causes of vulgar error.

His third chapter is about what he calls 'the erroneous disposition of the people'. It is a wise, thoughtful chapter and persuades the reader that this is indeed a perennial cause of the rise, spread and persistence of error. By 'the people' he does not mean any particular group in a class-structure, but:

whosoever shall resign their reasons, either from the Root of deceit in themselves, or inability to resist such trivial deceptions from others, although their condition and fortunes may place them many Spheres above the multitude, yet are they still within the line of Vulgarity, and Democratical enemies of truth [I, 3].

In the main, however, ch. 3 is about the populace who are 'the most deceptible part of Mankind and ready with open armes to receive the encroachments of Error'. This, he explains, is inevitable for a number of reasons; they have no criterion by which to distinguish truth from falsehood: 'their uncultivated understandings, scarce holding any theory, they are but bad discerners of verity.' It follows that they are the victims of their own sense impressions and: 'conceive the Earth far bigger than the Sun, the fixed Stars lesser than the Moon, their figures plain, and their spaces from Earth equidistant. For thus their sense informeth them, and herein their reason cannot Rectifie them....' As well as being the slaves of their own senses they are easily deluded by words; a piece of rhetoric, a fable, or a proverb, may be taken by them for literal truth. They are so little acquainted with the uses of language that, when they read the Bible: 'Their apprehensions are commonly confined unto the literal sense of the Text; from whence have ensued the gross and duller sort of Heresies.' The populace has no notion of what modern critics call 'ambiguity', or what Browne more specifically describes as 'Superconsequencies, Coherencies, Figures, or Tropologies; and are not sometime perswaded by fire beyond their literalities'. They will go to the stake for their misreadings. Browne is always impressed and appalled by men's willingness to be martyred for a belief, but in this context his stress falls upon the errors generated by such literal-mindedness. It has led men to:

the dulness of Idolatry. A sin or folly not only derogatory unto God but men; overthrowing their Reason, as well as his Divinity. In brief, a reciprocation, or rather, an inversion of the Creation, making God one way, as he made us another; that is after our Image, as he made us after His own.

The judgment of the vulgar is also likely to be clouded by their appetites, as was well understood, Browne says, by Mahomet, who invented a heaven to satisfy their desires.

But the wisdom of our Saviour, and the simplicity of his truth proceeded another way; defying the popular provisions of happiness from sensible expectations; placing his felicity in things removed from sense, and the intellectual enjoyment of God.

In a measure, Browne believes, this felicity can be enjoyed on earth, for we can attain some degree of awareness of God by studying his creation. Therefore Christians will welcome the advancement of knowledge; the religion of Christ (unlike that of Mahomet) 'was never afraid of universities'. Of course Browne knew that this was an account of what should be rather than of what is; he was well aware that some pious people were opposed to the new learning, fearing that it threatened their faith. Any Baconian work, such as he had undertaken, was likely to encounter traditionalist criticism. He is asserting that this will not come from thoughtful and intelligent Christians. There is no danger, he argues, that the new learning will undermine essential beliefs. Galen (A.D. 129–200) had questioned some that are not essential:

Galen doth sometimes nibble at Moses, and, beside the Apostate Christian [Julian] some Heathens have questioned his Philosophical part, or treaty of the Creation: Yet there is surely no reasonable Pagan, that will not admire the rational and well-grounded precepts of Christ; whose life, as it was conformable unto his Doctrine, so was that unto the highest rules of Reason; and must therefore flourish in the advancement of learning, and the perfection of parts best able to comprehend it.

Browne himself sometimes 'nibbles at Moses', though with the discretion of one who had decided to 'follow the great Wheel of the Church'. Galen must have been a very congenial author to him. He was the founder of experimental physiology and he shared Browne's basic belief in the wisdom of the Creator. His thought, like Browne's, was rooted in the Aristotelian conception *Natura nihil agit frustra*. Professor Charles Singer, introducing his translation of Galen's anatomical writings, says that *De Usu Partium* 'might be described as a long hymn to Divine Wisdom in fitting the hand for its functions'. A similar teleological approach to knowledge of the created world is fundamental throughout *Pseudodoxia*. From this point of view Browne resembles Aristotle and Galen rather than Bacon, for Bacon in *The Advancement of Learning* had repudiated questions about design or purpose as impediments to knowledge, whereas Browne never maintains any separation between the physical and the metaphysical cause; for him the question how things are is indissolubly linked with the question why; his avowed motive for studying nature is his belief that it reveals the mind of God, though he was also impelled by indefatigable curiosity.

He has not of course lost sight of the subject of his chapter, the proneness of the vulgar to adopt and spread error. He goes on to show that, if they are easily deceived individually, they are even more apt to be misled when they are herded together, all their imperfections are 'enlarged by their aggregation'. He gives instances from Scripture of the irrational behaviour of crowds, concluding that 'certainly he that considereth these things in God's peculiar people, will easily discern how little of truth there is in the waies of the Multitude; and though sometimes they are flattered with that Aphorism, will hardly believe, The voice of the people to be the voice of God'.

Moreover, a crowd is easily swayed by oratory and deceived by quacks of all kinds: 'Thus having been deceived by themselves and continually deluded by others, they must needs be stuffed with errors, and even over-run with these inferior falsities.'

In the following chapter [I, 4] Browne considers causes of

error which operate upon 'the wiser sort' as well as the less wise. The first of these is misapprehension, as for instance when a misapprehension of what was seen occasioned belief in the existence of centaurs:

when some young Thessalanians on horseback were beheld afar off, while their horses watered, that is while their heads were depressed, they were conceived by the first Spectators, to be but one animal; and answerable hereunto have their pictures been drawn ever since.

Browne derived this, and other, rationalizations of pagan myths from 'Palephatus, his Book of Fabulous Narrations'.[1] Alexander Ross directs a many-sided and confused attack upon this apparently harmless piece of scepticism in *Arcana Microcosmi*. First he says that there undoubtedly are centaurs; many travellers have seen them, they are monstrous births, brought about by

the influence of the stars, and partly by other causes, as the ill position of the matrix, the bad temperature of the seed, the perverse inclination of the woman, the commixion of seeds of divers kinds, sudden fear, bad diet, unwholesome air, untimely Venus [Book II, ch. III, sect. i].

These monsters, Ross assures us, have no souls and therefore are not men. Next he reproduces Browne's account of the origin of the myth about centaurs though without acknowledging that Browne is his source. There are also, he says, tropological centaurs; the poetic meaning is 'lascivious and voluptuous men, who by Hercules, that is men of courage, wisdom and strength, were subdued and brought to civilitie'. Puffed up by his skill in interpretation, Ross now accuses Browne of failing to make 'a distinction between Poetical fictions and real truth'. As to 'real truth' Ross will later assert that creatures with the torso of a man and the body of a horse in fact exist, no less than the monstrous births he has previously described. Meanwhile, he

[1] He gives a reference to his work in Bk I, ch. 6, and adds a note: 'An Ancient author who writ *de Incredibilibus* whereof some part is still extant.'

overlooks all that Browne here writes about mistaking allegory for history, irony for statement and metaphor for assertion. He would have his readers believe that Dr Browne, and not he, is liable to confuse fiction with fact. It would obviously have been vain to attempt argument with such a protean adversary.

To return to Browne's fourth chapter; he says that if we avoid misapprehension of things seen, and misunderstanding of things read, we may still be drawn into errors by fallacious reasoning. Aristotle, Browne says, names six types of false reasoning which he will reduce to four: first, '*Petitio principii*... Briefly, where that is assumed as a Principle to prove another thing, which is not conceded as true itself'; second, '*A dicto secundum quid ad dictum simpliciter*, when from that which is but true in a qualified sense, an inconditional and absolute verity is inferred'; third, '*A non causa pro causa*, when that is pretended for a cause which is not, or not in that sense which is inferred,'....'The fourth is, the Fallacy of the Consequent; which...may be a fallacious illation in reference unto antecedency or consequency.' And of each of these defects in reasoning he gives examples.

Chapter v is entitled *Of Credulity and Supinity*, by which he means, on the one hand, too easy credence of customary beliefs, and, on the other, an obstinate or lazy incredulity about new discoveries: 'As credulity is the Cause of Error, so Incredulity often times of not enjoying truth.' He chooses, as his example of 'supinity', refusal to countenance the idea that the earth moves round the sun. Men had indeed been slow to credit this discovery; Copernicus had published his theoretical proof in *De Revolutionibus Orbium Coelestium* in 1543, one hundred and three years before Browne published *Vulgar Errors*; it was now thirteen years since Galileo had been condemned by the Roman Catholic Church for affirming, on the evidence of what he saw through his telescope, that the Copernican theory corresponded to the facts. But Browne, and others of comparable intellect and learning, found it hard to credit. He is, however, aware that to assert that this cannot be true, because it is hard to imagine, would be an obstinate clinging to error:

> And therefore if any affirm, the earth doth move, and will not believe with us, it standeth still; because he hath probable reasons for it, and I no infallible sense, nor reason against it, I will not quarrel with his assertion [I, 5].

It is admirable, and it is characteristic of Browne, to have chosen this example, and it is noteworthy that he draws attention to his own position by using the first person. The Ptolemaic universe and all that went with it was deeply planted in Browne's imagination; it had been part of his thinking from his youth upward and was assumed by most of the authors he had read. Yet he was sufficiently aware of the challenge to it to know that it might not correspond with fact. Therefore he will not assert its truth nor obstinately refute the 'New Philosophy'; to do so would, he recognizes, disqualify him as a truth seeker. He does not, however, pretend to be convinced; he says only that he will quarrel with no one for asserting what he cannot disprove. He immediately contrasts this receptiveness with the attitude he would adopt to any assertion that affronts common sense. The example he gives is one of Zeno's paradoxes:

> But if, like Zeno, he shall walk about, and yet deny there is any motion in Nature, surely that man was constituted for Anticera,[1] and were a fit companion for those, who having a conceit they are dead, cannot be convicted into the society of the living.

The pre-Socratic philosopher, Zeno, is probably best known to modern readers for his paradox of Achilles and the tortoise. Browne is impatient with such logic-chopping.

It is no easy matter to decide whether Browne's response to Copernicus and Galileo was old-fashioned in 1646; was he retarded in that he imagined a Ptolemaic universe, or was he in the vanguard because he was prepared to learn from recent

[1] Anticera is a place where hellebore, the reputed cure for madness, grows in abundance.

discoveries? Simon Wilkin, editing *Pseudodoxia* in the 1830's, found a copy of the first edition that had been owned and annotated by Sir Christopher Wren, the father of the architect. He prints some of these notes and among them the comment upon Sir Thomas Browne's readiness to believe that the earth moves: Sir Christopher Wren wrote:

In the booke of God, from Moses unto Christ, there are no less than eighty and odd expresse places, affirming in plaine and overt termes the naturall and perpetuall motion of the sun and the moon...others (as expressly) the impossibility of any other motion in the earth than that terrible and pænal motion of his shaking itt, that made it....Soe that were it nothing else than the veneration and firme beliefe of that Word of His, which the penmen thereof spake not of themselves, but by inspiration of the Holy Ghost, they that profess Christianitye should not dare, much less adventure to call the letter thereof in question concerning things soe plainly, frequently, constantly, delivered: should tremble at that curse which is denounced against those that add anything to itt: or diminish any tittle of itt: should feare to raise such a hellish suspition in vulgar mindes, as the Romish church, by under-valewing the majesty and authority thereof, hath done; should bee affrighted to follow that audacious and pernicious suggestion, which Satan used, and thereby undid us all in our first parents; that God had a double meaning in his commands, in effect condemning God of amphibologye.[1]

Born in 1591, Sir Christopher Wren senior was fourteen years older than Browne. However, his belief in the literal and factual truth of whatever the Bible contains had more than two hundred years of life ahead of it. On the same grounds many were still opposing Darwin in the late nineteenth century. Sir Thomas Browne, however, had drawn attention in his third chapter to that 'amphibologye' in the inspired word of God which Wren thinks it would be an insult to imagine.

He thought that, if we wish to destroy errors, we have to ally ourselves with those who are advancing knowledge. Certainly he meant to be in the vanguard, as much so as his gifts and his

[1] Wilkin, vol. II, p. 210.

situation would allow. He is severe with those who do not contribute what they can to the increase of knowledge, although he sympathizes with anyone who, having chosen a studious life, labours in vain because of incapacity:

Now as there are many great Wits to be condemned, who have neglected the increment of Arts, and the sedulous pursuit of knowledge; so are there not a few very much to be pitied, whose industry being not attended with natural parts, they have sweat to little purpose, and rolled the stone in vain [1, 5].

The subject of the next chapter [1, 6] is *of adherence unto Antiquity* as a cause of error. Browne is assuredly Bacon's disciple when he writes: 'But the mortallest enemy unto knowledge, and that which hath done the greatest execution upon truth, hath been a peremptory adhesion unto Authority, and, more especially, the establishing of our belief upon the dictates of Antiquity.' Here he explicitly takes his stand with the Moderns in that curious war between Ancients and Moderns to which Bacon's *Advancement of Learning* was the bugle call and in which Swift fought the last lively battle for the Ancients in his *Battle of the Books* (1704). In a sense the war can be thought of as perpetual, for there are always some who overrate past literature, art and learning at the expense of present, and others who admire nothing that is not new. But it is evident in all Browne's writings that he relished both. He is not contemptuous of ancient learning; only of the notion that its conclusions are final. He points out that these admired ancients had no inhibitions about opposing their forerunners: 'Thus Hippocrates about 2000 years ago, conceived it no injustice either to examine or refute the Doctrines of his Predecessors: Galen the like, and Aristotle the most of any.' Moreover, ancient authors can often be shown, by any observant countryman, to be wrong about the facts. For example, horses and cows are as liable to cough as men are, asses and horses to belch, and horses, dogs and foxes to grow grey with age, even though Aristotle believes the contrary.

Browne follows this by affirming that many of the old writers were merely copying from one another, without re-examining the evidence:

Thus may we perceive the Ancients were but men, even like ourselves. The practice of transcription in our days, was no Monster in theirs: Plagiarie had not its Nativitie with Printing, but began in times when thefts were difficult, and the paucity of Books scarce wanted that Invention.

He has now given us three reasons for accepting ancient writers with caution: (1) we thereby enslave the future to the past; (2) neither error nor vice is confined to any one time; (3) the ancients can be shown to have made mistakes.

In his second edition, 1650, Browne inserted what is now his fourth reason for wariness: the Greeks were much addicted to the invention of fables. He instances a number of Greek myths and, with the help of Palephatus's *De Incredibilibus*, assigns to each a probable origin similar to the one whereby he accounted for centaurs in his fourth chapter:

That Fable of Orpheus who by the melody of his Musick, made Woods and Trees to follow him, was raised upon a slender foundation; for there were a crew of mad women, retired unto a Mountain from whence being pacified by his Musick, they descended with boughs in their hands, which unto the fabulosity of those times proved a sufficient ground to celebrate unto all posterity the Magick of Orpheus' Harp, and its power to attract the senseless Trees about it.

In like manner the story 'that Medea the famous sorceress could renew youth'; or of the three-headed Gerion and Cerberus; or of Hercules's descent into Hell; or of Briareus's hundred arms, and many more are given an origin agreeable to common sense. The point is not that Browne misunderstands poetry, but that he knows how many, like Alexander Ross, cannot distinguish between fact and fable. Simple-minded faith in ancient writings can thus be a cause of vulgar errors; therefore he seeks to undermine such literal belief in mythical tales.

A fifth way in which we allow ancient authors to enslave our minds is, Browne says, by unnecessary reverence for their moral philosophers. Such famous axioms as Thales's *Nosce teipsum* (know thyself), or Cleobulus's *Nihil nimis* (nothing too much), and several more are not, he thinks, beyond the reach of a modern man. Still less need we quote ancient authors in support of truisms; an author he happened to be reading at the time of writing this chapter quoted 'Apolonius Thyaneus' to confirm the obvious truth that nothing is more natural than the desire to preserve life. Others seem to require the authority of Euclid to declare that a whole is larger than its parts. Such pedantry, he thinks, fosters the belief that ancient writers are the source of all wisdom and knowledge.

In ch. 7, headed *Of Authority*, Browne's main endeavour is to demonstrate that authority, even when the authoritative word is alleged to be that of an eyewitness, is always less reliable than sound reasoning. For some kinds of knowledge, Browne says, it is obvious that authority is irrelevant; no geometrician, for instance, asserts propositions on authority, they require demonstrative and rational proof. Similarly, no good astronomer will believe that the sun is bigger than the earth merely because Ptolemy said so. It is in general foolish to depend upon authority in any inquiry into the laws of nature; Aristotle himself never did so.

Morality, rhetoric, law and history are less independent of testimony than are the natural sciences. But even in these fields, says Browne, everything will depend upon the quality of the witnesses: 'the solid reason of one man, is as sufficient as the clamor of a whole Nation; and with unprejudicate apprehensions begets as firm a belief as the authority or aggregated testimony of many hundreds.' This is a wiser opinion than that of Joseph Glanvill who, in *Philosophical Considerations concerning Witches and Witchcraft* (1666), asserts the existence of such beings on the grounds that: 'in things of Fact, the People are as much to be believed, as the most *subtle Philosophers* and *Speculators*, since here sense is the

Judge.' Browne was never so simple-minded. His own belief in witches was based in part on his theology and in part on medical cases for which he and his professional colleagues could find no other explanation. He knew that a witness must be trusted only according to his ability to discriminate in the matters of which he speaks:

So if Lactantius affirm the Figure of the Earth is plain, or Austin deny there are Antipodes; though venerable Fathers of the Church, and ever to be honoured, yet will not their Authorities prove sufficient to ground a belief thereon [I, 7].

But if, instead of assertion about matters the writer has not studied, we find either reasoned argument or 'confirmed experience', we may be convinced even by the assertions of an amateur.

So Raymund Sebund, a Physitian of Tholouze, besides his learned Dialogues *De Natura humana*, hath written a natural Theologie, demonstrating therein the Attributes of God, and attempting the like in most points of Religion. So Hugo Grotius, a Civilian, did write an excellent Tract of the verity of the Christian Religion. Wherein most rationally delivering themselves, their works will be embraced by most that understand them, and their reasons enforce belief even from prejudicate Readers.

In matters of history we value affirmative testimony, but must not attempt to prove a negative on account of its absence. Browne chooses an example from his own field of medicine and once again runs up against the Unicorn and provokes Alexander Ross. We cannot deduce that: 'Because Dioscorides hath made no mention of Unicorn's horn, there is therefore no such thing in Nature.' Since Dioscorides set out to give a full account of medical materials his omission makes it likely that the Ancients did not use this horn in medicine; but we cannot infer that it did not exist. Dioscorides does not mention a number of other simples which certainly must have existed, such as 'Senna, Rhubarb, Bezoar and Ambergris'. The paragraph closes with a further tribute to reason since a syllogism, unlike testimony, can prove a negative as well as an affirmative.

Browne uses the example of the Unicorn's horn (that supposedly sovereign remedy) as a good illustration of his point. His point is that, though unmentioned, it may have existed. It is clear that, on other grounds which emerge in a later book, Browne does not believe it did exist.

It will be well at this point to sum up and finish with the Unicorn controversy between Browne and Ross. In Book III, ch. 23 we discover Browne's doubts and the reasons for them. First, there are a number of animals with one horn which may have given rise to a belief in this magical and majestic creature; Browne names five of them. Secondly, the animal with the alleged magical properties is described in a variety of ways which cannot all point to a single species. Thirdly, the powder sold as Unicorn's horn at this time cannot be that of which we read; ours is usually white, the records usually describe a black powder; Scaliger saw five kinds, one light red and two almost red—none was white. Fourthly, the horn sold as Unicorn's horn today comes from several kinds of animal—he describes the differing shapes and sizes of these animals. Fifthly, some powders, alleged to be of Unicorn's horn, are not obtained from horns at all; some are minerals, some fossils; one kind is a substance harder than bone, that is, parts of the tooth of a Moose or Sea-horse, which 'being burnt becomes a good remedy for fluxes: but antidotally used, and exposed for Unicorn's horn, it is an insufferable delusion'. Sixthly, even if we had the Unicorn's horn it would be absurd to suppose it was an antidote, since the Ancients asserted no such thing. Finally, suppose we could obtain Unicorn's horn and allowed it some virtue as an antidote (such as some horns and hoofs possess) it would certainly be irrational to claim for it as many diverse powers as are claimed. And ch. 23 of Book III ends with a paragraph characteristic of Browne's ironical style:

Since therefore there be many Unicorns; since that whereto we appropriate a Horn is so variously described, that it seemeth either never to have been seen by two persons, or not to have been one animal; Since though they agreed in the description of the animal, yet is not the Horn we extol the same with that of the Ancients; Since what Horns soever they be that pass among us, they are not the Horns of one, but several animals. Since many in common use and high esteem are no Horns at all: Since if there were true Horns, yet might their vertues be questioned: Since though we allowed some vertues, yet were not others to be received: with what security a man may rely upon this remedy, the mistress of fools hath already instructed some, and to wisdom (which is never too wise to learn) it is not too late to consider.

It is worth recording, in this context, that members of the Royal Society were interested as late as 1661 in the properties of Unicorn's horn. On 24 July of that year 'a circle was made with powder of Unicorn's horn, and a spider set in the middle of it, but it immediately ran out. The trial being several times repeated, the spider once made some stay on the powder.' There is no indication which of the several powders of horn was used in this experiment; the record suggests a simple-minded faith, fifteen years after the publication of *Pseudodoxia*, that they were using the horn of a genuine Unicorn.

Alexander Ross had not been very clear-headed about Browne and the Unicorn in his third chapter of the second book of *Arcana*; he returns to it in ch. 6, but to no better effect. He admits with Browne that there are a number of creatures with one horn, but (having apparently abandoned or forgotten his idea of monstrous births in ch. 3) he describes, and apparently accepts as accurate, Cardan's assertion that 'the true Unicorn hath the proportion and bignesse of an Horse, the head, legs and feet of a Stagge, and the mane of a Horse, he hath a horn in his forehead, (saith Cardan) three cubits long; two of these Unicorns were seen at Mecha, of which see Parry in his Twenty first Book of poisons'. Ross relies on several other named authorities, among them 'Vertomanus, Justin Martyr, Basil and other of the Fathers', and says that: 'I therefore make no question of the true Unicorn, as he is commonly painted—Yea, the holy scriptures seem to favour this description.' He is also convinced of the medical properties of Unicorn's horn, especially as a cure for fevers and an antidote against poison, and he explains how true Unicorn's horn can be distinguished from false: 'The means to discriminate the true Unicorn's horn from the false are two, to wit, if it cause the liquor, into which it is put, to bubble; and secondly, if it sweat when the poison is near it, as Baccius tells us.' It would be hard to find a better example of indiscriminate subservience to authorities. It is amusing that Ross has, if we take account of both passages, produced three incompatible lines of argument against Browne's scepticism: (1) the unicorn of myth was never meant to be mistaken for a real animal; (2) unicorns exist, but they are monstrous births; (3) the unicorn of myth and picture exists and his horn has the properties ascribed to it.

In the seventh chapter of Book I Browne was only using the Unicorn's horn to illustrate his point that absence of testimony does not prove non-existence. Next he makes a list of some incredibles to which the Ancients testify: if they did not attempt to counteract poison or allay fever with the powdered horn of a unicorn, they advocated other cures which Browne considers no more propitious, for example:

It were methinks but an uncomfortable receit for a Quartane Ague (and yet as good perhaps as many others used) to have recourse unto the Recipe of Sammonicus; that is, to lay the fourth Book of Homer's *Iliads* under one's head, according to the precept of that Physitian and Poet, *Mœoniæ Iliados quartum suppone trementi*. There are surely few who have belief to swallow, or hope enough to experiment the Collyrium of Albertus; which promiseth a strange effect, and such as thieves would count inestimable, that is, to make one see in the dark: yet thus much, according unto his receit, will the right eye of an Hedge-hog boiled in oyl, and preserved in a brazen vessel effect. As strange it is, and unto vicious inclinations were worth a night's lodging with Lais, what is delivered in Kiranides; that the left stone of a Weesel wrapt up in the skin of a she Mule, is able to secure incontinency from conception.

If such remedies were valid, Browne concludes, the 'first and most uncomfortable Aphorism of Hippocrates' (*Ars longa, Vita brevis*) would be erroneous, 'for surely that Art were soon attained, that hath so general remedies; and life could not be short, were there such to prolong it'.

In the two following chapters (8 and 9) Browne considers some authors, much read in his day, who, though in some respects excellent, have 'given authority' to vulgar errors. In so far as any such errors derive from Herodotus, the readers, he says, are at fault rather than the historian who: 'as well intending the delight as benefit of his Reader, hath besprinkled his work with many fabulosities'—these were not meant to deceive; but Sir John Mandeville in his travels includes many fabulous stories derived from Ctesias which readers accept as factual; Dioscorides and other ancient authors who wrote of *Materia Medica* must be read with caution and Browne, using his favourite form, the ironical subjunctive, illustrates his point:

It had been an excellent Receipt, and in his time when Saddles were scarce in fashion of very great use, if that were true which he delivers, that Vitex, or Agnus Castus, held only in the hand, preserveth the rider from galling. It were a strange effect, and Whores would forsake the experiment of Savine, if that were a truth which he delivereth of Brake or female Fearn, that onely treading over it, it causeth a sudden abortion. It were to be wished true, and women would idolize him, could that be made out which he recordeth of Phyllon, Mercury and other vegetables, that the juice of the male Plant drunk, or the leaves but applied unto the genitals, determines their conceptions unto males [I, 8, sect. iv].

As to Pliny 'there is scarce a popular error passant in our days, which is not either directly expressed, or diductively contained in this Work'. But here too Browne blames the readers rather than the author: 'for commonly he nameth the Authors from whom he received those accounts, and writes but as he reads....' Claudius Ælianus, whose *History of Animals* and *Varia Historia* are 'in the hands of everyone', includes doubtful, false, or impossible assertions more confidently than Pliny, many of which are taken over from Ctesias. Julius Solinus, although, Browne says, his *Polyhistor* is little more than 'Pliny varied is now likely, and deserves indeed to live for ever; not only for the elegancy of the Text, but the excellency of the Comment, lately performed by Salmasius, under the name of *Plinian-Exercitations*'. Browne highly praises Athenaeus, 'a delectable Author, very various, and justly stiled by Casaubon, Graecorum Plinius'. But, much as he enjoys reading him, he warns the reader against uncritical acceptance of what he writes, 'for such as amass all relations, must erre in some, and may without offence, be unbelieved in many'.

Next he names a number of poets who recounted the marvels of nature in hexameters or iambics and can be read with pleasure, but must not on that account be believed.

He closes this chapter with a warning to his readers that even learned and revered bishops can mislead in matters of natural history, as they frequently rely on ancient authors rather than on their own observation. Similarly, he cautions the reader against uncritical reading of occultist authors 'who pretend to write of Secrets, to deliver Antipathies, Sympathies, and the occult abstrucities of things'. Such works, he says, contain 'various delectable subjects', but if we accept them as authorities we 'thereby omit not onely the certainty of Truth, but the pleasure of its experiment'.

After these pages, which are as characteristic in their obvious relish for lively reading matter as in their warning against credulity, Browne, no less characteristically, reminds us that his own book also needs to be read with caution:

> Thus, I say, must these Authors be read, and thus must we be read our selves; for discoursing of matters dubious, and many controvertible truths; we cannot without arrogancy entreat a credulity, or implore any farther assent, then the probability of our Reasons, and verity of experiments induce [I, 8].

In ch. 9 Browne talks of the unintended perpetuation of errors by moralists and preachers. The heritage of error is used by 'Writers, Preachers, Moralists, Rhetoricians, Orators and Poets' to 'illustrate matters of undeniable truth'. Unfortunately, the illustrations also are liable to be accepted as true, it may even be supposed that the truth illustrated depends upon the truth of the illustration. Alexander Ross provides evidence that such supposition was not confined to the simple. He defends the whole fable of the Phoenix, for instance (against Sir Thomas Browne's argument in Book III), and among his many reasons is his assurance that to doubt the factual resurrection of the Phoenix would imply doubt of that which it has been used to illustrate; he writes that:

> The testimony of so many Writers, especially of the Fathers proving by the Phoenix the Incarnation of Christ, and his Resurrection, and withall our resuscitation in the last day, doe induce me to believe there is such a bird, else their arguments had been of small validity among the Gentiles, if they had not believed there was such a bird. What wonder is it, saith Tertullian, for a virgin to conceive, when the Eastern bird is generated without copulation.... Shall men utterly perish (saith he) and the birds of Arabia be sure of their resurrection? [*Arcana*, Book II, ch. XXI, sect. 12.]

This curious piece of circular argumentation justifies, perhaps, Browne's sternly Baconian conclusion to ch. 9, in which he seems to wish that paintings and poems could be destroyed rather than continue to impede the advancement of learning:

> For were a pregnant wit educated in ignorance hereof, receiving only impressions from realities; upon such solid foundations, it must surely raise more substantial superstructions, and fall upon very many excellent strains, which have been jusled off by their intrusions [I, 9].

Browne opened his account of the general causes of error with the Fall of man and in the last two chapters of Book I he turns again to the Devil's activities as the 'Promoter of false Opinions'. Just as, in ch. 1, he admitted that mankind might have sinned without Satan since, as Milton was to state it: 'The first sort by their own suggestion fell. Self-tempted, self-depraved'; so in ch. 10 he admits that once the Fall had taken place mankind would continue to err without Satan's intervention. Nevertheless, Browne accepts the church's teaching; he accepts both the temptation in the Garden of Eden and Satan's subsequent activity in the world. He ascribes to Satan's active malice false beliefs about God; Satan has tried, he says, five different ways to undermine faith. He has suggested that there is no God, he is merely 'an invention of the creature'; that, if there is a God, he does not govern the world; that if he governs the world he cares only for species, not individuals. Since these three suggestions fail, and few become atheists, Satan inculcates the alternative suggestion that there are many Gods, and that, Browne argues, is equivalent to atheism; 'for Unity is the inseparable and essential attribute of the Deity', as Socrates, Plato and Aristotle knew. Or, fifthly, he has tried to persuade mankind that he himself is God; this he has done by claiming foreknowledge (speaking through Oracles) and omnipotence (performing wonders through magicians).

Browne reminds his readers of the performance of Pharaoh's magicians recorded in Exodus:

> To this effect [that is, to prove his omnipotence] his insolency was not ashamed to play a solemn prize with Moses; wherein although his performance were very specious, and beyond the common apprehension of any power below a Deity, yet was it not such as could make good his Omnipotency. For he was wholly confounded in the conversion of dust into lice.

Browne's thought here may not be easy for a modern reader to follow, but it is characteristic and worth unravelling. We may need to remind ourselves of the sequence of events in Exodus vii–x, as well as of the belief that all wonder-working in the pre-Christian era, unless it was the work of Jehovah, was believed by Christians to be Satan's work. In the Exodus story the Egyptian magicians could at first match the wonders performed by Moses; they changed rods into serpents and water into blood; they produced a plague of frogs, but they could not produce lice out of the dust of the earth. Browne writes, of this wonder worked by Moses, that it was:

> An act Philosophy can scarce deny to be above the power of Nature, nor upon requisite predisposition beyond the efficacy of the Sun.

Wherein notwithstanding the head of the old Serpent was confessedly too weak for Moses' hand, and the arm of his Magicians too short for the finger of God.

This is not an easy sentence to construe. It would seem to mean that producing lice out of dust is more than Nature can do or the sun effect. It is not likely that Browne did mean this. As late as 1662 the Royal Society was ready to believe that the sun engendered not only lice but bees. We read in the *Transactions* of that year that 'Mr Hoskyns related an experiment of the production of bees out of dead bullocks'. Browne meant, I think, that philosophers could not be sure that this metamorphosis was beyond the power of nature or that it could not be effected by the sun. It was, however, beyond the powers of Satan and his agents the magicians. God enabled Moses to make use of a law of nature that eluded Satan, just as it puzzled seventeenth-century natural scientists.

Another miraculous power to which Satan lays claim is 'that he can raise the dead'. This belief, Browne says, was inconsistent with most ancient philosophies, and

More inconsistent with these opinions, is the Error of Christians, who holding the dead do rest in the Lord, do yet believe they are at the lure of the Devil; that he who is in bonds himself commandeth the fetters of the dead, and dwelling in the bottomless lake, the blessed from Abraham's bosome, that can believe the real resurrection of Samuel: or that there is anything but delusion in the practice of Necromancy[1] and popular raising of Ghosts [I, 10].

Browne has a serene confidence that death is a 'country from whose bourne no traveller returns'.

Another Satanic trick is to delude us in our dreams, seeming to give foresight or knowledge beyond the reach of our waking consciousness. But, Browne asserts, it is not hard to distinguish such illusory visions from those in which 'it hath pleased Almighty God, sometimes to reveal himself'. Revelations from heaven 'are conveyed by new impressions, and the immediate illumination

[1] 'Divination by the dead' (Sir Thomas Browne's own gloss).

of the soul', but the Devil's predictions in our dreams are no more than a compound of images already existing in the mind.

Browne makes fun of Satan's pretence to omniscience when he spoke through oracles by showing that much of what was foretold or advised was not beyond the reach of common sense. For instance, Caracalla consulted the oracle for a remedy for the gout, and he 'received no other counsel than to refrain cold drink; which was but a dietetical caution, and such as without a journey unto Aesculapius, culinary prescription and kitchin Aphorisms might have afforded at home'. However, although he mocks at the Devil's claims to omniscience, he does not doubt that he knows more than we do:

> being a natural Magician he may perform many acts in ways above our knowledge, though not transcending our natural power, when our knowledge shall direct it.... I hardly believe he hath from elder times unknown the verticity of the Loadstone; surely his perspicacity discerned it to respect the North, when ours beheld it indeterminately. Many secrets there are in Nature of difficult discovery unto man, of easie knowledge unto Satan; whereof some his vain glory cannot conceal, others his envy will not discover.

Here again the effect is to belittle this mere 'Magician'; he cannot control the laws of Nature but, being a spirit, he must know of forces in Nature which men have not yet discovered. This knowledge may account for some of his wonders. Being both proud and envious it is to be expected that Satan will sometimes display his knowledge and sometimes hide it.

It will be noticed that, although Browne does not doubt the menacing existence of Satan, he has argued throughout the chapter against his possession of powers usually ascribed to him. He has been showing that the Devil claims more and greater powers than he owns. But, he now says, Satan also deludes us by a contrary stratagem,

> yet would he also perswade our beliefs, that he is less than Angels or men; and his condition not onely subjected unto rational powers, but

the actions of things which have no efficacy on our selves. Thus hath he inveigled no small part of the world into a credulity of artificial Magick.

Hence have arisen such dangerous beliefs as that devils

stand in awe of Charms, Spels, and Conjurations; that he is afraid of letters and characters, of notes and dashes, which set together do signifie nothing, not only in the dictionary of man, but the subtiler vocabulary of Satan.

Browne lists a long series of beliefs about how men may subjugate Satan to their will, or scare him from his own purposes; such beliefs as that the name of God, the sign of the Cross, or words from holy Scripture will overcome him. The notion of his own weakness is inculcated by the Devil to entrap us; we should suspect an 'Ambuscado':

Whereby to confirm our credulities, he will comply with the opinion of such powers, which in themselves have no activities. Whereof having once begot in our minds an assured dependence, he makes us relie on powers which he but precariously obeys; and to desert those true and only charms which Hell cannot withstand.

Browne brings ch. 10 to an end with Satan's ultimate ruse: 'Lastly, To lead us farther into darkness, and quite to lose us in this maze of Error, he would make men believe there is no such creature as himself; and that he is not only subject unto inferiour creatures, but in the rank of nothing.'

If Satan can persuade mankind that he does not exist, he will not only produce a false sense of security but 'he annihilates the blessed Angels and Spirits in the rank of his creation' (that is to say, he breaks a link in the chain of being and destroys the order of the cosmos). To effect this Satan may try to persuade us that:

Apparitions, and such as confirm his existence are either deceptions of sight, or melancholly depravements of phansie. Thus when he had not only appeared but spake unto Brutus; Cassius the Epicurean was ready at hand to perswade him, it was but a mistake in his weary imagination, and that indeed there were no such realities in nature. Thus he endeavours to propagate the unbelief of Witches, whose concession infers his co-existency; by this means also he advanceth the opinion of total death, and staggereth the immortality of the soul; for, such as deny there are spirits subsistent without bodies, will with more difficulty affirm the separated existence of their own [I, 10].

If Browne's scepticism about the Devil's powers, or about the powers of magic to control him, has suggested that he is akin to a modern sceptic or agnostic, this passage reminds us how wide is the gulf between. We must not, however, leap to the conclusion that Browne's credulity was antiquated in his own day. His conviction that disbelief in the devil and witches would lead to atheism was asserted nineteen years later by Joseph Glanvill, Fellow of, and energetic apologist for, the Royal Society. In 1666 Glanvill wrote of Satan:

His influence is never more dangerous than when his agency is least suspected...he cannot expect to advantage himself more than by insinuating the belief, that there is no such thing as himself, but that fear and fancy make Devils now, as they did Gods of old.—And when men are arrived at this degree of dissidence and infidelity, we are beholden to them if they believe either Angel, or Spirit, Resurrection of the body, or Immortality of Souls. These things hang together in a Chain of Connection, at least in those mens Hypothesis; and 'tis but an happy chance if he that hath lost one link holds another [*Philosophical Considerations concerning Witches*...].

Consequently, Glanvill argues, it is well to believe in witches, if only in order to retain our belief in God. Here, as in Glanvill's earlier work, *The Vanity of Dogmatizing* (1661), one can detect the influence of Browne in the organization of ideas and in the style. (In *The Vanity of Dogmatizing* Glanvill expressed his admiration for the author of *Pseudodoxia*, although, when he revised this work in 1665, he tried to make his style more 'plain and natural', as was proper for the apologist of the Royal Society.) However, the idea that there is a vital connection between belief in the Devil and belief in God was not invented by Browne, nor did its continuance depend upon Glanvill's agreement.

In ch. 11, Browne illustrates further how Satan is a cause of human error. He says that most Christians have escaped the theological traps described in ch. 10; but many are deluded by alleged predictions, or cures, and many are beguiled into impieties by speculations of which Satan is the source. When men are persuaded that natural phenomena 'proceed from supernatural powers', Satan is often at work inculcating superstition; a little more knowledge would enlighten his victims:

> To behold a Rainbow in the night, is no prodigy unto a Philosopher. Then Eclipses of Sun or Moon, nothing is more natural. Yet with what superstition they have been beheld since the Tragedy of Nicias and his Army, many examples declare.

Nevertheless, Browne adds, these 'natural productions from second and settled causes' sometimes coincide with events in human history in a way that 'admits a further consideration'. It is the hand of God, not of Satan, that he thinks may be detected in such coincidences.

If Satan sometimes blinds the eyes of men so that they cannot recognize natural cause and effect (such as philosophers discern), even more often he makes them suppose a causal relation where there is none. For example:

> When Augustus found two galls in his sacrifice, the credulity of the City concluded a hope of peace with Anthony; and the conjunction of persons in choler with each other. Because Brutus and Cassius met a Blackmore, and Pompey had on a dark or sad coloured garment at Pharsalia; these were presages of their overthrow. Which notwithstanding are scarce Rhetorical sequels; concluding Metaphors from realities, and from conceptions metaphorical inferring realities again.

In similar fashion Satan deceives men about cause and effect in the cure of disease:

> He deludeth also by Philtres, Ligatures, Charms, ungrounded Amulets, Characters, and many superstitious ways in the cure of common diseases: seconding herein the expectation of men with events of his own contriving.

Browne does not doubt that Satan has magical powers (how extensive remains obscure), but he is sure he will not use them for good ends. To resort to magical cures is to put ourselves in the Devil's power:

For thereby he begets not only a false opinion, but such as leadeth the open way of destruction. In maladies admitting natural reliefs, making men rely on remedies, neither of real operation in themselves, nor more than seeming efficacy in his concurrence. Which whensoever he pleaseth to withdraw, they stand naked unto the mischief of their diseases; and revenge the contempt of the medicines of the Earth which God hath created for them. And therefore when neither miracle is expected, nor connection of cause unto effect from natural grounds concluded; however it be sometime successful, it cannot be safe to rely on such practises, and desert the known and authentick provisions of God. In which rank of remedies, if nothing in our knowledge of their proper power be able to relieve us, we must with patience submit unto that restraint, and expect the will of the Restrainer.

Here, and in the ensuing examples and discussion of magical cures, it is easy to discern Browne's intention, but hard to follow his reasoning. I expect it was not so difficult for his contemporary readers; he was making the orthodox distinction between the Devil's wonders and the miracles of God. William Perkins makes that distinction clear in *A Discourse of the Damned Art of Witchcraft* (published posthumously, 1608) where he writes: 'A true wonder is a rare worke, done by the Power of God simply, either above, or against nature, and is properly called a miracle' [p. 13]. On the other hand, wonders performed by satanic power 'be no miracles, because they are done by virtue of nature simply, but above and against the ordinary course thereof'. Browne expresses this distinction by saying of Satan: 'whether he worketh by causes which have relation or none to the effect, he maketh it out by secret and undiscerned ways of Nature.' Whereas about God's miracles Browne says:

But the effects of powers Divine flow from another operation; who either proceeding by visible means or not, unto visible effects, is able to conjoin them by his co-operation....And thus may he operate also from causes of no power unto their visible effects; for he that hath determined their actions unto certain effects, hath not so emptied his own, but that he can make them effectual unto any other.

God can contravene the laws because they are his own, Satan can only make clever use of them. But I suspect that Browne's clumsy writing here is the result of some discomfort. He accepts, but he does not enjoy the belief that God can change the relation between cause and effect. The miracle that commands his wonder and worship is the creation of an ordered universe.

Magical cures are not the only delusion proffered by the Devil. Innocent-seeming speculations can also serve his purposes; men have been led to worship false gods through the apparently 'innocent error, and harmless digression from truth' of supposing that sun, moon and stars were living creatures. By inculcating the belief that 'spirits are corporeal' Satan 'establisheth the Doctrine of Lustrations, Amulets and Charms', and of even graver consequence was the speculation 'that there are two principles of all things, one good, and another evil; from the one proceeding vertue, love, light and unity; from the other, division, discord, darkness and deformity'. (The strong hold this still has upon the imagination will be recognized by readers of Mr E. M. Forster's *A Passage to India*.) By means of this belief Satan 'obtained the advantage of Adoration...and therefore, not willing to let it fall, he furthered the conceit in succeeding Ages, and raised the faction of Manes[1] to maintain it'.

Among other speculative errors which, Browne shows, must be dear to the Devil is Aristotle's belief 'that the feminine sex have no generative emission, affording no seminal Principles of conception'. This, Browne says, is 'still maintained by some, and will be countenanced by him forever. For hereby he disparageth the fruit of the Virgin, frustrateth the fundamental Prophesie, nor can the seed of Woman then break the head of the Serpent.'

[1] Manes, or Manichæus, founder of the Manichæan sect.

As well as speculations that lead to infidelity or impiety, Satan delights to foster those that lead merely to imbecility:

> Thus if Xenophanes will say there is another world in the Moon; if Heraclitus with his adherents will hold the Sun is no bigger than it appeareth; if Anaxagoras affirm that Snow is black; If any other opinion there are no Antipodes, or that Stars do fall, he shall not want herein the applause or advocacy of Satan.

Satan delights to promote all types of errors because he is the enemy of God 'who is truth itself'.

At this point, however, Browne recollects that the Delphic Oracle did not always mislead; for example *Nosce teipsum*, 'the Motto of Delphos was a good precept in morality', and 'a just man is beloved of the gods, an uncontrolable verity'. But, he decides, if the Devil either speaks the truth, or performs humane acts (such as enabling Vespasian to cure a lame man), 'it is upon design, and a subtile inversion of the precept of God, to do good that evil may come of it'.

Moreover, so wide is the empire of truth that even the devils in Hell cannot wholly escape from it. Although they are deceivers they cannot, such is the nature of things, practise deceit within their own society: 'And so also in Moral verities, although they deceive us, they lie not unto each other; as well understanding that all community is continued by Truth, and that of Hell cannot consist with it.'

This characteristic piece of humorous but morally valid reasoning beguiles Browne into an even more startling paradox. Not only are devils forced to speak the truth in order to sustain their own society, but they also cannot avoid being 'well-wishers hereunto and in some sense do really desire its enlargement'. This turns out to mean that devils would like several propositions to be true that are in fact false:

> He cannot but wish he were as he professeth, that he had the knowledge of future events; were it in his power the Jews would be in the right,

and the Messias yet to come. Could his desires effect it, the opinion of Aristotle should be true, the world should have no end, but be as immortal as himself.

And thus he would escape punishment. But here Browne, as he very well knows, is merely playing with words and we need be no more patient with him than he was with Zeno. As he says in the next paragraph: 'If things were true which now are false, it were but an exchange of their natures, and things must then be false which now are true.'

This is in the last paragraph of Book I and Browne is leading up to his conclusion of 'the General Part'. He tells us how the fall of the Angels was caused by Satan's rejection of truth, that is to say of the order ordained by God:

> For whilest they murmur against the present disposure of things, regulating determined realities unto their private optations, they rest not in their established natures; but unwishing their unalterable verities, do tacitly desire in them a difformity from the primitive Rule, and the Idea of that mind that formed all things best. And thus he offended truth even in his first attempt; For not content with his created nature, and thinking it too low, to be the highest creature of God, he offended the Ordainer, not only in the attempt, but in the wish and simple volition thereof [I, 11].

By reminding us that Satan delighted in falsehood from the moment of his revolt, Browne reminds us also that when we attempt to dispel error we are opposing Satan and fulfilling God's will. He has established, both in general and in particular examples, the connection between Satan and all human error, so that his readers may gladly follow him in the remaining books when he attempts to confute particular errors.

CHAPTER VI

'PSEUDODOXIA' (BOOKS II–VII)

IN the opening and closing chapters of Book I Browne framed his inquiry. The frame is traditional, orthodox Christian belief. He glances in those first and last chapters at the Devil as the source of error and, particularly in ch. 10, of error about God and about his own supernatural powers. But in the body of his work Browne is not writing about theology. He had described his own faith in *Religio Medici*, Part I, and it is recognizably at the root of his conception of the created world; but he had no wish then and he has no wish now to engage in theological controversy. The subject of *Pseudodoxia* is widespread misconception about phenomena; he undertakes, as his subtitle declares: *Enquiries into Very many received Tenents, And commonly presumed Truths*, concerning, for the most part, matters of fact. He inquires into beliefs about certain minerals, vegetables, animals, or about mankind; and, in the last three books, he inquires into beliefs that arise out of myth, allegory, metaphor, or proverb. He hopes to contribute to the advancement of positive knowledge.

In writing about *Religio Medici* and Book I of *Pseudodoxia* I thought it best, even at the risk of tediousness, to follow very closely at the heels of the author. Admirers of Browne in the nineteenth and twentieth centuries have selected noble or amusing passages from his works; I believe that, although this has kept his name green and fostered appreciation of his style, it has not much helped the modern reader to discover what he was doing in his writings. By following the train of his thought and attempting, sometimes, to interpret his meaning I hoped to gain, and perhaps to impart, a fuller understanding of what Sir Thomas intended and of how his contemporaries understood him. However, to adopt the same method for *Pseudodoxia*, Books II–VII, would be to offer a very poor substitute for the work itself. Neither enjoyment nor understanding depends here upon following the order of Browne's chapters. Within each chapter there is order, but it is an obvious logical order; he examines the witnesses, the probability, the origins of each erroneous or dubious belief. There is no significant order in the sequence of chapters, or even of books, save for the decorous 'chain of being' arrangement of the first four.

Instead of following in Browne's footsteps through these books I hope to be able to discover something of his mind and of his art by raising in turn three separate questions: first, what is Browne's method and what are his assumptions in these inquiries into vulgar and common errors? Secondly, where does he stand, as seeker after knowledge, in relation to his contemporaries? Thirdly, what does *Pseudodoxia* tell us about the man himself? Do we find here that 'le style c'est l'homme même'?

I. METHOD AND ASSUMPTIONS

Browne was aware of three possible ways of arriving at the truth about phenomena: one could inquire what the books say (authority); one could consider probability (reason); or, in some cases, one could test by one's own senses (experiment). The adherents to antiquity, in the by then vigorous Ancients and Moderns controversy, gave most weight to the first; some of the admired Ancients had given most weight to the second; the Royal Society and its supporters—the Moderns—gave most weight to the third. Browne keeps all three in play as far as is appropriate or possible. He cites authorities *pro* and *con* the belief in question; he examines the belief by the light of reason; he refers to any experimental test he has been able to apply. His summing up may take the form of a question; but his own choice of an answer is made plain by the gradual accumulation of his three kinds of evidence. As an example of method I will choose the inquiry about the relative length of a badger's legs. I deliberately choose this one because Browne has often been accused of failing in this instance to see for himself, although dealing with a creature common in the English countryside.

This inquiry [III, 5] begins:

That a Brock or Badger hath the legs on one side shorter then of the other, though an opinion perhaps not very ancient, is yet very general; received not only by Theorists and unexperienced believers, but assented unto by most who have the opportunity to behold and hunt them daily. Which notwithstanding upon enquiry I find repugnant unto the three Determinators of Truth, Authority, Sense, and Reason.

As he indicates in this opening paragraph, he used all three 'determinators' in order to satisfy himself and convince his readers. First he quotes two great authorities on natural history, Albertus Magnus (1206–80, teacher of Aquinas and author of *Summa de Creaturis*) and Aldrovandus (1522–1605, professor of Natural History at Bologna from 1560). The former is doubtful and admits that he 'could not confirm the verity thereof'; the second plainly says that no such inequality is observable. This then is not a matter about which Browne has a weight of authority to contend with. When he has, he will often marshal six or more names on either side, as in the first error he discusses, 'The common Tenent that Chrystal is nothing else but Ice strongly congealed'. Having disposed of authorities about the badger's legs, Browne next refers to the experimental test; although he did not dissect a badger as his son Edward was to do eighteen years later, on 10 February 1664,[1] yet he carefully looked at one or more; he says: 'And for my own part, upon indifferent inquiry, I cannot discover this difference, although the regardable side be defined, and the brevity by most imputed unto the left.' It is a clumsy piece of prose, as Browne's expository prose sometimes is, but it is not, I think, difficult to construe. By 'indifferent inquiry' Browne does not mean, as I once thought, insufficient or slight inquiry, he means unbiased inquiry, and this links straight on to

[1] Wilkin, vol. I, p. 49.

what follows: he looked for a shorter pair of legs upon each side of the badger, although it was usually thought that the shorter legs were on the left side. Finally, at greater length and with obvious relish, Browne brings reason to bear on the question:

Again, It seems no easie affront unto Reason, and generally repugnant unto the course of Nature; for if we survey the total set of Animals, we may in their legs, or Organs of progression, observe an equality of length, and parity of Numeration; that is, not any to have an odd legg, or the supporters and movers of one side not exactly answered by the other.

Assumptions of some kind underlie all reasoning. What Sir Thomas Browne is assuming is that Nature is rationally planned and that we shall therefore expect something approaching uniformity of principle—if the belief about the badger's legs would make that creature unique among quadrupeds, it is probably erroneous. Of course Browne knows that other four-legged creatures, frogs, locusts, grasshoppers for instance, have legs of unequal length, but it is their hind legs, he points out, that are unequal to their forelegs. To suppose an inequality in the badger's legs on one side is irrational, not only because there is no example of such an arrangement, but because such an arrangement would be 'ill contrived':

Lastly, The Monstrosity is ill contrived, and with some disadvantage; the shortness being affixed unto the legs of one side, which might have been more tolerably placed upon the thwart or Diagonal Movers. For the progression of quadrupeds being performed *per Diametrum*, that is the cross legs moving or resting together, so that two are always in motion, and two in station at the same time; the brevity had been more tolerable in the cross legs. For then the Motion and station had been performed by equal legs; whereas herein they are both performed by unequal Organs, and the imperfection becomes discoverable at every hand.

In this instance Browne's three determinators all serve him well and point decisively to the overthrow of this vulgar error: There is no weight of authority to support it; the senses cannot discern it; it would be irrational to suppose it.

There are, of course, many vulgar errors for which one or

other of the determinators cannot be invoked. For example, experience cannot help us to decide for or against common opinion about the Phoenix, or about whether or not a peacock is ashamed when it looks at its legs. Browne discusses the former at length [III, 12], but the latter very briefly [III, 27, sect. 2]. He first cites two authorities, Cardan (1501–76), well known for his *De Subtilitate Rerum* and *De Varietate Rerum*, and Scaliger (1485–1558), who wrote a commentary on the former. It is worth remembering that great authorities on natural history who flourished in the sixteenth century were not as obviously outmoded for Browne, in the seventeenth, as a nineteenth-century authority would be for a twentieth-century naturalist. Advancement in scientific learning was not moving so rapidly then as now. Cardan affirms the predicament of the peacock; Scaliger reasons against it; so Browne allows the authorities to cancel one another. He then gives what seems to him a good reason against the belief: 'let them believe that hold specifical deformities; or that any part can seem unhandsome to their eyes, which hath appeared good and beautiful unto their makers.' And lastly, as he frequently does, he attempts to account for the origin of the belief. 'The occasion of this conceit, might first arise from a common observation, that when they are in their pride, that is, advance their train, if they decline their neck to the ground, the hinder grow too weak, and suffer the train to fall.' This evokes a vivid picture of the peacock's seeming embarrassment. Any country observer—either seriously or wittily—could have started a rumour which by the time of Montaigne (see *Essais*, Book III, ch. 4) had given rise to a proverb: 'Ce sont les pieds du paon qui abattent son orgueil.' But who can say whether a proverb points back to an observed moral analogue, or states the literal truth? Cardan and Scaliger had both thought the matter worth discussing; it is not surprising or 'quaint' that Sir Thomas Browne should devote a short paragraph to it.

If there are some beliefs that cannot be tested by experiment, so there are some that cannot be tested by reason. For example, there is no reason either for or against the belief that garlic hinders the attraction of the loadstone [II, 3]. The belief is affirmed by many 'grave and worthy writers' (he names eight of them): 'But that it is evidently false, many experiments declare.' He gives an account of three experiments. This error, which, as Browne says, is 'an effect as strange as that of Homer's Moly, and the Garlick that Mercury bestowed upon Ulysses', he disposes of in a paragraph occupying less than a third of a page in Keynes's edition (vol. II, p. 116). His discussion of more serious questions about the properties of the loadstone fills the rest of two long chapters. I chose the slight instance to illustrate the fact that there is no one of the three determinators that can always be called upon. Browne uses as many as are appropriate and prefers, if possible, to use all three.

II. BROWNE IN RELATION TO HIS CONTEMPORARIES

It is probably easier now than it was in the nineteenth century to avoid thinking of Sir Thomas Browne as 'quaint'. But it is not easy to decide just how serious his contribution to knowledge would have seemed to a contemporary, nor whether, in opinions, he was in advance of or behind the times, and it is certainly not easier today than it was in 1652 (when Alexander Ross published *Arcana*) to be sure how seriously Browne himself has entertained some of the errors he dispels. When possible it is worth while to find out what contemporaries thought of Browne or how they pursued inquiries similar to his. The publication of six editions of *Pseudodoxia* within Browne's lifetime is solid evidence that the book was in demand. Among contemporary witnesses to Browne's reputation the most intelligent and the most direct is the French doctor of medicine, Gui Patin (1602–72). A very brief sketch of Patin's career and character will suggest what weight should be given to his testimony. He was a humanist in the sense that Milton, or Browne himself, were humanists; he admired Plato, Aristotle, Virgil, Cicero and Galen among Ancients, and, among the Moderns, Scaliger, Erasmus, Salmasius (Milton's opponent) and the great French doctor of medicine Fernel; he calls Pliny's *Natural History* 'une grande mer dans laquelle il fait bon pêcher'. He was violently opposed to some new medical theories, including Harvey's discovery of the circulation of the blood. This does not mean that he was in general tied to the doctrine of the Ancients, but rather that he was a man of strong, idiosyncratic, eclectic views. He is best known to posterity by his letters to his friends which were posthumously published and were re-edited in three volumes in 1846. Sainte-Beuve wrote two *Causeries du Lundi* about Patin,[1] and pleaded for another and better annotated edition of the letters. He valued Patin both for his own lively and idiosyncratic character revealed in letters, where one finds 'le naturel, et rien que le naturel, avec tous ces hasards et ces crudités', and because 'un corps bien rédigé des Lettres de Gui Patin n'offrirait pas seulement un tableau de l'histoire de la médecine durant cinquante ans: on y verrait un coin très étendu des mœurs et de la littérature avant Louis XIV'. His beliefs, his outlook, his temperament and his tastes constitute him an ideal contemporary reader of Sir Thomas Browne. It is unfortunate that he seems to have read only *Religio Medici*. This, however, he relished and he refers to it in his letters on four separate occasions. On 21 October 1644 he writes that the book is:

> tout gentil et curieux, mais fort délicat et tout mystique; l'auteur ne manque pas d'esprit, vous y verrez d'étranges et ravissantes pensées. Il n'y a guère de livres de cette sorte. S'il était permis aux savants d'écrire librement on nous apprendrait beaucoup de nouveautés, il n'y eut jamais gazette qui valut cela; la subtilité de l'esprit humain se pourrait découvrir par cette voie.

Here Patin emphasizes the same qualities as strike a modern reader: wit, strange and beguiling sequences of thought and subtlety of mind.

[1] *Causeries du Lundi* (vol. VIII, 25 April and 2 May 1853. 3rd edition, pp. 88–133).

Five years later, speaking about Sir Kenelm Digby's *Observations on Religio Medici*, Patin says: 'J'ai bonne opinion de ces deux esprits, encore que je ne voudrais pas jurer qu'en tout deux il n'y eut quelques extravagances' [26 July 1650]. After three more years had passed he wrote a little censoriously of the author's melancholy; he was discussing a translation into Latin with notes by Nicholas von Moltke. Patin says of von Moltke: 'C'est un maître homme qui a de l'esprit et du mérite de son original, en faisant abstraction des mauvaises qualités que cet Anglais a dans sa cervelle mélancholique' [21 October 1653].

However, four years later, 19 June 1657, Patin came across a ham-fisted German translation with notes and, as he perused it, his former delight in Browne's book revived, quickened by his contempt for the annotator; he says:

> Ce livre n'aurait pas besoin de tels écoliers. Personne n'était capable de traduire ce livre s'il n'avait l'esprit approchant de l'auteur, qui est gentil et éveillé. Le genre du premier auteur du livre vaut mieux que tous les commentaires, qui ne sont que la misérable pédanterie d'un jeune homme allemand qui pense être bien savant.

'Esprit gentil et éveillé'; 'quelques extravagances'; 'une cervelle mélancholique': all three expressions will strike the modern reader as appropriate to the author of *Religio Medici*, although the last does not seem to apply to the author of *Pseudodoxia*. Patin's comments suggest that, despite the lapse of time and all the changes in our thinking, Browne's first book has for us the same qualities that it had for this contemporary reader, whose own interests and gifts made it likely that he would read it intelligently.

As far as I know Gui Patin is the only contemporary who has left printed evidence that he read Sir Thomas Browne for pleasure and savoured the personality that the writing revealed. Glanvill, it is true, imitated Browne's style in his first published work, but he does not share, and perhaps does not notice, Browne's quizzical humour, just as he does not share Browne's 'negative capability'.[1] Glanvill writes always as a propagandist, advocating one point of view and decrying another. In *The Vanity of Dogmatizing* he is an advocate of open-mindedness, but the quality itself becomes less and less evident in his writings as the years pass. The two earnest controversialists, Joseph Glanvill and Alexander Ross, tell us nothing about Browne the 'man of achievement in literature'. They do, however, help us to assess his contemporary status as a contributor to the advancement of knowledge.

When Glanvill wrote *The Vanity of Dogmatizing*, first published 1661, he imitated the style of *Pseudodoxia* and often followed the order of Browne's arguments and examples. Clearly this young modernist (Glanvill was twenty years old in 1661) did not think of his predecessor as outmoded. When he revised his work four years later he made no change of substance although—faithful member of the Royal Society as he was—he apologized for his style and modified it here and there: in the address to the Royal Society prefaced to the edition of 1665 Glanvill says that:

perceiving that several ingenious persons whose assistance might be conducive to the Advance of real knowledge, lay under prejudices of Education and Customary Belief; I thought that the enlarging them to a state of more generous Freedom by striking at the root of Pedantry and opinionative Assurance would be no hinderance to the World's improvement. For such it was then that the ensuing Essay was designed; which therefore wears a dress, that possibly is not so suitable to the graver Geniusses, who have outgrown all gayeties of style and youthful relishes; but yet perhaps is not improper for the persons for whom it was prepared.

He proceeds to apologize for the style of his first edition and the unavoidable remaining evidence of it in the revised version. He says that he has grown to dislike the older way of writing; it is 'less agreeable to my present relish and Genius; which is more gratified with manly sense, flowing in a natural and unaffected eloquence, then with the musick and curiosity of fine Metaphors

[1] *The Letters of John Keats*, 21 December 1817.

and dancing periods'. Fashion in prose style had changed, the new had become the established between 1661 and 1665. The revised edition has a new title (*The Vanity of Dogmatizing* becomes *Scepsis Scientifica*), and a shorter and better subtitle, 'Confest Ignorance, the way to Science'; but nothing is altered in the substance of the book. The closeness of that to *Pseudodoxia* can be quickly illustrated by quoting, as an example, the title of Glanvill's chapter xv (it is identical in the two editions):

Our affections are engaged by our Reverence to Antiquity and Authority. This hath been a great hinderer of Theoretical improvements; and it hath been an advantage to the Mathematicks and Mechanicks Arts, that it hath no place in them. Our mistake of Antiquity. The unreasonableness of that kind of Pedantick Adoration. Hence the vanity of affecting impertinent quotations. The pedantry on't is derided; the little improvement of Science through its successive derivations, and whence that has hapned.

A comparison between this and *Pseudodoxia*, Book I, chapters 6 and 7, shows how closely Glanvill is following Browne. Both writers are indebted to Bacon's *Advancement of Learning* but, both in the title and in the chapter it describes, Glanvill follows closely enough in Browne's steps to suggest that he had *Pseudodoxia* open before him. Nearly all the points made in Browne's two chapters are made in *Scepsis*, XVII: modern reverence for antiquity, 'the *Golden Age* was never present'; the absurdity of 'impertinent citations; and inducing Authority in things neither requiring, nor deserving it'; the advantage of mathematics over other 'Sciences'. All these quotations are from Glanvill; their prototypes can all be found in Browne. Sometimes there is a difference of substance because Browne is more intelligent, or better informed, or less concerned with advocacy; for example, Aristotle is nothing but a whipping boy for Glanvill who omits Browne's point that none of the Ancients expected uncritical acceptance, and all of them 'examine and refute the Doctrines of their Predecessors... Aristotle the most of any'. It is only Browne who makes a point of the difference in kind which frees mathematics from the incubus of authority. Glanvill only thinks it probable that mathematics have 'got the start in growth of other Sciences because their progress hath not been retarded by that reverential awe of former discoveries, which hath been so great an hinderance to theoretical improvements', and he chooses an example which scarcely supports his optimism. '*Galilaeus* without crime out-saw all *Antiquity*, and was not afraid to believe his eyes, in spite of the Opticks of Ptolemy and Aristotle.'

It is not only in generalities that Browne shows a clearer intellect and more common sense than his younger contemporary. This is sometimes as obvious when both discuss the same particular beliefs. For example, Browne in Book II, ch. 3 of *Pseudodoxia* and Glanvill in ch. XXI of *The Vanity of Dogmatizing* discuss some of the alleged magical properties of the loadstone. Browne first warns the reader that:

> Herein relations are strange and numerous; men being apt in all Ages to multiply wonders, and Philosophers dealing with admirable bodies [phenomena that evoke wonder] as Historians have done with excellent men, upon the strength of their great atchievements, ascribing acts unto them not only false but impossible.

Among the 'impossible' beliefs about the loadstone which Browne considers and makes fun of are the following: (1) that by putting a loadstone under her pillow a man can discover whether his wife is incontinent; (2) that if thieves make a fire at four corners of a house and into it throw fragments of a loadstone, the fumes will be so disturbing that the occupants will desert the house; (3) that with the aid of a loadstone Helenus foresaw the Fall of Troy; (4) that water sprinkled on the loadstone causes it to 'emit a voice not unlike an infant'; (5) that the touch of a loadstone immunizes against pain from flesh wounds, and (6) that:

> a Loadstone preserved in the salt of a Remora, acquires a power to attract gold out of the deepest Wells. Certainly a studied absurdity,

not casually cast out, but plotted for perpetuity; for the strangeness of the effect ever to be admired, and the difficulty of the trial never to be convicted.

All this Glanvill omits; there is nothing intentionally amusing in *The Vanity of Dogmatizing*. He does, however, discuss the question to which Browne turns in his next paragraph. Browne begins by referring back to the absurdities mentioned above: 'These conceits are of such monstrosity that they refute themselves in their recitals.' He goes on to others, less obviously absurd, which Glanvill will find entirely credible.

There is another of better notice, and whispered thorow the World with some attention; credulous and vulgar auditors readily believing it, and more judicious and distinctive heads, not altogether rejecting it. The conceit is excellent, and if the effect would follow, somewhat divine; whereby we might communicate like spirits, and confer on earth with Menippus in the Moon. And this is pretended from the sympathy of two Needles touched with the same Loadstone, and placed in the centre of two Abecedary circles or rings, with letters described round about them, one friend keeping one, and another the other, and agreeing upon an hour wherein they will communicate. For then, saith Tradition, at what distance of place soever, when one Needle shall be removed unto any letter; the other by a wonderful sympathy will move unto the same. But herein I confess my experience can find no truth; for having expressly framed two circles of Wood, and according to the number of the Latine letters divided each into twenty three parts, placing therein two stiles or Needles composed of the same steel, touched with the same Loadstone, and at the same point: of these two, whensoever I removed the one, although but at the distance of half a span, the other would stand like Hercules' pillars, and if the Earth stand still, have surely no motion at all. Now as it is not possible that any body should have no boundaries, or Sphear of its activity, so it is improbable it should effect that at distance, which nearer hand it cannot at all perform [II, 3].

Glanvill, advocate of experiment though he is, ignores this paragraph and proceeds to quarrel only with the reasoned proof in the next, where Browne wrote:

Again, the conceit is ill contrived, and one effect inferred, whereas the contrary will ensue. For if the removing of one of the Needles from

A to B, should have any action or influence on the other, it would not intice it from A to B, but repell it from A to Z: for Needles excited by the same point of the stone, do not attract, but avoid each other, even as these also do, when their invigorated extreams approach unto one other.

To this Glanvill replies:

Now though there will be some ill contrivance in a circumstance of this invention, in that the thus *impregnate Needles* will not move to, but avert from each other (as ingenious Dr. Browne in his *Pseudodoxia Epidemica* hath observed:) yet this cannot prejudice the main design of this way of secret conveyance: Since 'tis but reading counter to the *magnetick* informer; and noting the letter which is most distant in the *Abecedarian circle* from that which the Needle turns to, and the case is not alter'd [CXXI, p. 204].

Again it is the younger author who is the more credulous.

Both authors go on to speak of another rumoured possibility of communication at a distance. However, the difference between them is again marked. Browne uses this rumour merely as an analogy with the unlikely belief he has been discussing:

And therefore the Sympathy of these Needles is much of the same mould with that intelligence which is pretended from the flesh of one body transmuted by insition into another. For if by the Art of Taliacotius, a permutation of flesh, or transmutation be made from one man's body into another, as if a piece of flesh be exchanged from the bicipital muscle of either partie's arm, and about them both, an Alphabet circumscribed; upon a time appointed as some conceptions affirm, they may communicate at what distance soever. For if the one shall prick himself in A, the other at the same time will have a sense thereof in the same part: and upon inspection of his arm perceive what letters the other points out in his. Which is a way of intelligence very strange: and would requite the lost Art of Pythagoras, who could read a reverse in the Moon [II, 3].

And thereupon Browne returns to the real and imagined properties of the loadstone. But Glanvill, instead of treating 'sympathized hands' as an analogy, to emphasize the improbability of the foregoing, takes this example as a probability; he writes: 'There is besides this another way, which is said to have advanced the *secret* beyond *speculation*, and compleated it in *practice*. That some have conferr'd at distance by *sympathized* hands, and in a moment have thus transmitted their thoughts to each other' [CXXI, p. 204].

He goes on to describe the transference of flesh 'from one into the other' and to imagine in detail a message given and received, adding: 'Now that there has been some such practises I have had a considerable relation, which I hold not impertinent to insert', and proceeds to tell his story. In his revised edition of 1665 he is a little more cautious, but still far more credulous than Browne.

In the next paragraph we find Glanvill accepting Sir Kenelm Digby's assurance that 'there is a magnetick way of curing *wounds* by annointing the *weapon* and that the wound is affected in like manner as is the *extravenate bloud* by the *Sympathetick Medecine*' (that is as the blood let out of the veins is affected by medicine which has a natural affinity with the disease).

Browne, whose common sense is unfailing whenever his own medical experience is relevant, had dismissed this in 1646, advising men to rely on Nature and 'ordinary Balsams, or common vulnerary plaisters'.

The third witness to Sir Thomas Browne's contemporary status, Alexander Ross, is almost as much inferior to Glanvill in intelligence as Glanvill is inferior to Browne. Glanvill was Browne's junior by twenty-nine years, Ross his senior by fifteen; Glanvill constituted himself champion of the Moderns, Ross fought sturdily for the Ancients. We have already sampled his attack on *Religio Medici* and his defence of Unicorns against Browne's scepticism in *Pseudodoxia*. For us Alexander Ross's attacks on Browne are of twofold value: they illustrate how a learned reader of his own day might resist and misconceive him; they are also an admirable foil to Browne's writings. The serious yet buoyant and amused unravelling of error in *Pseudodoxia* reveals its intellectual light more clearly against a background of Ross's plodding, obscurantist, self-contradictory arguments.

Two examples, in addition to the one given in the last chapter, will serve to illustrate Ross's methods when he tries to confute Browne; I have chosen one from *Pseudodoxia*, Book III, and one from Book V, because Ross encounters a different kind of inquiry in each. In the first Browne is disproving a current belief that 'A Bear brings forth her young informous and unshapen, which she fashioneth after by licking them over' [III, 6]. It is a good example of Browne at work on an error that did not seem at that time absurd on the face of it, was in fact widely believed, and was susceptible of convincing disproof. He uses all three of his 'determinators of truth', and closes with an account of how the error is likely to have arisen. Aristotle, he says, 'seems to countenance it' and it is affirmed by other 'authorities', but they prove to be those against whom Browne had warned his readers in Book I, ch. 8, such as Solinus, Pliny and Ælian. He also quotes Ovid; poets too were sometimes sources of misinformation. All these affirmations can, he explains, be disregarded, because three more recent and more reliable natural philosophers have demonstrated that the belief is contradicted by experience. Mathiolus dissected a she-bear and found cubs 'with all their parts distinct: and not without shape'. Scaliger reports that hunters in the Alps used the same method with the same result. Aldrovandus saw a cub: 'preserved in a Glass...taken out of a Bear, perfectly formed and compleat in every part'.

This is adequate disproof from recorded sense-experience; but Browne is concerned to show that the belief also offends against reason:

> It is moreover injurious unto Reason, and much impugneth the course and providence of Nature, to conceive a birth should be ordained before there is a formation. For the conformation of parts is necessarily required, not onely unto the pre-requisites and previous conditions of birth, as Motion and Animation: but also unto the parturition or very birth it self: Wherein not only the Dam, but the younglings play their parts; and the cause and act of exclusion proceedeth from them both.

For the exclusion of Animals is not meerly passive like that of Eggs, nor the total action of delivery to be imputed unto the Mother: but the first attempt beginneth from the Infant: which at the accomplished period attempteth to change his Mansion: and strugling to come forth, dilacerates and breaks those parts which restrained him before.

The belief was, he thought, irrational because it contradicted the laws of nature concerning the birth of mammals. It was also irrational because it belittled the Creator: 'imputing that unto the tongue of a Beast, which is the strangest Artifice in all the acts of Nature; that is the formation of the Infant in the Womb, not only in Mankind, but all viviparous Animals'. Since the belief has no weight of authority behind it, is contradicted by those who have put it to the test of experience, offends against the laws of probability, and slights the power of the Creator, Browne finds it worth while to suggest how it may have arisen. He explains that the cub is born enclosed in a tough membrane which the dam has to break. The beholder can easily believe that the she-bear is licking her cub into shape though in fact she 'only draws the curtain, and takes away the vail which concealed the piece before'.

Undeterred by this thorough demolition Alexander Ross, champion of all Ancients but especially Aristotle, proceeds (in his *Arcana Microcosmi*), to rescue the belief. First he repeats the substance of Browne's last paragraph, alleging that 'This is all that the Ancients meant, as appears by *Aristotle* (*Animalia* l. 6. c. 31) who says, that in some manner the young Bear is for a while rude, and without shape'. However, having stated this, Ross goes on to say that he himself is not convinced that the bear-cub is formed before birth:

If I should yeild that the cub is not perfectly articulated nor formed, till it be excluded, no Error will arise hence; for the plastick faculty which hath its original from the sperm, ceaseth not to operate after the generation of the young animal, but continueth working so long as it lives.

This he attempts to prove by examples of post-natal developments such as of teeth, hair, or new skin over a wound; moreover, he asks, what else is the process of nutrition but 'a continuall generation of lost substance'. By this time Ross has convinced himself that Browne has not proved his case. Presumably he decided to retain his defence of the Ancients in case bear-cubs are in fact born complete, but to claim for himself none the less the right to believe that they are not; he concludes:

Hence then it appears, that if the Ancients had held the young Bears to bee ejected without form, which afterwards they received by *Plastick* faculty, it had been no Error: and though some young Bears have been found perfectly formed in the womb of the Dam, it is a question whether all be formed and shaped so [Book IV, ch. 4, sect. iv].

My second example of Ross at work upon a confutation of Browne is of a different kind. The descriptive title of the relevant chapter in *Pseudodoxia*, Book V, is 'Of many things questionable as they are commonly described in Pictures'. In discussing this chapter, Ross tries to convict Browne of confusing hieroglyphs and emblems with records of fact. If he had read more carefully he would have noticed that this is precisely the confusion Browne is trying to dispel. In the Emblem Books of the period we find some emblems that are based upon fact (the compass is an emblem of fidelity because in fact it 'draws my circle just'), but some, such as that of the pelican opening its own breast to feed its young, have no basis in fact. Browne begins with the pelican; he notes that the emblem 'is set forth not only in common signs, but in the Crest and Scutcheon of many Noble families; had been asserted by many holy Writers, and was an Hieroglyphic of piety and pitty among the Aegyptians; on which consideration, they spared them at their tables' [V, I]. The ironical clause at the end is characteristic—Ross probably failed to see the point—also he either actually failed to notice that Browne is writing about emblems here, or he conveniently forgot; he counters the whole of this first chapter by saying that 'this and divers other pictures are rather Hieroglyphical and Emblematical, then truly Historicall'. However, we soon discover which of the two writers is the more literal-minded. In ch. 4 Sir Thomas entertains us with speculations about pictures that show the serpent in Eden with the face of a woman; he says it is traditional, but 'nevertheless is a conceit not to be admitted, and the plain and received figure, is with better reason embraced'. For this opinion he gives the following reasons: (1) Eve would have been more astonished and therefore better forearmed if she had met a serpent with a woman's face. (2) Satan had no reason so to adapt the figure of a serpent, since the creature itself could not alarm Eve: mankind before the Fall had no reason to fear any creature. (3) Satan could as easily speak through the mouth of a serpent as of a woman. (4) We have no reason to suppose that his doing so would surprise Eve since we have no reason to think she knew that animals cannot speak. Ross asserts (without explanation) that, as regards 1, Eve would have been less surprised to find herself addressed by a snake with a woman's head and, in answer to 4, he says that: 'She could not be so grossly ignorant in that happy state...as to think a serpent would speak and discourse rationally.' He is, moreover, sure that a woman-faced serpent would have caused her no surprise:

for divers other creatures have the form of humane faces, such as Baboons, Apes, Monkies, Satyrs, and that *American* beast mentioned by *Andrew Theret*, called *Haijt* by the Inhabitants and *Guedon* by the French; the picture whereof may be seen in *Gesner* [Book IV, ch. 11, sect. iii].

It is Ross's solemnity as much as his credulity that separates him from Browne. He illustrates vividly for the modern reader that even an educated man could in mid-seventeenth century mistake emblems and hieroglyphs for evidence of fact. Browne himself often selects them because they invite amusing speculation; he is as well aware as any modern reader that this question about the serpent's face is not worth serious inquiry. He elaborates partly for the fun of it and partly as a dissuasive from grave inquiries into matters of this kind. Here, for example, he takes the opportunity for sophisticated joking. If Satan had assumed the face of a woman he would not only have startled Eve and so strengthened her defences, but he would have given 'some excuse unto the woman, which afterwards the man took up with lesser reason; that is to have been deceived by another like himself'. (The implication is that Eve, being a mere woman, was less like Adam than a serpent with a woman's face was like Eve. Browne, despite his domestic happiness, could never resist an anti-feminist joke.) Next Browne amuses himself (as he will later when he discusses the Phoenix [III, 12]) with a *reductio ad absurdum*. The point to be established is that Eve would not have feared a snake in its natural shape. Browne assumes that there were only two of each kind in the Garden of Eden; it would have been absurd to fear the destruction of one, because that would have implied the destruction of a species; it would have, as Browne puts it: 'frustrated the command of multiplication, destroyed a species, and imperfected the Creation'. It follows that no creature needed to fear destruction by another, and Eve was not afraid of a snake.

Alexander Ross believes that all Browne's arguments are equally solemn and to be taken *au pied de la lettre*. Evidence to the contrary is abundant in all Browne's writings. Moreover, whereas Ross thought laughter a contemptible thing, Browne approved of it. He discusses laughter in Book VII, ch. 16 and is answered by Ross in *Arcana*, Book II, ch. 15. Browne says it is unlikely to be true, and if true it is deplorable, that Crassus only laughed once, and that was 'at an Ass eating thistles'.

For, if an indifferent and unridiculous object could draw his habitual austereness unto a smile: it will be hard to believe he could with perpetuity resist the proper motives thereof. For the act of Laughter which is evidenced by a sweet contraction of the muscles of the face, and a pleasant agitation of the vocal Organs, is not meerly voluntary, or totally within the jurisdiction of our selves: but as it may be constrained by corporal contaction in any, and hath been enforced in some even in their death; so the new unusual or unexpected jucundities, which present themselves to any man in his life, at some time or other will have activity enough to excitate the earthiest soul, and raise a smile from the most composed tempers. Certainly the times were dull when these things happened, and the wits of those Ages short of these of ours; when men could maintain such immutable faces, as to remain like statues under the flatteries of wit and persist unalterable at all efforts of Jocularity.

In the next paragraph Browne asserts that, despite what is often said, he is convinced that 'our blessed Saviour' could and did laugh.

It will be hard to conceive how he passed his younger years and childhood without a smile, if as Divinity affirmeth, for the assurance of his humanity unto men, and the concealment of his Divinity from the devil, he passed this age like other children.

Finally, bringing this inquiry to a conclusion, Browne says that we cannot infer that Christ did not laugh from the silence of Scripture on the matter:

The Scriptures being serious, and commonly omitting such Parergies, it will be unreasonable from hence to condemn all Laughter, and from considerations inconsiderable to discipline a man out of his nature. For this is by a rustical severity to banish all urbanity; whose harmless and confined condition, as it stands commended by morality; so is it consistent with Religion, and doth not offend Divinity [VII, 16].

But, for Alexander Ross, 'this act' of laughing 'is rather a property of levity and folly then of reason and humanity; therefore we see women more inclined to laughing then men, childhood then age, and fools then wise men'. Ross is sure that Christ never laughed [Book IV, ch. 15, sect. iii].

III. THE STYLE AND THE MAN

Browne's own humour more often provokes a smile than a laugh. It is sophisticated, subtle, quizzical; it will sometimes elude us if we are not vigilant. The reader needs to be flexible, ready to be either grave or gay; aware that either mode can serve a serious purpose, and yet not over-anxious to discern such a purpose where none is evident. It would obviously be a mistake to resist a smile when Browne discusses the alleged cause of the death of Aeschylus:

It much disadvantageth the Panegyric of Synesius [he supplies a note: 'who writ in praise of baldness'] and is no small disparagement unto baldness, if it be true what is related by Ælian concerning Æschilus, whose bald-pate was mistaken for a rock, and so was brained by a Tortoise which an Æagle let fall upon it. Certainly it was a very great mistake in the perspicacity of that Animal. Some men critically disposed, would from hence confute the opinion of Copernicus, never conceiving how the motion of the earth below, should not wave him from a knock perpendicularly directed from a body in the air above [VII, 18, 6].

Browne was not convinced by the Copernican theory though, as we have seen (p. 136), he was not prepared to oppose it. He can joke about the 'New Philosophy' because, as we shall see, it threatens no belief that he values (see p. 186). This might be called academic (or donnish) humour; it is funny at the expense of an erudition upon which also it depends. Similarly Browne, though he is often gravely polysyllabic, can sometimes enjoy the consequent absurdity. When he considers the belief that elephants have no joints, which was, as he says, 'an old and grey-headed error even in the days of Aristotle', he has a merry time with it, which begins with verbal extravagance. All creatures that move forward need joints:

Whereof though some want bones, and all extended articulations, yet have they arthritical Analogies, and by the motion of fibrous and musculous parts, are able to make progression. Which to conceive in bodies inflexible, and without all protrusion of parts, were to expect a Race from Hercules his pillars; or hope to behold the effect of Orpheus his Harp, when trees found joints, and danced after his Musick [III, 1].

The polysyllables lead on to the comical use of mythology, after which, with seeming gravity, he adduces three good reasons for rejecting the erroneous belief; it is only after disproving the error by means of two determinators of truth that he clinches the matter with the third; those who believe it:

forget or consult not experience, whereof not many years past, we have had the advantage in England, by an Elephant shewn in many parts thereof, not only in the posture of standing, but kneeling and lying down.... This being not the first that hath been seen in England; for (besides some others) as Polydore Virgil relateth, Lewis the French King sent one to Henry the third, and Emanuel of Portugal another to Leo the tenth into Italy, where notwithstanding the errour is still alive and epidemical, as with us.

This kind of delaying tactic is Browne's most usual type of humour. He loves to accumulate evidence, making a vulgar error seem more and more absurd, and then to conclude with a pretended uncertainty, leaving the reader to deduce that the belief is ridiculous. For example, he plays for many pages with beliefs about the Phoenix [III, 12]. These beliefs were that 'there is but one Phoenix in the World, which after many hundred years burneth it self, and from the ashes thereof ariseth up another'. His principal method of demolition here depends upon cumulative argument; the joke culminates when, after disproving the story in eleven paragraphs which take very full account of all three 'determinators', he writes:

Since therefore we have so slender grounds to confirm the existence of the Phoenix, since there is no ocular witness of it, since as we have declared, by Authors from whom the story is derived, it rather stands rejected; since they who have seriously discoursed hereof, have delivered themselves negatively, diversely, or contrarily; since many others cannot be drawn into Argument, as writing Poetically, Rhetorically, Enigmatically, Hieroglyphically; since Holy Scripture alledged for it duly perpended, doth not advantage it; and lastly, since so strange a generation, unity and long life, hath neither experience nor reason to confirm it, how far to rely on this tradition, we refer unto consideration.

He then closes the chapter, in his character of doctor of medicine, with some ironic reflections on the folly of relying upon parts of a unique creature, the Phoenix, for cures, or suspecting them of causing physical ills. It is for him axiomatic that, if there exists a unique creature, it cannot be destroyed.

Both the joke and the proof are dependent on the self-evidence of the proposition (as Browne thought) that God would not permit his six days' work of creation to be impaired. If the Phoenix had been part of it, he would necessarily have been indestructible and no part of him could have either fed us or healed us.

A briefer example of proof by demonstrating logical absurdity occurs in a paragraph about the Amphisbæna, an animal reputed to have two heads [III, 15]; Browne argues that:

Were there any such species or natural kind of animal, it would be hard to make good those six positions of body, which according to the three dimensions are ascribed unto every Animal: that is, *infra*, *supra*, *ante*, *retro*, *dextrosum*, *sinistrosum*: for if (as it is determined) that be the anterior and upper part, wherein the senses are placed, and that the posterior and lower part which is opposite thereunto, there is no inferiour or former part in this Animal; for the senses being placed at both extreams, doth make both ends anterior, which is impossible; the terms being Relative, which mutually subsist, and are not without each other. And therefore this duplicity was ill contrived to place one head at both extreams, and had been more tolerable to have setled three or four at one. And therefore also Poets have been more reasonable then Philosophers, and Geryon or Cerberus less monstrous than *Amphisbæna*.

After which he proceeds through several paragraphs to his conclusion that:

The ground of the conceit was the figure of this Animal, and motion oft-times both ways; for described it is to be like a worm, and so equally framed at both extreams, that at an ordinary distance it is no easie matter to determine which is the head.

This description exactly corresponds to the definition in the *Oxford Dictionary* beginning: 'A worm-like lizard found in America.'

Sometimes Browne begins a chapter with pedantry and punning, for the joy of it, before settling down gravely to dispel and explain a mistake. Book III, ch. 19 'Of Lampries' begins:

Whether Lampries have nine eyes, as is received, we durst refer it unto Polyphemus, who had but one, to judg it. An error concerning eyes, occasioned by the error of eyes; deduced from the appearance of diverse cavities or holes on either side, which some call eyes that carelessly behold them; and is not only refutable by experience but also repugnant unto Reason.

In Book V, ch. 22 we find a graver play upon words than this light mockery on the organ of sight, that inadequate 'determinator of truth'. Chapter 22 is a long one in which, as the chapter-heading explains, he writes: *Compendiously of many questionable Customs, Opinions, Pictures, Practices, and Popular Observations.* Several of these depend upon mistaking a trope for a fact, and it is in handling such errors as these that Browne most needs to draw attention to the multiple meanings of words. Paragraph 16 begins: 'We shall not, I hope, disparage the Resurrection of our Redeemer, if we say the Sun doth not dance on Easter day.' There is, he says, no scriptural record of this miracle:

And if metaphorical expressions go so far, we may be bold to affirm, not only that one Sun danced, but two arose that day: That light appeared at his nativity, and darkness at his death, and yet a light at both; for even that darkness was a light unto the Gentiles, illuminated by that obscurity. That 'twas the first time the Sun set above the Horizon; that although there were darkness above the earth, there was light beneath it, nor dare we say that hell was dark if he were in it.

This warning against mistaking trope for statement is the obverse, or parody, of the type of wit with which we are familiar in some 'metaphysical' poems.

In a different style, economically, sententiously, using cadence to enliven common sense, Browne ridicules those who mistake tropes for facts in Book III, ch. 4 concerning the belief: 'that a Bever to escape the Hunter, bites off his testicles'. He writes:

But if any shall positively affirm this act, and cannot believe the Moral, unless he also credit the Fable; he is surely greedy of delusion, and will hardly avoid deception in theories of this Nature. The Error therefore and Alogy in this opinion, is worse then in the last;[1] that is, not to receive Figures for Realities, but expect a verity in Apologues; and believe, as serious affirmations, confessed and studied Fables.

Even more tersely the same point is made concerning proverbs, in Book II, ch. 6:

But although Proverbs be popular principles, yet is not all true that is proverbial; and in many thereof, there being one thing delivered, and another intended; though the verbal expression be false, the Proverb is true enough in the verity of its intention.

Some of the pleasure to be derived from reading *Pseudodoxia* depends upon various kinds of humour or wit; but more, I think, depends on the reader's growing confidence in Browne's basic good sense. Two related instances of this may be especially valued by a reader of this century: Browne's discussion of errors about Jews and about Negroes. They are not contiguous chapters as they would probably be today, they are not even in the same book: the first comes under the heading of 'Tenents concerning Man', the second under 'Tenents Geographical and Historical'. In both Browne, by means of grave and careful argument, destroys the ugly and dangerous error of those who despise a race. In the first he disproves the vulgar error 'that Jews stink naturally'; he begins with four historical paragraphs showing that there is no such thing as an unmixed race of Jews. Next he affirms that Jews, with their strict diet-rules and severe laws with regard to 'generations and conceptions', are the most unlikely of races to be so afflicted. 'Lastly,' he says, 'Experience will convict it; for this offensive odour is no way discoverable in their Synagogues where many are, and by reason of their number it could not be concealed.' In the concluding paragraph of this closely argued chapter he writes: 'Assenting hereto, many difficulties must arise: it being a dangerous point to annexe a constant property unto any Nation...' [IV, 10].

[1] 'The last' was about the dove, and the figurative intention of the statement is that it has 'no gall'.

There are two chapters about the blackness of Negroes; the first [VI, 10] is mainly the work of Browne the naturalist, interested in the cause of the pigmentation. In the second [VI, 11] he raises the moral issues; the chapter opens with the sentence: 'A second opinion there is, that this complexion was first a curse of God derived unto them from Cham, upon whom it was inflicted for discovering the nakedness of Noah.' The whole chapter is devoted to a refutation of this absurdity. After four reasons against it, based upon Biblical history and its interpretation, Browne adds:

Lastly, Whereas men affirm this colour was a Curse, I cannot make out the propriety of that name, it neither seeming so to them, nor reasonably unto us; for they take so much content therein, that they esteem deformity by other colours, describing the Devil, and terrible objects, white.

and he goes on to consider several theories of beauty. There are many, he says:

which place it not only in proportion of parts, but also in grace of colour. But to make Colour essential unto Beauty, there will arise no slender difficulty: For Aristotle in two definitions of pulchritude, and Galen in one, have made no mention of colour. Neither will it agree unto the Beauty of Animals: wherein notwithstanding there is an approved pulchritude. Thus horses are handsome under any colour, and the symmetry of parts obscures the consideration of complexions... we measure not their Beauty thereby: for if a Crow or a Black-bird grow white; we generally account it more pretty; And in almost a monstrosity descend not to opinion of deformity. By this way likewise the Moors escape the curse of deformity: there concurring no stationary colour, and sometimes not any unto Beauty.

There are some who believe that beauty depends neither upon proportion nor upon colour:

As M. Leo the Jew[1] hath excellently discoursed in his *Genealogy of Love*, defining beauty a formal grace, which delights and moves them to love which comprehend it. This grace say they, discoverable outwardly, is the resplendor and Ray of some interiour and invisible Beauty

[1] Leo the Jew was a pseudonym for Judah Abramel who wrote a work entitled *Dialogi d'Amore* (1535).

and Browne goes on to say that: 'by this consideration of Beauty, the Moors also are not excluded, but hold a common share therein with all mankind.'

Moreover, Browne adds, whatever theory of beauty we select, we must recognize that choice of examples will depend upon taste:

For Beauty is determined by opinion, and seems to have no essence that holds one notion with all; that seeming beauteous unto one, which hath no favour with another; and that unto every one, according as custome hath made it natural, or sympathy and conformity of minds shall make it seem agreeable.

Finally, with regard to this vulgar error of a curse, Browne emphasizes that 'refuge unto Miracles' or to 'immediate contrivance, from the insearchable hands of God' is a way to impede the advance of knowledge and to preserve ignorance permanently: 'Thus in the conceit of the evil odor of the Jews, Christians without a farther research into the verity of the thing, or inquiry into the cause, draw up a judgement upon them from the passion of their Saviour.'

The good sense and good feeling in these two chapters are ubiquitous in Browne's writings and often they are allied to his particular kind of scepticism or open-minded inquiry. His defence of Epicurus from the vulgar opinion about him is an example. He was to write again about this 'Virtuous heathen' in *Urne-Buriall*. In *Pseudodoxia* he devotes a paragraph to him:

Who can but pitty the vertuous Epicurus, who is commonly conceived to have placed his chief felicity in pleasure and sensual delights, and hath therefore left an infamous name behind him? How true, let them determine who read that he lived seventy years, and wrote more books than any Philosopher but Chrysippus, and no less than three hundred, without borrowing from any Author. That he was contented with bread and water, and when he would dine with Jove, and pretend unto epulation,[1] he desired no other addition then a piece of Cytheridian cheese. That shall consider the words of Seneca, *Non dico, quod plerique*

[1] 'The action of feasting or indulging in dainty fare' [*O.E.D.*].

nostrorum, sectam Epicuri flagitiorum magistrum esse: sed illud dico, male audit infamis est, et immerito. Or shall read his life, his Epistles, his Testament in Laertius, who plainly names them Calumnies, which are commonly said against them [VII, 17].

Ross, characteristically, tries to destroy this rehabilitation.

Similarly charitable—especially from a Baconian in mid-seventeenth century—is Browne's rejection of a belief in Aristotle's suicide. He was alleged to have drowned himself in Euripus, because he despaired of finding a reason for its 'ebb and flow seven times a day'. Browne exposes the improbability and makes this an opportunity for a fine panegyric:

However therefore Aristotle died, what was his end, or upon what occasion, although it be not altogether assured, yet that his memory and worthy name shall live, no man will deny, nor grateful Scholar doubt, and if according to the *Elogy* of Solon, a man may be only said to be happy after he is dead, and ceaseth to be in the visible capacity of beatitude, or if according unto his own *Ethicks*, sense is not essential unto felicity, but a man may be happy without the apprehension thereof; surely in that sense he is pyramidally happy; nor can he ever perish but in the Europe[1] of Ignorance, or till the Torrent of Barbarism overwhelmeth all [VII, 13].

Humour, wit and generous common sense are prevailing characteristics of *Pseudodoxia*. Those who prefer Browne's grand style will find it more often in his next work *Urne-Buriall*; it is the style he uses when he writes of mortality and immortality; of time and eternity. To convey what he feels about these he requires the imagery and cadence which bring some of his best prose close to poetry. For example, there is a sentence about the Last Judgment which can bear comparison with Donne's Holy Sonnet VII ('At the round earth's imagin'd corners') upon the same theme. Browne writes: 'For then indeed shall men rise out of the earth: the graves shall shoot up their concealed seeds, and in that great Autumn, men shall spring up, and awake from their chaos again'

[1] Euripus was a channel credited with violent and dangerous currents; the word was used metaphorically for a dangerous strait [see *O.E.D.*].

[VI, 5]. But the sustained image, the plain diction, the firm cadence are not common in *Pseudodoxia*. If by a great prose style we mean a style of such lucid grace we cannot claim that Browne is often a great stylist in this work. He is so only when what he has to say requires it.

In *Pseudodoxia* Browne is, for the most part, constructing arguments; he can be witty, ingenious, ironical and, not seldom, he can be awkward in his constructions, grammatically contorted and obscure. He enjoys recondite words, archaic or new-fangled (many were used by him for the first time and of these some were short-lived), and he enjoys far-fetched conceits and elaborate jokes. For the most part he sustains the tone of a detached, impartial inquirer, amused at the proneness of men to believe so much more than they have grounds for. But, underlying all the amusement and all the arguments, is Browne's faith in the wisdom of God and his conviction that, with every advance in knowledge, it will be more fully revealed. When he writes of this faith directly, his style becomes measured, grave and lucid; as it is, for instance, in that characteristic and curious chapter 5 of Book VI: '*A Digression of the Wisdom of God in the site and motion of the Sun.*' For ten paragraphs Browne praises the wonderful contrivance of the relation between the earth and the sun, conceived as Ptolemy had conceived it. He admires the complexity and intellectual beauty of the pattern and then, at the close of the chapter, when the modern reader may be wondering whether the advance of knowledge had not already undermined this argument for God's providence, he adds:

> Now whether we adhere unto the hypothesis of Copernicus, affirming the earth to move, and the Sun to stand still; or whether we hold, as some of late have concluded, from the spots in the Sun, which appear and disappear again; that besides the revolution it maketh with its Orbs, it hath also a dinetical motion, and rowls upon its own Poles, whether I say we affirm these or no, the illations before mentioned are not thereby infringed.

All the inferences he has drawn from the Ptolemaic account are equally valid for the Copernican:

We therefore conclude this contemplation, and are not afraid to believe, it may be literally said of the wisdom of God, what men will have but figuratively spoken of the works of Christ; that if the wonders thereof were duly described, the whole world, that is, all within the last circumference, would not contain them. For as his Wisdom is infinite, so cannot the due expressions thereof be finite, and if the world comprise him not, neither can it comprehend the story of him.[1]

[1] When my own book was already in page proof I read Mr Frank Livingstone Huntley's *Sir Thomas Browne*, which contains an especially valuable chapter on *Pseudodoxia*.

CHAPTER VII

'HYDRIOTAPHIA, URNE-BURIALL'

IN 1658, twelve years after the first edition of *Pseudodoxia*, *Hydriotaphia* and *The Garden of Cyrus* were published in one volume. The volume included two dedicatory epistles, one for *Hydriotaphia* addressed to Thomas le Gros, and one for *The Garden of Cyrus* addressed to Nicholas Bacon. Both are dated 1 May. Internal evidence, however, indicates that *Urne-Buriall* was written two years earlier, in 1656. No reader of *Religio Medici* and *Pseudodoxia* can doubt that Sir Thomas Browne enjoyed writing; he must have rejoiced when, ten years after he had completed his *magnum opus*, the discovery of the urns at Old Walsingham offered him a subject so appropriate to his interests and his gifts; the work strikes a buoyant note despite the funereal subject; it conveys his delight in speculation and in the craft of writing, and its central theme is not death but immortality and the manifold follies of men as revealed in their burial customs.

The work concludes with a paragraph towards which he had been moving, with many undulations, in five chapters; the paragraph is among the often-quoted passages upon which his fame as a great prose stylist rests.

To subsist in lasting Monuments, to live in their productions, to exist in their names, and praedicament of Chymera's, was large satisfaction unto old expectations and made one part of their Elyziums. But all this is nothing in the Metaphysicks of true belief. To live indeed is to be again our selves, which being not onely an hope but an evidence in noble beleevers, 'tis all one to lie in St. Innocent's Church-yard, as in the Sands of Ægypt: Ready to be anything, in the extasie of being ever, and as content with six foot as the Moles of Adrianus.

This is indeed splendid rhetoric, but the modern reader who contents himself with the sounds and the verbal associations may miss its intention. Rhetoric was a means of communication and Sir Thomas Browne was expressing himself with precision as well as elegance. He wished to be understood. To this end he supplied two annotations: one, a gloss on 'St Innocent's Church-yard', reads: 'In Paris where bodies soon consume'; another, glossing 'the Moles of Adrianus', reads: 'A stately Mausoleum or sepulchral pyle built by Adrianus in Rome, where now standeth the Castle of St Angelo.' The *Oxford Dictionary* reminds us that *mole* could mean 'a Roman form of Mausoleum' and was so used up till the middle of the nineteenth century. Clearly Sir Thomas Browne consulted his ear when he chose the monosyllabic word, but he ran no risk of obscuring his contrast between six foot of earth and Adrian's mighty monument. Some modern editors deprive their readers of Browne's notes, but this can mean that they deprive them of his sense; today we are likely to need more, not fewer, notes than the author provided for his first readers. For instance, a modern reader might not recognize 'praedicament' as a term in logic, meaning that which is predicated or asserted; and, if he does not, the phrase 'and praedicament of Chymera's' becomes little more than well-sounding verbiage, whereas to find 'large satisfaction' in the assertion of (as the *Oxford Dictionary* has it) 'an unreal creature of the imagination' makes a point which is precise, relevant and comical. It has long been customary to praise Sir Thomas Browne for his style and to find in *Urne-Buriall* some of its finest examples. Mr John Carter, introducing his edition (shorn of notes) of *Urne Buriall and The Garden of Cyrus* (1958), reminds us of the line of distinguished critics who have recognized this value, and he refuses to compete with them:

> Where Johnson and Coleridge, Pater and Saintsbury, and (perhaps the most perceptive of all) Lytton Strachey, have praised and analysed, there is not much left to say about Sir Thomas Browne's style in general, nor about these two masterpieces in particular, that has not been said better before.

He attempts no eulogy or criticism, neither shall I; but I shall point to Browne's style in use and in context. Examples chosen to indicate what Browne is saying will, I think, demonstrate that his prose style in *Urne-Buriall* varies in quality and in kind. He does not always write as a master of the English language; he can command it for some purposes, for others he comes near to being defeated by it. Both his successes and his failures result from his endeavour to communicate meaning.

In a field at Old Walsingham in Norfolk forty or fifty urns had been unearthed; they contained burnt remains of human bones. Sir Thomas Browne in his epistle-dedicatory explains that he does not write about them because he takes pleasure in antiquarian studies:

We were hinted by the occasion, not catched the opportunity to write of old things, or intrude upon the Antiquary. We are coldly drawn unto discourses of Antiquities, who have scarce time before us to contemplate new things, or make out learned Novelties. But seeing they arose as they lay, almost in silence among us, at least in short account suddenly passed over; we were very unwilling they should die again, and be buried twice among us.

Then he draws attention, humorously, to the relation between the subject and his medical profession:

Beside, to preserve the living, and make the dead to live, to keep men out of their Urnes, and discourse of humane fragments in them, is not impertinent unto our profession; whose study is life and death, who daily behold examples of mortality, and of all men least need artifical *memento's*, or coffins by our bed side, to minde us of our graves.

And he gives a reason, though not perhaps the most convincing one, why he feels it incumbent on him to write about these antiquities:

'Tis opportune to look back upon old times, and contemplate our Forefathers. Great examples grow thin, and to be fetched from the passed world. Simplicity flies away, and iniquity comes at long strides upon us. We have enough to do to make up our selves from present and passed times, and the whole stage of things scarce serveth for our instruction. A compleat peece of vertue must be made up from *Cento's* of all ages, as all the beauties of Greece could make but one handsome Venus.

It is not convincing, because he will not use these relics as examples of virtue, although he will take occasion to moralize upon them. In fact he needed no excuse for welcoming the theme offered by the Norfolk urns. It appealed to him because it allowed him to make use of his miscellaneous knowledge, gave him ample scope for quizzical comment on human vagaries, and offered him a fresh opportunity to define the area of his scepticism and to declare his faith.

Sir Geoffrey Keynes says [IV, vii] of the composition of both *Urne-Buriall* and *The Garden of Cyrus* that they were no doubt 'supplemented according to Browne's habit, from his accumulated notes, but they are both fashioned more in the round than most of his other works, and were evidently more consciously "composed" and in a shorter time'. The principle of their composition is association rather than logic; a thought suggests another or an example leads into a new train of thought. However, each of the five chapters in *Urne-Buriall* has a main direction; and the streams of thought in each of the first four chapters conjoin and flow together in the fifth.

The first chapter gives a general account of the burial customs of mankind; these are illustrated from the Bible, the Apocrypha, Homer's *Iliad*, Calaber's continuation of it and other ancient writings. It is a learned chapter and Browne supplies marginal references where he thinks his source will be unfamiliar. Other characteristics, however, besides his recondite learning, are evident both in the matter and the manner: there is his relish for the oddity of human beliefs; his delight in exploring the reasons that give rise to them and his own sceptical, amused detachment from them. In the closing paragraph he considers whether animals as well as men have burial customs; those who write of civil law think not:

Civilians make sepulture but of the Law of nations, others do naturally found it and discover it also in animals. They that are so thick skinned as still to credit the story of the Phœnix, may say something for animal burning: More serious conjectures finde some examples of sepulture in Elephants, Cranes, the Sepulchral Cells of Pismires and practice of Bees; which civil society carrieth out their dead, and hath exequies; if not interrments.

Probably he thought of Alexander Ross when he described those who still believed in the Phoenix (thick-skinned then meant obtuse rather than insensitive).

In ch. II Browne narrows his attention on to the Norfolk urns and does what he can to identify them. We now know that they must have been Saxon urns, but Browne gives his reasons for supposing them to be Roman and indicates the various lines of inquiry he pursued in his endeavour to date them. More than a hundred and twenty years after Browne wrote his chapter, Sir John Evans[1] identified and dated the urns from Browne's description. There is a moment when Browne himself seems to be on the verge of recognizing that they are not Roman:

Some men considering the contents of these Urnes, lasting peeces and toyes included in them, and the custome of burning with many other Nations, might somewhat doubt whether all Urnes, found among us, were properly Romane Reliques, or some not belonging unto our Brittish, Saxon or Danish Forefathers [p. 19].[2]

However, he presently decides that 'the most assured account will fall upon the Romanes, or Brittains Romanized'. But he is characteristically undogmatic, aware of good arguments on both sides. He knows that urns have been found elsewhere which are certainly not Roman; he has seen drawings of urns found in Norway and Denmark, nor does he decide about the origins of other urns found in various places in England. He loves to speculate and is 'content to be in uncertainties'; he is Keats's 'man of achievement in literature'; but he is also scholarly in that he treats with respect all the available knowledge without drawing from it a hasty conclusion.

In his third chapter the thought flows over a wider area to em-

[1] *Hydriotaphia*, with introduction and notes by Sir John Evans (1893).
[2] The page references in this chapter are to Keynes, vol. IV.

brace burial customs in general; the particular Norfolk urns begin to recede and perplexing questions about mortality move forward. Although he is still attentive to matters of detail concerning these and other sepulchral urns, he does not resist digression. Describing the usual shape of urns, for instance, he allows his imagination to play over his anatomical knowledge, adding a note referring the reader to the sixty-third Psalm: 'The common form with necks was a proper figure, making our last bed like our first; nor much unlike the Urnes of our Nativity, while we lay in the nether part of the earth, and inward vault of our Microcosme' [p. 23].

Presently, he allows himself another interlude; he imagines the urns decked with flowers and this reminds him of stranger recorded tributes to the dead:

> We conceive not these Urnes to have descended thus naked as they appear, or to have entred their graves without the old habit of flowers. The Urne of Philopœmen was so laden with flowers and ribbons, that it afforded no sight of it self. The rigid Lycurgus allowed Olive and Myrtle. The Athenians might fairely except against the practise of Democritus to be buried up in honey; as fearing to embezzle a great commodity of their Country, and the best of that kinde in Europe. But Plato seemed too frugally politick, who allowed no larger monument then would contain four Heroic verses, and designed the most barren ground for sepulture: Though we cannot commend the goodnesse of that sepulchral ground, which was set at no higher rate then the mean salary of Judas [p. 26].

Sir Thomas gives a reference to Plutarch for 'the old habit of flowers', but supplies no other references: either he expects his reader to know in what work Plato lays down his strict rule, and who has reported the spendthrift practice of Democritus, or he sees that he need not know. The passage is a characteristic Brownian arabesque, such as are to be found in all his major works. He is not furthering an argument; he is enjoying a flight of fancy. He finds, whether in his notebooks or in his memory, these strange examples concerning burial, and he weaves a pattern with them for his own and his reader's entertainment.

In this passage Browne is not making any moral or theological comment; but sometimes a digression indicates his moral taste. It is evident throughout the work that he is not over-solemn about the disposal of dead bodies; but there is one kind of humour which he has read of with disgust:

Antiquity held too light thoughts from Objects of mortality, while some drew provocatives of mirth from Anatomies, and Juglers shewed tricks with Skeletons. When Fidlers made not so pleasant mirth as Fencers, and men could sit with quiet stomacks while hanging was plaid before them [p. 27].

He supplies a reference and also a marginal note of his own which explains the sadistic amusement to which the text refers:

A barbarous pastime at Feasts, when men stood upon a rolling Globe, with their necks in a Rope fastned to a beame, and a knife in their hands, ready to cut it when the stone was rolled away, wherein if they failed, they lost their lives to the laughter of their spectators.

In this third chapter the central motif of the whole work emerges clearly in a contrast between the Emperor Trajan and the originals of these rural ashes: 'He that lay in a golden Urne eminently above the earth, was not like to finde the quiet of these bones.' This is not, however, the prelude to a prose poem, but to a sardonic commentary on human cupidity:

Many of these Urnes [that is of such gaudy ones] were broke by a vulgar discoverer in hope of inclosed treasure. The ashes of Marcellus were lost above ground, upon the like account. Where profit hath prompted, no age hath wanted such miners. For which the most barbarous Expilators found the most civil Rhetorick. Gold once out of the earth is no more due unto it; What was unreasonably committed to the ground is reasonably resumed from it: Let Monuments and rich Fabricks, not Riches adorn men's ashes, the commerce of the living is not to be transferred unto the dead: It is not injustice to take that which none complaines to lose, and no man is wronged where no man is possessor [p. 28].

He does not countenance these rationalistic excuses, and such crude cupidity brings to his mind other 'barbarous expilators' of tombs and another kind of treasure. In the next paragraph he is writing of necromancy; he turns back to the Norfolk urns and says:

What virtue yet sleeps in this *terra damnata* and aged cinders, were petty magick to experiment; These crumbling reliques and long fired particles superannuate such expectations: Bones, hairs, nails, and teeth of the dead, were the treasures of old Sorcerers. In vain we revive such practices; Present superstition too visibly perpetuates the folly of our forefathers, wherein unto old Observation this Island was so compleat, that it might have instructed Persia.

Here speaks the sceptical and rational doctor who hoped to destroy vulgar errors.

Soon we find him comparing the advantages of burning with those of burial and, parenthetically, setting on one side the religious argument against the former: 'Christians dispute how their bodies should lye in the grave. In urnal enterrment they clearly escaped this Controversie: Though we decline the Religious consideration' [p. 31]; and he goes on to talk of the problems of space and position in graveyards. Moreover, cremation at least spares us from Yorick's fate: 'To be gnaw'd out of our graves, to have our sculs made drinking bowls, and our bones turned into Pipes, to delight and sport our Enemies, are Tragical abominations, escaped in Burning Burials' [p. 32]. This Jacobean sentence, a paragraph by itself, is followed by a long historical and anatomical paragraph about what in fact happens, in the way of corruption or of accidental preservation, to entombed human bodies. It includes an observation of his own which made a contribution to knowledge for which he is commended by his learned editor of 1893:

In an Hydropical body ten years buried in a Church yard, we met with a fat concretion, where the nitre of the Earth, and the salt and lixivious liquor of the body, had coagulated large lumps of fat, into the consistence of the hardest Castle-soap; whereof part remaineth with us.

Sir John Evans comments:

Here as in some other cases, Sir Thomas Browne was in advance of his time. The substance like Castile soap into which the muscles and albuminoid portions of the body are converted under certain circumstances is now well known under the name of 'adipocere', or 'adipocire', a name which appears to have been given to it in 1787 by MM. Fourcroy and Thouret, who are commonly regarded as the first discoverers of this peculiar chemical compound.

In the last paragraph of this chapter Browne returns to what has been its principal theme, the disposal of man's mortal remains, and he touches upon the relevance of this to Christian belief concerning the resurrection of the body. He had already 'declined the Religious consideration' when writing of 'urnal enterrment' or cremation. Now he includes (without obtruding) his own belief that this mortal body, whether burnt or buried, is not relevant to our resurrection.

Severe contemplators observing these lasting reliques, may think them good monuments of persons past, little advantage to future beings. And considering that power which subdueth all things unto it self, that can resume the scattered Atomes, or identifie out of any thing, conceive it superfluous to expect a resurrection out of Reliques. But the soul subsisting, other matter clothed with due accidents, may salve the individuality [p. 34].

In ch. v he will reiterate his doubt of 'the resurrection of the body'.

The main theme of ch. IV is burial in relation to conceptions of immortality. In close relation with the end of ch. III it begins with:

Christians have handsomely glossed the deformity of death, by careful consideration of the body, and civil rites which take off brutal terminations. And though they conceived all reparable by a resurrection, cast not off all care of enterrment [p. 35].

He continues his train of thought in the next paragraph which begins: 'Christian invention hath chiefly driven at Rites, which speak hopes of another life, and hints of a Resurrection', and goes on to show, drawing upon many examples, that Pagans too surmised that the soul was immortal. The paragraph closes with three contrasting Pagan attitudes to burial, illustrating three different conceptions of immortality:

> The Stoicks who thought the souls of wise men had their habitations about the Moon, might make slight account of subterraneous deposition; whereas the Pythagorians and transcorporating Philosophers, who were often to be buried, held great care of their enterrment. And the Platonicks rejected not a due care of the grave, though they put their ashes to unreasonable expectations, in their tedious term of return and long set revolution.

These two paragraphs strike the keynote of ch. IV; they are characteristic of their author both in matter and manner; as always he enjoys his erudition and the juxtapositions and connections it affords. But intellectual amusement is only a part of his intention; whatever strange forms belief in immortality may assume, its continual recurrence implies that the belief is natural in man. Convinced of this, he makes merry with the aberrations that it can give rise to:

> Men have lost their reason in nothing so much as their Religion, wherein stones and clouts make Martyrs; and since the Religion of one seems madness unto another, to afford an account or rational of old Rites, requires no rigid Reader [p. 36].

Being himself anything but rigid he proceeds to assemble many surprising varieties of ceremonial practice in interments, briefly indicating what may have been the reason for them.

As his list of examples draws to a close, he mentions four practices of which, for various reasons, he does not approve. The first of these he thinks unwise on medical grounds: 'That they sucked in the last breath of their expiring friends, was surely a practice of no medical institution.' In the second he recognizes a practical point; but condemns the ensuing superstitions:

> That they powred oyle upon the pyre, was a tolerable practise, while the intention rested in facilitating the accension; But to place good Omens in the quick and speedy burning, to sacrifice unto the winds for a dispatch in this office, was a low form of superstition [p. 38].

(An example not only of Browne's good sense but of his occasionally clumsy prose.) He is more severe upon a third example:

The Archimime or Jester attending the Funeral train, and imitating the speeches, gesture, and manners of the deceased, was too light for such solemnities, contradicting their funeral Orations, and doleful rites of the grave.

While a fourth custom is condemned as foolish, but admitted to have value for posterity:

That they buried a peece of money with them as a Fee of the Elysian Ferriman, was a practise full of folly. But the ancient custome of placing coynes in considerable Urnes, and present practise of burying medals in the Noble Foundations of Europe, are laudable wayes of historical discoveries, in actions, persons, Chronologies; and posteritie will applaud them.

The next eight paragraphs read as though they might have been found among Browne's notebooks; they are records of fact, little elaborated or integrated; sometimes he records them as questions to which he offers no answer, for instance: 'Why the Female Ghosts appeared unto Ulysses before the Heroes and masculine Spirits?' [p. 39], and other such matters out of Homer which as he says 'cannot escape some doubt'. Then from Homer he turns to Dante, and the quality of his prose alters; soon he is fully engaged in complex discourse provoked by the Christian poet's judgments on ancient philosophers. Browne's prose becomes tightly woven and the meaning so close-packed in the first sentence that the grammar barely conveys it.

Pythagoras escapes in the fabulous Hell of Dante, among that swarm of Philosophers, wherein whilest we meet with Plato and Socrates, Cato is to be found in no lower place then purgatory. Among all the set, Epicurus is most considerable, whom men make honest without an Elyzium, who contemned life without encouragement of immortality, and making nothing after death, yet made nothing of the King of terrours [p. 40].

Already in *Pseudodoxia* Browne had expressed his admiration for Epicurus, whose noble stoical philosophy had been so misconceived. Now he defends him against Dante's condemnation, but before he does that he argues (perhaps with himself as much as with his reader) about the relative courage of Pagans and Christians in the face of death. The former die bravely without being assured of resurrection (though some, as he has previously said, are hopeful). The latter, certain of immortality, would, if they fully imagined what that means, prefer death to life. Browne begins by praising the amazing courage of Pagans:

> Were the happinesse of the next world as closely apprehended as the felicities of this, it were a martyrdome to live; and unto such as consider none hereafter, it must be more then death to die, which makes us amazed at those audacities, which durst be nothing, and return into their Chaos again [p. 40].

And yet, he argues, the courage of Pagans is not superior to that of Christians. He crosses swords with Machiavelli and argues for the exceptional courage of those who, in old age, were martyred for the Christian faith. The argument becomes complex to the verge of obscurity. He is contemplating the relevance to voluntary death of an assured hope of immortality; martyrdom amazes him and had occupied his thoughts when he wrote *Religio Medici* some twenty years earlier. His paragraph goes straight on from 'and return into their Chaos again'.

> Certainly such spirits as could contemn death, when they expected no better being after, would have scorned to live had they known any. And therefore we applaud not the judgement of Machiavel, that Christianity makes men cowards, or that with the confidence of but half dying, the despised vertues of patience & humility, have abased the spirits of men, which Pagan principles exalted, but rather regulated the wildnesse of audacities, in the attempts, grounds, and eternal sequels of death, wherein men of the boldest spirits are often prodigiously temerarious [p. 40].

But this argues only that the Christian hope will curb an overbold disregard of life: there will be fewer suicides. As yet Browne has said nothing to prove that Christians face death with as much courage as Pagans. For that he turns to the martyrs and counters a possible argument that there is little valour in giving up a mere remnant of life.

> Nor can we extenuate valour of ancient Martyrs, who contemned death in the uncomfortable scene of their lives, and in their decrepit Martyrdomes did probably lose not many moneths of their dayes, or parted with life when it was scarce worth the living. For (beside that long time past holds no consideration unto a slender time to come) they had no small disadvantage from the constitution of old age, which naturally makes men fearful; complexionally superannuated from the bold and couragious thoughts of youth and fervent years. But the contempt of death from corporal animosity,[1] promoteth not our felicity. They may set in the Orchestra, and noblest Seats of Heaven, who have held up shaking hands in the fire, and humanely contended for glory [p. 41].

Here Browne is asserting that the courage of the ancient martyrs is far greater than that of men whose physical courage, in the vigour of their youth, enabled them to face death unflinchingly. These old men who trembled, but nevertheless endured their painful martyrdom, are much more to be commended. However, there is a gap in his argument, for in asserting the courage of the martyrs he appears to have forgotten the opening clause of his paragraph. 'Were the happiness of the next world as closely apprehended as the felicities of this, it were a martyrdom to live.' But if the logical structure of the two paragraphs is imperfect, the feeling expressed is clear. It involves a characteristic ambivalence; he has no wish to praise either Pagan or Christian at the expense of the other. This becomes apparent when, in the next paragraph, he returns to Dante and Epicurus.

> Mean while Epicurus lies deep in Dante's hell, wherein we meet with Tombs enclosing souls which denied their immortalities. But whether the virtuous heathen, who lived better than he spake, or erring in the principle of himself, yet lived above Philosophers of more specious Maximes, lie so deep as he is placed; at least so low as not to rise against

[1] *Animosity*: 'High spirits, courage, bravery' [*O.E.D.*].

Christians, who beleeving or knowing that truth, have lastingly denied it in their practise and conversation, were a quæry too sad to insist on [p. 41].

By beginning with the poet's 'fabulous hell' and ending with a refusal to ask the question, Browne expresses both his intellectual doubt and his emotional conviction. Theological orthodoxy may support Dante, but Browne's own feeling (or moral taste) opposes him. He feels that the virtue of Epicurus is not diminished, but rather enhanced by his unawareness of immortality. In the whole of this argument Browne's mastery of English prose is questionable. He uses the language in a way that expresses his own processes of thought and feeling; if that is mastery, he has it here. But he does not write here either with perfect lucidity or with eloquence. He cannot, because ambivalence is a part of what he has to express. He is not writing to persuade an audience, but to raise in the reader's mind his own hestitations and doubts.

When, however, he reaches the close of ch. IV, he ends it with a paragraph which is masterly in every sense. Its argument is coherent and closely knit. Familiar and latinate words are juxtaposed to build clauses both lucid and harmonious. No parenthetic doubt separates the opening from the concluding clause towards which the argument advances with accumulating reasons and evidence. Here, writing upon a theme he has long considered and committing himself to nothing of which he is not fully persuaded, his tool, the rich flexible English language of his day, is wholly under his control:

It is the heaviest stone that melancholy can throw at a man, to tell him he is at the end of his nature; or that there is no further state to come, unto which this seemes progressional, and otherwise made in vain; Without this accomplishment the natural expectation and desire of such a state, were but a fallacy in nature. Unsatisfied Considerators would quarrel the justice of their constitutions, and rest content that Adam had fallen lower, whereby by knowing no other Original, and deeper ignorance of themselves, they might have enjoyed the happiness of inferiour Creatures who in tranquility possess their constitutions, as having not the apprehension to deplore their own natures. And being framed below the circumference of these hopes, or cognition of better being, the wisdom of God hath necessitated their contentment: But the superiour ingredient and obscured part of our selves, whereunto all present felicities afford no resting contentment, will be able at last to tell us we are more then our present selves; and evacuate such hopes in the fruition of their own accomplishments [p. 42].

Sir Thomas Browne's religion, as we discover it in his writings, is eclectic and personal. In *Religio Medici*, despite his declared intention to 'follow the great wheel of the Church', he claimed a wide area of liberty for his 'private reason'. When that leads him to doubts, or to beliefs that would offend the orthodox, he does not suppress them, but neither does he flaunt them. They are there for those who care to find them, but they can easily be overlooked. His belief in the immortality of the soul is in accordance with the teaching of his church, but it is not dependent on it. He recognizes that faith is made easy by Christian revelation: 'Happy are they, which live not in that disadvantage of time, when men could say little for futurity, but from reason.' Nevertheless, in that last paragraph of ch. IV he offers a reasoned argument for the belief and does not invoke the revealed promise. As one would expect from all that he had written, the argument rests upon the nature of man; man's nature includes aspirations that can never be satisfied in this mortal world. It would be 'a fallacy in nature' if that hope were chimerical. And Browne is consistently certain that there are no such fallacies; 'no grotesques in Nature', nothing made in vain.

In ch. V *Urne-Buriall* culminates in an essay on time and eternity. A high proportion of what might be called purple patches, and what are at any rate well-known anthology pieces, occur in this chapter. Phrases recall them to our minds: 'Time which antiquates Antiquities'; 'that duration, which maketh Pyramids pillars of snow, and all that's past a moment'; 'But the iniquity of oblivion blindly scattereth her poppy'; 'Darkness and light divide the course of time, and oblivion shares with memory, a great part even of our living beings'; 'Life is a pure flame, and we live by an invisible Sun within us'. They are splendid phrases, deservedly remembered. They are of course also meaningful; pearls strung upon the thread of the argument. That argument is stated in the opening paragraph:

Now since these dead bones have already out-lasted the living ones of Methuselah, and in a yard under ground, and thin walls of clay, out-worn all the strong and specious buildings above it; and quietly rested under the drums and tramplings of three conquests; What Prince can promise such diuturnity unto his Reliques, or might not gladly say,

Sic ego componi versus in ossa velim. [p. 43]

And that argument is clinched in the final paragraph, already quoted (p. 188). Tombs and monuments cannot even keep our memories green; the humblest urn may outlast the grandest monument, and neither is of moment in 'the Metaphysicks of true belief', because 'To live indeed is to be again our selves'.

Fourteen paragraphs intervene between the first and last in ch. v; they are not solely occupied with saying the same thing in different ways, although that is a proper and welcome part of the art of rhetoric. But Sir Thomas also manages to define points that he has not before made clear, for instance his doubt about the body's resurrection.

There is nothing strictly immortal, but immortality; whatever hath no beginning may be confident of no end (all others have a dependent being, and within the reach of destruction); which is the peculiar of that necessary essence that cannot destroy it self; And the highest strain of omnipotency to be so powerfully constituted, as not to suffer even from the power of it self. But the sufficiency of Christian Immortality frustrates all earthly glory, and the quality of either state after death makes a folly of posthumous memory. God who can onely destroy our souls, and hath assured our resurrection, either of our bodies or names hath directly promised no duration. Wherein there is so much of chance that the boldest expectants have found unhappy frustration; and to hold long subsistence, seems but a scape in oblivion. But man is a noble Animal, splendid in ashes, and pompous in the grave, solemnizing Nativities and Deaths with equal lustre, nor omitting Ceremonies of bravery, in the infamy of his nature [p. 48].

The heresy is not obtruded; for most of the paragraph he invites us to consider the transience of 'gloria mundi'. But the parenthesis in the first sentence and the statement that there is no promise of the duration of our bodies are at odds with a clause in the Apostles' Creed. His scepticism adds point to the irony of the magniloquent final sentence. It is in fact doubtful whether Browne is ever merely magniloquent. The paragraph following this opens with the famous sentence: 'Life is a pure flame, and we live by an invisible Sun within us', but how much more significant is that Heraclitean image of the soul in the context of what precedes it. In *Urne-Buriall*, as everywhere else, Browne uses rhetoric to communicate feeling and thought. It is only by following his meaning that we can fully enjoy his style and, by its means, discover his wisdom, humour and good sense.

CHAPTER VIII

'THE GARDEN OF CYRUS'

IF we accept Sir Geoffrey Keynes's suggested dating, *The Garden of Cyrus* was the last work that Sir Thomas Browne prepared for the press. He had no obvious reason for writing books for publication; his life was full and busy, he was practising medicine, he was head of a large family, he was busy with experiments and he was an omnivorous reader. He was certainly not driven to write by excess of leisure, nor, I think, by ambition; he enjoyed writing, he was addicted to it. Jotting down his thoughts in notebooks did not always satisfy his craving; he needed to weave some of those notes into compositions, or ordered sequacious reflections. It would seem that, a year or more after completing *Urne-Buriall*, his notebooks and his meditations suggested the new theme. In his dedicatory letter: 'To my Worthy and Honoured friend, Nicholas Bacon', he apologizes for writing about gardens, being himself no gardener; he explains that he is not writing a 'Herball', for of these there are already enough and Sir Nicholas is familiar with them; he is not expecting to add to knowledge about botany; he is merely seeking a field of inquiry that has not already been fully cropped; he says to his learned friend:

You have been so long out of trite learning, that 'tis hard to finde a subject proper for you; and if you have met with a Sheet upon this, we have missed our intention. In this multiplicity of writing, bye and barren Themes are best fitted for invention; Subjects so often discoursed confine the Imagination, and fixe our conceptions unto the notions of fore-writers. Beside, such Discourses allow excursions, and venially admit of collaterall truths, though at some distance from their principals. Wherein if we sometimes take wide liberty, we are not single, but erre by great example.[1]

[1] Browne's marginal note reads: 'Hippocrates, *De superfœtatione, de dentitione*.'

So Browne chose his 'barren theme' in order to leave his imagination unconfined and his area of inquiry little restricted. What this theme was, he indicates in the subtitle: 'The Quincuncial Lozenge, or Net-work Plantations of the Ancients, Artificially, Naturally, Mystically Considered.' It may not look promising to a modern reader; but when Sir Thomas Browne brings to bear on it his great range of reading and his habit of perceiving connections, it proves to be bewilderingly fruitful. He calls it a 'spruce' subject, which then meant *lively*, and so it proves, and he says he has not, in handling it, 'affrighted the common reader with any other Diagramms, than of itself', that is to say of a *Quincunx* or network. But one wonders what sort of a 'common reader' he had in mind. One, presumably, who read encyclopaedias with the same avidity as today he might read anthropological or sociological handbooks, and one who also enjoyed literary skill. He must have had in mind as well some readers who can, I think, never have been common, those who would want either to check up or to explore further, since once again Sir Thomas supplies references. His reader would not have needed, and luckily does not now need, to be himself a polymath. Browne had read the Greek and Latin philosophers, historians and poets; he had read contemporary works in English and in Latin, especially works about travel or biology; he was well acquainted with the history of Christian thought (enough at any rate to have considered some of the principal heresies); he had read some Cabbalistic and some Neoplatonic writings; he was familiar, of course, with the Bible (surprisingly, he sometimes, but not always, used the Douay version). This list is not meant to be exhaustive, but only to suggest the width of knowledge that he draws on in *The Garden of Cyrus*. It would require an uncommonly learned reader to appraise the accuracy and depth of Browne's knowledge; for an ordinary reader the interest is in how he uses it.

Browne thinks of the ancient gardens, with the trees arranged in squares (like a continuous pattern of fives on a die), and he first thinks of them historically. Characteristically he amuses himself with the question: Was gardening the first of the crafts? He decides that it was:

For though Physick may pleade high, from the medicall act of God, in casting so deep a sleep upon our first Parent; And Chirurgery finde its whole art [a note explains how] in that one passage concerning the Rib of Adam, yet is there no rivality with Garden contrivance and Herbary. For if Paradise were planted the third day of the Creation, as wiser divinity concludeth, the Nativity thereof was too early for Horoscopie; Gardens were before Gardiners, and but some hours after the earth [p. 69].[1]

This strikes the dominant note; it is not solemn, not even always serious; often it merely invites the reader to share a scholar's pastime, the making of mosaic patterns with fragments of knowledge. That knowledge may be familiar to all his readers, as when it is drawn from the Bible.

Nebuchodonosor,[2] whom some will have to be the famous Syrian King of Diodorus, beautifully repaired that city; and so magnificently built his hanging gardens, that from succeeding writers he had the honour of the first. From whence over-looking Babylon, and all the Region about it, he found no circumscription to the eye of his ambition, till over-delighted with the bravery of this Paradise; in his melancholy metamorphosis he found the folly of that delight, and a proper punishment in the contrary habitation, in wilde plantations and wandrings of the fields [p. 70].

Or the fragments of knowledge may be more recondite. If we merely glance down the margins at the reference notes supplied by the author we find that these (with quotations sometimes in Greek, often in Latin) are from learned works of at least eight different kinds: philosophical, topographical, architectural, logistic, piscatorial, botanical, medical and, of course, horticultural.

The first chapter is an historical and geographical survey;

[1] The page references in this chapter are to Keynes, vol. IV.

[2] Douay version's spelling for Nebuchadnezzar. The story, in either version, is contained in Daniel iv.

Sir Thomas takes us to Babylon, Persia, Greece, India, Judea and finally back to where his chapter began, the Garden of Eden in which he finds evidence of the quincuncial figure: 'Since even in Paradise itself, the tree of knowledge was placed in the middle of the Garden, whatever was the ambient figure; there wanted not a centre and rule of decussation' [p. 76].[1]

The second chapter is about the same figure in works of art or craft—Sir Thomas Browne calls them 'artificial contrivances and manual operations'. The third illustrates the recurrence of the figure in nature. After these first three chapters, one introductory and two under the general title, *The Quincunx Naturally considered*, there are two chapters under the title, *The Quincunx Mystically considered*. The difference of substance is that in chs. II and III he is mainly pointing to how things are; in IV and V he is conjecturing about causes and significance.

The Garden of Cyrus is, I think, the least important of the works published in Browne's lifetime; the subject is far less interesting, the thought less profound and the composition less close-woven than in *Religio Medici*; he reveals less of himself, is less concerned to enlighten his reader, and has a less serious intention than in *Pseudodoxia*; the subject stimulated his imagination less, and affects the general reader less, than that of *Urne-Buriall*. No one would choose it in order to introduce a new reader to Browne. But, for those who already know his works, it illustrates many of his attractive characteristics. Among the most prevalent, here and elsewhere, is his delighted response to marvels in the natural world; the sense of wonder, which some think of as the prerogative of childhood, was undimmed in him in his fifties and probably remained so to the end. For example, in ch. II, when he writes of the recurrence of intersecting lines in many crafts, such as stone-cutting, perspective pictures or 'neat and curious textures' woven by American Indians, suddenly he remembers an exception—that natural craftsman the spider weaves his web without

[1] Decussation, i.e. intersection or crossing.

decussation. Delightedly, and irrelevantly, he includes him in the paragraph:

But this is no law unto the woof of the neat Retiarie Spider, which seems to weave without transversion, and by the union of right lines to make out a continued surface, which is beyond the common art of Textuary, and may still nettle Minerva, the Goddesse of that mystery [p. 79].

He gives a note to remind his reader of 'the contention between Minerva and Ariachne'. Then he adds an invitation to other observers which many boys would find irresistible:

And he that shall hatch the little seeds, either found in small webs, or white round Egges, carried under the bellies of some Spiders, and behold how at their first production in boxes, they will presently fill the same with their webbs, may observe the early, and untaught finger of nature, and how they are natively provided with a stock, sufficient for such Texture [p. 80].

The same wonder, this time expressed in an evocative image, is evident when he writes, in ch. III, of the habitation of a maggot, found, so he tells us, on almost every head of the Teazell (or thistle).

The *Arbustetum* or Thicket on the head of the Teazell, may be observed in this order: [the quincuncial] and he that considereth that fabrick so regularly palisadoed, and stemm'd with flowers of the royal colour, in the house of the solitary maggot, may finde the *Seraglio* of Solomon [p. 86].

Again, and characteristically, he had not been content with aesthetic delight alone; he is still the Baconian author of *Pseudodoxia* and he tells us that he:

could with much inquiry never discover any transfiguration in this abstemious insect, although we have kept them long in their proper houses, and boxes, where some, wrapped up in their webbs, have lived upon their own bowels, from September unto July.

Enhancing the wonder for Browne, in this as in all his works, is the conviction that what he sees is the controlled design of the great Artificer. When, in ch. IV, he writes of the sensuous effects of the quincuncial disposition of trees, he more than once declares this faith; the prose glows with it: 'And therefore providence hath arched and paved the great house of the world, with colours of mediocrity, that is, blew and green, above and below the sight, moderately terminating the *acies* of the eye' [p. 113]. Soon after, with the same keen appreciation of the contrivance, he describes the effect of Nature's ubiquitous provision of shade:

Nor are only dark and green colours, but shades and shadows contrived through the great Volume of nature, and trees ordained not onely to protect and shadow others, but by their shades and shadowing parts, to preserve and cherish themselves. The whole radiation or branchings shadowing the stock and the root, the leaves, the branches and fruit, too much exposed to the windes and scorching Sun. The calicular leaves inclose the tender flowers, and the flowers themselves lie wrapt about the seeds, in their rudiment and first formations, which being advanced the flowers fall away; and are therefore contrived in variety of Figures, best satisfying the intention; Handsomely observable in hooded and gaping flowers, and the Butterfly bloomes of leguminous plants, the lower leaf closely involving the rudimental Cod, and the alary or wingy divisions embracing or hanging over it [p. 114].

In this passage, although a feeling of delighted admiration permeates it, the prose is not lyrical. It is subdued to its business of description. But the subject of his contemplation leads on to one of his deservedly famous prose poems:

Light that makes things seen, makes some things invisible; were it not for darknesse and the shadow of earth, the noblest part of the Creation had remained unseen, and the Stars in heaven as invisible as on the fourth day, when they were created above the Horizon, with the Sun, or there was not an eye to behold them. The greatest mystery of Religion is expressed by adumbration, and in the noblest parts of Jewish Types, we finde the Cherubims shadowing the Mercy-seat: life it self is but the shadow of death, and souls departed but the shadows of the living: all things fall under this name. The Sun it self is but the dark *simulachrum*, and light but the shadow of God [p. 115].

However, no less characteristic than his sense of the marvellous and intricate design of the world is his delight in speculation that leads nowhere. In ch. v, for example, there is a series of paragraphs entirely composed of queries and ending with such sentences as: 'We leave it unto Arithmetical Divinity, and Theological explanation.' Or he may begin his paragraph: 'Yet if any delight in new Problemes' and, after suggesting a number that seem chosen only to puzzle the mind, end with: 'He may meet with abstrusities of no ready solution.' Here, as everywhere, Browne is in no hurry to find certainty; he enjoys the process of inquiry and expects that others will do the same.

As his discourse nears its conclusion he hands over the mysteries of the quincunx to his successors as though he were making them a handsome present; he has found plenty of questions for them, attractive, he feels, because they are unexplored and difficult:

> And these we invent and propose unto acuter enquirers, nauseating crambe verities and questions over queried. Flat and flexible truths are beat out by every hammer; But Vulcan and his whole forge sweat to work out Achilles his armour [p. 124].

And then Browne once again declares his own allegiance to the Baconian method of inquiry to which, despite his teleological convictions, he has always been faithful. Convinced that what we shall discover will reveal purpose and design, he points to observation or experiment as the road to discovery. Unlike Bacon, Browne has no fear that teleology is misplaced in natural philosophy; neither does he seem to share Bacon's expressed motive 'to harness nature to our use'. There appears to be no division for Browne between useful and useless knowledge. So he passes on to his readers the (as he feels) alluring task of further exploring the Quincuncial order.

> A large field is yet left unto sharper discerners to enlarge upon this order, to search out the *quarternio's* and figured draughts of this nature, and moderating the study of names, and meer nomenclature of plants, to erect generalities, disclose unobserved proprieties, not only in the vegetable shop, but the whole volume of nature; affording delightful Truths, confirmable by sense and ocular Observation, which seems to

me the surest path, to trace the Labyrinth of truth. For though discursive enquiry and rationall conjecture, may leave handsome gashes and flesh-wounds; yet without conjunction of this, expect no mortal or dispatching blows unto errour.

These then are some of the characteristics Browne's readers will expect, and will find in *The Garden of Cyrus*: wonder, a quest for the purposes of God, delight in speculation, and trust in observation and experiment as the gateways to knowledge. But hardly less characteristic is his common sense, which sets a limit to speculation. In this work it shows itself in his deliberate avoidance of the mysticism of numbers. Chapter v begins: 'To enlarge this contemplation unto all the mysteries and secrets, accomodable unto this number, were inexcusable Pythagorisme....' He does not totally resist the temptation; he 'cannot omit the ancient conceit of five, surnamed the number of justice, as justly dividing between the digits, and hanging in the Centre of Nine', with a diagram in the margin to explain the conception, though he does not think it necessary, as I have done, to emphasize the point by enlarging the fifth dot. He adds a few amusing and intelligible points about the number five and then he calls a halt: 'Many expressions of this Number occurre in Holy Scripture, perhaps unjustly laden with mystical Expositions and little concerning our order' [p. 121]. He proceeds to show how some of them can be understood by practical good sense:

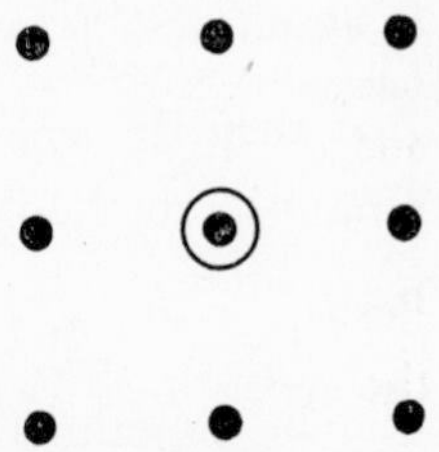

> That the Israelites were forbidden to eat the fruit of their new planted Trees, before the fifth yeare, was very agreeable unto the naturall Rules of Husbandry; Fruits being unwholesome, and lash, before the fourth, or fifth Yeare.

However, he indulges himself in speculations about why on the second day of the Creation we are not told that 'God saw that it was good', whereas on the third day we are twice told so; to follow his train of thought here it may be helpful to recall Donne's poem,

The Primrose; being at Montgomery Castle,
upon the hill, on which it is situate.

of which I quote the last stanza:

> Live Primrose then, and thrive
> With thy true number five;
> And women, whom this flower doth represent,
> With this mysterious number be content;
> Ten is the farthest number; if halfe ten
> Belonge unto each woman, then
> Each woman may take halfe us men;
> Or if this will not serve their turne, Since all
> Numbers are odde, or even, and they fall
> First into this, five, women may take us all.

Browne writes:

> In the second day, or Feminine part of five, there was added no approbation. For in the third or masculine day, the same is twice repeated; and a double benediction inclosed both Creations, whereof the one, in some part was but an accomplishment of the other [p. 121].

Perhaps this makes some amends for his derogatory comment on the creation of woman in *Religio Medici* [II, 9]. Here at least he sees the feminine and masculine as equally essential parts of one whole: it would have been easy, had he wished, to turn the conceit another way. For the rest of his paragraph he substitutes a rational for a mystical explanation of the number five in various Biblical contexts; for instance, 'That the Trespasser was to pay a fifth part above the head or principall, makes no secret in this Number, and implied no more then one part above the principall; which being considered in four parts, the additionall forfeit must bear the Name of a fifth'. Similarly, the number five in I Samuel vi. 4, where 'five golden mice' had to be offered by the Philistines in token of penitence, can be accounted for by common sense; five mice because there were five 'princes' (in the Douay version five provinces, in King James' Bible five lords, of the Philistines). Nor do we need a mystical explanation of the number five when we read: 'That five should put to flight an hundred...considering a rank of Souldiers could scarce consist of a lesser number'. And finally, when St Paul says that he would rather speak 'five words in a known then ten thousand in an unknown tongue', common sense and grammar can account for the choice of this supposedly mysterious number: 'that is as little as could well be spoken. A simple proposition consisting of three words, and a complexed one not ordinarily short of five.'

Sir Thomas Browne delights in the marvellous but not in mystery. He notices, in his next paragraph, some occurrences in the Bible of the number five that he cannot so easily account for, such as the five thousand fed with five barley loaves; the five changes of raiment offered by Joseph for Benjamin, or the five pebbles with which David attacked Goliath, but says: 'We leave it unto Arithmetical Divinity, and Theological explanation.' He does not take such matters seriously and he goes on immediately to the series of insoluble riddles that he bequeaths to future inquirers.

The Garden of Cyrus, like Browne's other published works, contains examples of bad prose as well as good. Browne is a great master of an elaborate style; but he has no assured mastery of a plain style and when, for clear exposition, he needs that, he is often clumsy and sometimes barely intelligible. The opening paragraph of ch. II is a characteristic example of awkward sentence structure; it begins:

Nor was this only a form of practise in Plantations, but found imitation from high Antiquity, in sundry artificial contrivances and manual operations. For to omit the position of squared stones, *cuneatim* or wedgewise in the walls of Roman and Gothick buildings; and the *lithostrata* or figured pavements of the ancients, which consisted not all of square stones, but were divided into triquetrous segments, honey-combs, and sexangular figures, according to Vitruvius; The squared stones and bricks in ancient fabricks, were placed after this order. And two above or below conjoyned by a middle stone or *Plinthus*, observable in the ruines of Forum Nervae, the Mausoleum of Augustus, the Pyramid of Cestius, and the sculpture draughts of the larger Pyramids of Ægypt. And therefore in the draughts of eminent fabricks, Painters do commonly indicate this order in the lines of their description [p. 77].

The paragraph can be construed, but it does not yield its meaning easily, and nothing is gained by the difficulty; there is no intended ambiguity or tension between argument and feeling, such as accounted for complex structure in a passage quoted from *Urne-Buriall*, ch. IV. Here Browne is only endeavouring to inform his reader of a number of facts, some of them indicating the prevalence of quincuncial arrangement and some pointing to variants from it. For this purpose he had no prose style at his command. The prose is bad because the sentences are ill-constructed.

The fault in style that Dr Johnson points to is Browne's overfondness for recondite words. In his *Life of Sir Thomas Browne*, the passage concerning style concentrates mainly upon this; Johnson says:

He fell into an age, in which our language began to lose the stability which it obtained in the time of Elizabeth; and was considered by every writer as a subject on which he might try his plastick skill, by moulding it according to his own fancy. Milton, in consequence of this encroaching licence, began to introduce the Latin idiom: and Browne, though he gave less disturbance to our structures and phraseology, yet poured in a multitude of exotick words; many indeed useful and significant, which, if rejected, must be supplied by circumlocution, such as 'commensality' for the state of many living at the same table; but many superfluous, as 'a paralogical', for an unreasonable doubt; and some so obscure, that they conceal his meaning rather than explain it, as 'arthritical analogies' for parts that serve some animals in the place of joints. [*Christian Morals* (1756).]

Certainly Browne had no qualms about augmenting the language, although for almost a century writers of rhetoric manuals had attacked the practice. (Johnson's 'stability...obtained in the time of Elizabeth' is an illusion.) Browne's use of a word is frequently the first example given in the *Oxford Dictionary*; it is, however, very seldom the last, and many of his inventions have become an accepted part of the language. No one at the time, or even when Dr Johnson wrote *The Life* in 1756, could be certain which word would be absorbed into it. Dr Johnson was nearly, but not quite right about the particular words he chose; *commensality* was neither new when Browne used it nor, according to the *Oxford Dictionary*, has it become obsolete. *Paralogical* is obsolete and *The Garden of Cyrus* provides the first, and Dr Johnson's citation from it the second example in the *Dictionary*. However, *paralogism* was used almost a century earlier and is not obsolete. Quite often all that Browne does is, by a change of termination, to derive an adjective or verb from an existing noun.

It will be worth while to look for a moment at a paragraph from *The Garden of Cyrus*, made hideous by the number of strange polysyllables:

> Physicians are not without the use of this decussation in several operations, in ligatures and union of dissolved continuities. Mechanicks make use hereof in forcipal Organs, and Instruments of incision; wherein who can but magnifie the power of decussation, inservient to contrary ends, solution and consolidation, union and division, illustrable from Aristotle in the old *Nucifragium*, or Nutcracker, and the Instruments of Evulsion, compression, or incision; which consisting of two *Vectes* or armes, converted towards each other, the innitency and stresse being made upon the *hypomochlion*, or fulciment in the decussation, the greater compression is made by the union of two impulsors [p. 80].

It is rare to find a passage quite so cluttered; it might stand as a warning to those who today are tempted to multiply strange technical terms. I found eight words that I needed to look up; some readers would find fewer, possibly some would find more. But even this passage illustrates the element of chance in word-survival. The word *decussation* is not defined as rare or obsolete in the *Oxford Dictionary*, but the earliest illustration given is from Sir Thomas Browne. *Mechanic*, in the sense here meant, has become rare, but it preceded Browne by a century and we meet it in Shakespeare. *Forcipal*, meaning 'of the nature of a forceps', is not described as obsolete, but the quotation from Browne is the only one given. *Inservient* is obsolete; it has been replaced by *subservient*. Browne's *Pseudodoxia* supplies the earliest illustration of the former; there is none earlier than 1632 for the latter: it must have been even chances which would survive. *Impulsor*, 'one who impels', is obsolete, but was not apparently invented by Browne, although the earliest illustration is 1653. It might have remained, and so might *illustrable*, which is easier to say than is the survivor *illustratable*; however, Browne alone is cited and the word is obsolete. *Hypomochlion* is italicized, which may mean that Browne meant only to use a Greek word transliterated; however, it survived long enough to be used by Coleridge; it means a fulcrum. *Fulciment*, a prop or support, was almost new; there is a 1648 illustration, not from Browne. It seems to have died out after 1759. *Innitency*, 'a pressing upon', was a rare word which soon became obsolete.

Dr Johnson's conclusion on this matter cannot easily be improved upon:

> His style is a tissue of many languages; a mixture of heterogeneous words, brought together from distant regions, with terms originally appropriated to one art, and drawn by violence into the service of another. He must, however, be confessed to have augmented our philosophical diction; and in defence of his uncommon words and expressions, we must consider, that he had uncommon sentiments; and was not content to express in many words that idea for which any language could supply a single term.

We should not still be reading Browne and consequently he would not have 'augmented our philosophical diction', if he had usually erred as badly as in the paragraph last quoted. It is of course exceptional. Nor must it be supposed that he never writes well when he writes simply. *Christian Morals* will prove the contrary. Moreover, the most memorable and often quoted lyrical passages in *The Garden of Cyrus*, though they are complex in structure and subtle in feeling, are predominantly simple in diction. I am thinking especially of the three valedictory paragraphs at the close of the work. The first of these tells us that it is night time and that Browne does not want to dream of Quincunxes. It is a miniature essay on dreams and he gives it four learned notes: one explains what he means by 'The Quincunx of Heaven'; one gives the title of a work by Hippocrates to which he refers; one names the Oneirocriticall Masters [authors who have written about dreams], and the last reminds us that the Bed of Cleopatra was strewed with roses. But the little essay is not bookish; he is thinking of his own experience of dreaming and, except for oneirocritical[l], there are no rare words:

> But the Quincunx of Heaven runs low, and 'tis time to close the five ports of knowledge. We are unwilling to spin out our awaking thoughts into the phantasmes of sleep, which often continueth præcogitations, making Cables of Cobwebbes and Wildernesses of handsome Groves. Beside Hippocrates hath spoke so little, and the Oneirocriticall Masters have left such frigid Interpretations from plants, that there is little encouragement to dream of Paradise it self. Nor will the sweetest delight of Gardens afford much comfort in sleep; wherein the dulnesse of that sense shakes hands with delectable odours; and though in the Bed of Cleopatra, can hardly with any delight raise up the ghost of a Rose.

The second valedictory prose poem gives another reason why he lays down his pen at the approach of night.

> Night, which Pagan Theology could make the daughter of Chaos, affords no advantage to the description of order: Although no lower then that Masse can we derive its Genealogy. All things began in order, so shall they end, and so shall they begin again; according to the ordainer of order and mystical Mathematicks of the City of Heaven.

Again, although there is wit, learning and religion in the content, the diction is plain and the structure lucid. Finally, and again in plain English idiom, he writes of sleep overcoming him and, by occasion, he writes of the relativity of time, and of his assurance of an eternal future.

Though Somnus in Homer be sent to rowse up Agamemnon, I finde no such effects in the drowsie approaches of sleep. To keep our eyes open longer were but to act our Antipodes. The Huntsmen are up in America, and they are already past their first sleep in Persia. But who can be drowsie at that howr which freed us from everlasting sleep? or have slumbring thoughts at that time, when sleep it self must end, and as some conjecture all shall awake again?

In each of these valedictory paragraphs the diction is plain and familiar, the grammar lucid, the rhythm varied and harmonious, the imagery witty and apt. It is because *The Garden of Cyrus* contains prose of this order that the work will continue to be read, or at any rate browsed in, although it is, as Dr Johnson said, little more than 'a sport of fancy'.

CHAPTER IX

POSTHUMOUS WORKS

THERE are only two more works sufficiently continuous, complete and of human interest to count among the literary remains of Sir Thomas Browne. These are *Christian Morals*, and *A Letter to a Friend upon Occasion of the Death of his Intimate Friend.* Both were published posthumously, and composed, Sir Geoffrey Keynes thinks, in the early 1670's, when Sir Thomas was over seventy years old. They neither of them suggest continuous composition or that they had reached their final form; they are made up of separate passages, sometimes paragraphs, sometimes brief essays which would have been susceptible of additions, removals or transpositions. *A Letter to a Friend* has slightly more continuity in that it keeps returning to its occasion (real or ostensible), the recent death of his patient, the friend of his correspondent.

There are three possible accounts that might be given for the existence of this letter among Browne's posthumous papers. (1) That it was a copy of a real letter that had been sent to the friend of a deceased patient; (2) that it was a literary composition in a traditional form; (3) that it originated as a real letter and developed into a literary composition. I incline to the third view; there seem to me to be indications of an actual event, details hardly to be accounted for in a wholly conventional letter about disease and death. If this view is correct the opening paragraph could be part of the originating letter; it appears to be written in answer to an inquiry:

> Give me leave to wonder that News of this nature, should have such heavy Wings, that you should hear so little concerning your dearest Friend, and that I must make that unwilling Repetition to tell you,
>
> *Ad portam rigidos calces extendit,*
>
> that he is Dead and Buried, and by this time no Puny among the mighty Nations of the Dead; for tho he left this World not very many

days past, yet every hour you know largely addeth unto that dark Society; and considering the incessant Mortality of Mankind, you cannot conceive there dieth in the whole Earth so few as a thousand an hour [p. 165].[1]

To modern readers this may seem too frigid for a genuine letter breaking the news of the death of a 'dearest Friend'. But the omnipresence of death had long been among the commonplaces of consolation; Seneca had used it, and Jeremy Taylor, to allay the fear of death, vividly presented the same thought in *Holy Dying* [1651]:

It is the same harmless thing that a poor shepherd suffered yesterday, or a maid-servant today; and at the same time in which you die, in that very night a thousand creatures die with you, some wise men, and many fools; and the wisdom of the first will not quit him, and the folly of the latter does not make him unable to die [ch. III, sect. VII, 4].

It is, in any case, obvious throughout the letter that Browne is not expressing overwhelming grief or pity. These would not have seemed to him the appropriate feelings. As a Christian he was assured of the immortality of the soul; as a physician he was accustomed to the mortality of the flesh. If we keep this in mind the disengaged tone of the letter ceases to surprise; we need not suppose that the old man has forgotten what friendship meant to him in his youth, nor need we necessarily think that the two young men of the letter were never other than imaginary.

The second paragraph of the letter is either an answer to a real inquiry in which the correspondent assumed that if his friend had died he would have intuitively known it, or else the question was invented to give an opportunity for the sceptical reply:

Altho at this distance you had no early Account or Particular of his Death, yet your Affection may cease to wonder that you had not some secret Sense or Intimation thereof by Dreams, thoughtful Whisperings, Mercurisms, Airy Nuncio's, or sympathetical Insinuations, which many seem to have had at the Death of their dearest Friends [p. 165].

[1] The page references in this chapter are to Keynes, vol. I.

With characteristic scepticism about peripheral mysteries, Browne says that we 'must rest content with the common Road and Appian Way of Knowledge by Information'.

A doctor, however, may be unmistakably warned by the patient's symptoms; in the seventeenth century he would have no difficulty in predicting imminent death in an advanced case of pulmonary tuberculosis. Browne knows that the sufferer is usually hopeful, but he is surprised that the friend shared this hope:

That you should be so little acquainted with Plautus's sick Complexion, or that almost an Hippocratical [moribund] Face should not alarum you to higher fears, or rather despair of his Continuation in such an emaciated State, wherein medical Predictions fail not, as sometimes in acute Diseases, and wherein 'tis as dangerous to be sentenced by a Physician as a Judge [p. 166].

The fictitious name suggests that the whole situation was imaginary and that Plautus and his friend were invented for an exercise in the art of letter-writing upon a theme appropriate to the Doctor's profession. But if this was so, one wonders why *A Letter* is not a more successful composition. Sir Thomas had read good models, yet his letter is an ill-coordinated patchwork. And then too there are details, such as the patient's increasing resemblance to his uncle, which seem irrelevant to the theme and dependent upon the particular circumstances. Browne says:

Upon my first Visit I was bold to tell them who had not let fall all hopes of his Recovery, That in my sad Opinion he was not like to behold a Grashopper, much less to pluck another Fig; and in no long time after, seemed to discover that odd mortal Symptom in him not mention'd by Hippocrates, that is, to lose his own Face, and look like some of his near Relations; for he maintained not his proper Countenance, but looked like his Uncle, the Lines of whose Face lay deep and invisible in his healthful Visage before; for as from our beginning we run through variety of Looks, before we come to consistent and settled Faces; so before our End, by sick and languishing Alterations, we put on new Visages; and in our Retreat to Earth, may fall upon such Looks, which, from community of seminal Originals, were before latent in us [p. 166].

Although Defoe or Swift might have invented just such a detail as this resemblance, merely to add verisimilitude, this would be a surprising technical trick for Browne to use in the 1670's. On the other hand his elaboration upon what he had observed and the general reflections arising from it would be appropriate either in the originating letter or in the letter designed for later publication. If this describes what Sir Thomas actually noticed as he watched a particular patient on his death-bed, the use of the Latin name needs explaining. My supposition is that Browne had a copy of an actual letter, which became the nucleus of the literary exercise, and that, as soon as he contemplated eventual publication, he eliminated the real name. The bibliographical evidence is not incompatible with this conjecture. In Sir Geoffrey Keynes's *A Bibliography of Sir Thomas Browne* we read that the *Letter* was first published in a pamphlet by the author's son Edward in 1690, including the twenty paragraphs at the close which reappear, slightly altered, in *Christian Morals*. Browne's excellent nineteenth-century editor, Simon Wilkin, collated the pamphlet with the manuscript in the British Museum. He printed it without the twenty paragraphs, because they were included in *Christian Morals*, and he also printed 'three additional passages among his footnotes: another fragment concerning consumptions, apparently composed for this work but not used, which has been recently discovered in a commonplace book which once belonged to Browne's daughters'.[1] This fragment Sir Geoffrey Keynes included in his limited edition of *The Commonplace Book of Elizabeth Lyttleton, daughter of Sir Thomas Browne* (1919). The facts support the theory that *A Letter* was the result of accretions and that Browne worked over it, and wrote from time to time pieces that he might include in it; they do not rule out the possibility that his starting-point was an actual letter.

If so, passages intimately concerned with the dead friend and passages directly offering consolation are the ones most likely to have existed in the first draft.

[1] Keynes, *Bibliography*, p. 90.

After the account of his own prognosis when he first saw the patient, Browne tells of fruitless hopes raised by some who suggested that a change of air would be beneficial. It was tried, but 'he lived not unto the middle of May'. So far a particular patient seems to be in his mind and the details (though not given without some literary embroidery) are such as a friend might wish to know. The paragraph, however, goes on to give Browne's opinion about the relation between climates and diseases, which is more appropriate to a medical treatise than to a letter of condolence.

This is followed by a paragraph which could well have found a place in the original letter; it offers one of the few comforts that can, in all ages, give some relief to the bereaved. The young man died peacefully and without pain.

Tho we could not have his Life, yet we missed not our desires in his soft Departure, which was scarce an Expiration; and his End not unlike his Beginning, when the salient Point scarce affords a sensible motion; and his Departure so like unto Sleep, that he scarce needed the civil Ceremony of closing his Eyes; contrary unto the common way, wherein Death draws up, Sleep lets fall the Eye-lids. With what strif and pains we came into the World we know not; but 'tis commonly no easie matter to get out of it: yet, if it could be made out that such who have easie Nativities have commonly hard Deaths, and contrarily, his Departure was so easie, that we might justly suspect his Birth was of another nature, and that some Juno sat cross-legg'd at his Nativity [p. 167].

Another comfort that can be offered to the bereaved is the thought that the disease was incurable; prolongation of life could only have meant a longer test of endurance. With this the next paragraph begins, although it too broadens out into a wide-ranging speculation:

Besides his soft Death, the incurable state of his Disease might somewhat extenuate your Sorrow, who know that Monsters but seldom happen, Miracles more rarely, in Physick. Angelus Victorius gives a serious Account of a Consumptive, Hectical, Pthysical Woman, who was suddenly cured by the Intercession of Ignatius. We read not of any in Scripture who in this case applied unto our Saviour, tho some may be contained in that large Expression, that *He went about Galilee, healing all manner of Sickness and all manner of Diseases.* Amulets, Spells, Sigils and Incantations, practised in other Diseases, are seldom pretended in this; and we find no Sigil in the *Archidoxis* of Paracelsus to cure an extreme Consumption or Marasmus, which, if other Diseases fail, will put a period unto long Livers, and at last make dust of all. And therefore the Stoicks could not but think that the firy Principle would wear out all the rest, and at last make an end of the World; which notwithstanding, without such a lingring period, the Creator may effect at his Pleasure: and to make an end of all things on Earth, and our Planetical System of the World, he need but put out the Sun [p. 167].

The expansion is so characteristic, and, from Browne's point of view, so germane to the subject, that it is equally likely to have occurred while he was writing a letter or when, from that letter, he compiled a literary work. The word consumption, used for the particular disease, would almost inevitably suggest to Browne the thought that, however long a man lives and whatever the cause of death, the body will be consumed at last. And from that to the consuming of the world by fire is a step of the mind he would not easily miss. Characteristic also is the detached, sceptical tone of the last clause. All speculation about how or when the world will end is a vain amusement of the mind; at the will of the Creator it could so easily be annihilated at any time.

The next paragraph mentions the time of the young man's death and weaves a pattern of reflections about times and seasons of dying which leads on to a sceptical piece about astrological predictions. He returns to the particular patient and says that:

he died in the dead and deep part of the Night, when *Nox* might be most apprehensibly said to be the Daughter of *Chaos*, the Mother of *Sleep* and *Death*, according to the old Genealogy; and so went out of this World about that hour when our blessed Saviour entred it, and about what time many conceive he will return again unto it [p. 168].

Later he says that 'Plautus' died fifteen days after the date of his birth, and this is one of the details that suggest the origination of the letter in an actual event.

A later paragraph, although it describes a particular death, has a dry tone, and a coldly cerebral wit which seems inappropriate to a letter of condolence:

In this consumptive Condition and remarkable Extenuation, he came to be almost half himself, and left a great part behind him which he carried not to the Grave. And tho that Story of Duke John Ernestus Mansfield [Knolles, *Turkish History* (1638)] be not so easily swallowed, that at his Death his Heart was found to be not so big as a Nut; yet, if the Bones of a good Sceleton weigh little more than twenty pounds, his Inwards and Flesh remaining could make no Bouffage, but a light bit for the Grave. I never more lively beheld the starved Characters of Dantë in any living Face; an *Aruspex*[1] might have read a Lecture on him without Exenteration, his Flesh being so consumed, that he might, in a manner, have discerned his Bowels without opening of him: so that to be carried, *sexta cervice*, to the Grave, was but a civil unnecessity; and the Complements of the Coffin might out-weigh the Subject of it [p. 170].

To write in this manner of 'shells of fledged soules left behind'[2] is characteristic of Browne and of the period, but more likely (supposing there was a real letter) to have been added later; it is a little essay on the frailty of the body which could have been suggested by the particular corpse.

In the next six paragraphs there is nothing that obviously belongs to the original letter. A man who died of consumption is here at most the occasion, not the subject. Browne is writing of physiological observations he has made during many years of medical practice. He displays his customary pleasure in accumulating and displaying pieces of knowledge, and he makes occasional pedantic jokes: for instance about the well-preserved teeth he has noticed in Egyptian mummies:

The Egyptian Mummies that I have seen, have had their Mouths open, and somewhat gaping, which affordeth a good opportunity to view and observe their Teeth, wherein 'tis not easie to find any wanting or decayed: and therefore in Egypt, where one Man practised but one

[1] A Roman soothsayer.

[2] George Herbert, *Death*.

Operation, or the Diseases but of single Parts, it must needs be a barren Profession to confine unto that of drawing of Teeth, and little better than to have been Tooth-drawer unto King Pyrrhus, who had but two in his Head [p. 171].

This is followed by three paragraphs concerning medical history, all manifestly inappropriate to a real letter of condolence.

After these, there are three paragraphs about dreams, a theme to which Browne frequently refers in his works. From *Religio Medici* onward we find references to dreams, in all of which he is sceptically amused by the various current theories concerning them. The topic is abruptly introduced here without any link to the preceding paragraph; but the last of the three paragraphs introduces some women who attended the young man's death-bed and were 'irrationally curious so strictly to examine his Dreams, and in this low state to hope for the Fantasmes of Health'. They were worried because he dreamt of his dead friends, but Browne says: ''Twas too late to dream of Flying, of Limpid Fountains, smooth Waters, white Vestments, and fruitful green Trees, which are the Visions of healthful Sleeps, and at good distance from the Grave' [p. 174].

Part, but not I think all, that occurs in these paragraphs about dreams could have been in a personal letter. The next paragraph could have been either that, or could have been invented for the published work, both as a seemly condolence (praise of the deceased) and as a physician's warning:

He was willing to quit the World alone and altogether, leaving no Earnest behind him for Corruption or Aftergrave, having small content in that common satisfaction to survive or live in another, but amply satisfied that his Disease should dye with himself, nor revive in a Posterity to puzzle Physick, and make sad Memento's of their Parent hereditary [p. 175].

This is the prelude to a series of five paragraphs in praise of the dead friend. When that series ends, Sir Thomas has included in his letter all the consolations that can be offered to the bereaved, both those that are equally suited to Pagans or Christians, and those that belong especially to the latter. For Christians there is the consolation of immortality; for all men it is consoling to know that their friend died peacefully, that return to health was impossible, and that he was ripe in virtue.

Browne specifies some of Plautus's virtues; he was not only free from covetousness but 'big with desires unto publick and lasting Charities' although not wealthy enough to carry out his wishes. This laudatory paragraph ends with a moral essay which uses the language of the Schools to express the conclusions of common sense:

> In brief, his Life and Death were such, that I could not blame them who wished the like, and almost to have been himself: almost, I say; for though we may wish the prosperous Appurtenances of others, or to be an other in his happy Accidents, yet so intrinsecal is every Man unto himself, that some doubt may be made, whether any would exchange his Being, or substantially become another Man [p. 177].

Next in praise of the dead friend we learn that, although little more than thirty, he had learnt the lesson that Rasselas mastered after many adventures: 'He had wisely seen the World at home and abroad, and thereby observed under what variety Men are deluded in the pursuit of that which is not here to be found.' Thus, free from the illusion that happiness is to be found in this world, Browne says that 'to be dissolved and be with Christ was his dying ditty'; and that in this he went beyond the Stoic precept: 'Not to fear death nor desire it.' This is a cue for Browne to pursue a favourite inquiry; how do Stoic and Christian attitudes to death compare with one another for courage? He interpolates an essay on the subject—a fresh attempt to say something that he had fumbled at in *Urne-Buriall*. It is interpolated between the paragraph just quoted from and three more about Plautus beginning: 'His willingness to leave this World about that Age when most Men think they may best enjoy it....' There can, I think, be no doubt that 'interpolation' is the right word, and that the structure here exemplifies the patchwork method of composing the letter.

In *Urne-Buriall* Browne paid homage to the courage of Pagans who 'durst be nothing, and return into their Chaos again', although he attempted to prove that the courage of Christian martyrs was equal or superior. But here he implies that Stoic suicide was a kind of cowardice:

> Not to be content with Life is the unsatisfactory state of those which destroy themselves [and in a note he quotes the passage from Lucan, against which he had warned his son Tom]; who being afraid to live, run blindly upon their own Death, which no Man fears by Experience: and the Stoicks had a notable Doctrine to take away the fear thereof; that is, In such Extremities to desire that which is not to be avoided, and wish what might be feared; and so made Evils voluntary and to suit their own Desires, which took off the terror of them.
>
> But the ancient Martyrs were not encouraged by such Fallacies; who, tho they feared not Death, were afraid to be their own Executioners; and therefore thought it more Wisdome to crucifie their Lusts than their Bodies, to circumcise than stab their Hearts, and to mortifie than kill themselves [p. 178].

I prefer his 'fumbling' in *Urne-Buriall* to this more lucid rhetoric. To clear his mind he has a little hardened his heart.

Two more eulogistic paragraphs bring the letter to a close, save for the nineteen paragraphs that overlap with *Christian Morals*. These are a series of noble precepts more appropriate in the longer work than in *A Letter* which is, in its published form (however it came into being), a curious miscellany even without this addition. About a third of the letter could be thought of as a model letter of condolence from a Christian physician. Another portion of similar length is a record of medical experience; the rest consists of moral reflections: these topics are not treated separately, but intermixed, and the effect is of gradual accretion of matters Browne thought relevant to the theme of *A Letter*. Sir Thomas must at some time have thought of adding the twenty paragraphs, for he invented a convenient link; after the final praise of the friend he adds, 'which affords me an hint to proceed in these good Wishes and few *Mementos* unto you'. These mementoes are the germ of *Christian Morals*.

When the first collected edition of Browne's works was published in 1686 it contained neither *A Letter to a Friend* nor *Christian Morals*; the former was published separately four years later, the latter had been mislaid. Dr Edward Browne had lent a box of his father's manuscript papers to Dr Thomas Tenison (subsequently Archbishop of Canterbury). When Elizabeth Lyttleton, Sir Thomas's daughter, fetched the box for her brother, he complained that 'he missed the choicest papers, which were a continuation of *Religio Medici*'. These, the most valuable of the literary remains, were eventually found and were published separately in 1716 under the title *Christian Morals*.

In his prefatory note to *A Letter to a Friend* Sir Geoffrey Keynes writes: 'The shorter work printed under this title is believed to have been written about ten years before the author's death and shortly after *Christian Morals*' [p. xi]. My own view is that *A Letter* was written before *Christian Morals*, and that the passages common to both works—the moral advice which makes up the last nineteen paragraphs of *A Letter* and recurs with minor changes in Part I of *Christian Morals*—show Sir Thomas Browne carefully revising his own prose. The only way in which I can indicate how I arrived at this conclusion is by juxtaposing some of the passages in which revision seems to me to be demonstrable. This is, I think, of interest not so much because it may establish that *Christian Morals* was the last of Browne's literary works, as because it illustrates the way in which Browne revised, and thereby allows us to watch the artist at work. The nineteen paragraphs in *A Letter*, beginning with 'Tread softly and circumspectly...', all find a place in *Christian Morals*, Part I; some are substantially changed, all are changed in some degree. It is because the versions in *Christian Morals* are invariably improvements that I conclude that this was the later work. I believe that juxtaposed passages will make it impossible to believe that he was revising from *Christian Morals* when he wrote the last paragraphs of *A Letter*. Moreover, in that work the moral essays seem to be tacked on to a letter of condolence somewhat arbitrarily. After concluding the praise of Plautus, Browne says that all this 'affords me an hint to proceed in these good wishes and few *Mementos* unto you'. I suggest that the *Mementos* may have already existed in his notebooks; he wanted to incorporate them in a work which would eventually be published. Later he decided to compose an entire work on the theme of Christian morals. This is conjecture; but that when he composed *Christian Morals* he revised those passages that he had meant to incorporate in *A Letter to a Friend* appears to me to be certain.

The difference between the opening of *Christian Morals* and the start of the moral essays that conclude *A Letter* could be accounted for by appropriateness to context. In *A Letter* they begin 'Tread softly and circumspectly in this funambulous[1] Track and narrow Path of Goodness: pursue virtue virtuously'; and there is no change in *Christian Morals* except that funambulous becomes funambulatory. In *A Letter* he goes on to speak of virtue in relation to health, and of the proper motive for avoiding sickness: 'In one Word, that you may truly serve God, which every Sickness will tell you, you cannot well do without Health.' And the relations between health and virtue are elaborated. In *Christian Morals* the advice to treat the tight-rope that leads to virtue circumspectly leads into a brief paragraph warning against doing the right thing for the wrong reason. Nothing is said about health. The next paragraph is almost exactly the same in both works, but in the third paragraph revision is, I believe, evident enough for it to be worthwhile to juxtapose the versions.

A Letter	*Christian Morals*
In this virtuous Voyage let not disappointment cause Despon-	In this virtuous Voyage of thy Life hull not about like the Ark

[1] *Funambulous*: 'Obs. Rare. Of or pertaining to a tight-rope' [*O.E.D.*].

dency, nor difficulty Despair. Think not that you are sailing from Lima to Manillia, wherein thou may'st tye up the Rudder, and sleep before the Wind; but expect rough Seas, Flaws, and contrary Blasts; and 'tis well if by many cross Tacks and Verings thou arrivest at thy Port. Sit not down in the popular Seats and common Level of Virtues, but endeavour to make them Heroical. Offer not only Peace-Offerings but Holocausts unto God. To serve him singly to serve our selves, were too partial a piece of Piety, nor likely to place us in the highest Mansions of Glory [p. 180].	without the use of Rudder, Mast, or Sail, and bound for no Port. Let not Disappointment cause Despondency, nor difficulty Despair. Think not that you are sailing from Lima to Manillia, when you may fasten up the Rudder, and sleep before the Wind; but expect rough Seas, Flaws, and contrary Blasts; and 'tis well if by many cross Tacks and Veerings you arrive at the Port; for we sleep in Lyons' Skins in our Progress unto Virtue, and we slide not, but climb unto it [I, i, para. 3]. Sit not down...

In *Christian Morals* Browne introduces his sailing imagery at the start of the paragraph. There is also a slight change within the extended metaphor, the change from *wherein* to *when*. *Wherein* was misleading, the sailor is not *in* port when he sails between Lima and Manila, but he can 'tye up the rudder, etc.', because, as Browne explains in a note, there is a constant gale from the east. The change, throughout the passage, from 'thou' to 'you' conforms to current usage; the second person singular was old-fashioned even in 1660. In *Christian Morals* the new metaphor 'Sit not down...' opens a new paragraph. On the other hand Browne introduces two new metaphors in his first paragraph: 'for we sleep in Lyons' skins' and 'we slide not but climb unto' virtue. Doctor Johnson, in his edition of *Christian Morals*, supplies a note to 'Lyons' skins': 'That is in armour, in a state of military vigilance. One of the Grecian chiefs used to represent open force by the lion's skin, and policy by the fox's tail.' There are some further changes after 'Sit not down...': 'popular Seats' becomes 'popular Forms', doubtless for the value of the double meaning of the word *form*. 'But endeavour to make them Heroical' is eliminated, presumably because 'Lyons' Skins' has already made that point. Instead, after 'Offer not only Peace-Offerings but Holocausts unto God', Browne introduces a Biblical image that neatly sums up the sense of the two paragraphs: 'Where all is due make no reserve, and cut not a Cummin seed with the Almighty.' In the last sentence there are two minor improvements: 'To serve him singly to please our selves, were too partial a piece of Piety, nor likely to place us in the highest Mansions of Glory' becomes, in *Christian Morals*, 'To serve him singly to please our selves, were too partial a piece of Piety, not like to place us in the illustrious Mansions of Glory'.

The two paragraphs printed below show again unmistakably successful revision:

A Letter	*Christian Morals*
If Avarice be thy Vice, yet make it not thy Punishment: miserable men commiserate not themselves, bowelless unto themselves, and merciless unto their own Bowels. Let the fruition of Things bless the possession of them, and take no satisfaction in dying but living rich. For since thy good Works, not thy Goods, will follow thee; since Riches are an Appurtenance of Life, and no dead Man is rich; to famish in Plenty and live poorly to dye rich, were a multiplying improvement in Madness, and Use upon Use in Folly [p. 181].	If Avarice be thy Vice, yet make it not thy Punishment. Miserable men commiserate not themselves, bowelless unto others, and merciless unto their own bowels. Let the fruition of things bless the possession of them, and think it more satisfaction to live richly than dye rich. For since thy good works, not thy goods, will follow thee; since wealth is an appertinance of life, and no dead Man is Rich; to famish in Plenty, and live poorly to dye Rich, were a multiplying improvement in Madness, and use upon use in Folly [I, 7].

The significant changes occur in the second and third sentences. Whereas in *A Letter*: *Bowels unto themselves, and merciless unto their own bowells* is tautological, the change in *Christian Morals* makes the point that a miser ('miserable man'—the word then meant both what it now means and also miserly) has no pity either on others or on himself. The change in the next sentence is an improvement both in sense and in grammar. In *A Letter* we are advised to take satisfaction in living rich, rather than in dying. Browne evidently realized that this jejune advice was not what he intended, but what he did intend is clearly expressed in *Christian Morals*: 'think it more satisfaction to live richly than dye rich'. Perhaps the following is an even more evident improvement by revision:

A Letter

Persons lightly dip'd, not grain'd in generous Honesty, are but pale in Goodness, and faint hued in Sincerity. But be thou what thou virtuously art, and let not the Ocean wash away thy Tincture. Stand magnetically upon that Axis where prudent Simplicity hath fix'd thee; and let no Temptation invert the Poles of thy Honesty: and that Vice may be uneasie, and even monstrous unto thee, let iterated good Acts and long confirmed Habits make Vertue natural, or a second Nature in thee. And since few or none prove eminently vertuous but from some advantageous Foundations in their Temper and natural Inclinations, study thy self betimes, and early find what Nature bids thee to be, or tells thee what thou may'st be. They who thus timely descend into themselves, cultivating the good Seeds which Nature hath set in them, and improving their prevalent Inclinations to Per-

Christian Morals

Persons lightly dipt, not grain'd in generous Honesty, are but pale in Goodness, and faint hued in Integrity. But be thou what thou vertuously art, and let not the Ocean wash away thy Tincture. Stand magnetically upon that Axis, where prudent simplicity hath fixt thee; and let no attraction invert the Poles of thy Honesty. That Vice may be uneasy and even monstrous unto thee, let iterated good Acts and long confirmed habits make Virtue almost natural, or a second nature in thee. Since virtuous superstructions have commonly generous foundations, dive into thy inclinations, and early discover what nature bids thee to be, or tells thee thou may'st be. They who thus timely descend into themselves, and cultivate the good seeds which nature hath set in them, prove not shrubs but Cedars in their generation; and to be in the form of the best of the Bad, or

fection, become not Shrubs but Cedars in their Generation; and to be in the form of the best of the Bad, or the worst of the Good, will be no satisfaction unto them [p. 182].

the worst of the Good,[1] will be no satisfaction unto them [I, 9].

In the first sentence there is one change only, the change of the word *sincerity* into *integrity*. The gain is considerable. Browne is not talking of a particular virtue (such as sincerity) but of virtue comprehensively. In his time the word *sincerity* could have a broader meaning than now; it could mean 'freedom from adulteration', but the narrower modern meaning of the word, 'freedom from dissimulation, honesty, genuineness', had already been current for more than a century and was beginning to exclude the other. On the other hand the word *integrity*, which even in its modern sense would be an obviously fitter choice, was in Browne's time richer in relevant implications than it now is; it meant not only 'moral principle in relation to truth and fair dealing', but also the state of being 'undivided; unimpaired; innocent; sinless' [*O.E.D.*]. It was in short precisely the word required by the context. In the sentence (a clause in the letter) beginning: 'Stand magnetically', Browne has substituted the word *attraction* for the word *Temptation*; by doing so he retains continuity in his metaphor of magnetism, which attracts but cannot be said to tempt. The next sentence in *Christian Morals* is altered in such a way that the sense is improved, both logically and theologically. The introduction of the word *almost* removes a difficulty in both kinds. Habit cannot, in reason, be said to make virtue natural; and, from the point of view of theology Virtue cannot be natural (although Browne suspected that it sometimes is, as is plainly implied in *Religio Medici*, Part II). However, habit, and the grace of God, can make virtue *almost* natural. The change in the next sentence improves the quality of the writing rather than alters the meaning. The sentence in *A Letter* from 'And since few' to 'what thou may'st

[1] *Optimi malorum pessimi bonorum* (Browne's note; it is not added to *A Letter* but only to *Christian Morals*).

be' is comparatively clumsy. The 'advantageous Foundations', surrounded as they are by abstract generalities, have no metaphoric life. In revision, the metaphor bears the weight of the meaning from the start 'Since virtuous superstructions have commonly generous foundations'. In *A Letter* the close of the sentence loses what impact its opening had; it 'drags its slow length along'. In *Christian Morals* Browne enlivens it by introducing another metaphor; in place of 'study thy self betimes, and early find...' we have 'dive into thy inclinations, and early discover...'—self-discovery is felt as action. A similar increase in vitality results from the small changes in the final sentence; the participles *cultivating* and *improving* go out; the first is replaced by *cultivate*, the second is eliminated, so that he can write 'prove not shrubs' instead of 'become not shrubs'. This also makes more sense, for a seedling cannot become either shrub or cedar tree; it can only prove to be one or the other.

The next example I choose is one of the famous pieces of Browne's prose. It may be familiar to some readers who are not widely acquainted with his work:

A Letter	*Christian Morals*
Let not the Sun in Capricorn go down upon thy Wrath, but write thy Wrongs in Water. Draw the Curtain of Night upon Injuries, shut them up in the Tower of Oblivion, and let them be as tho they had not been. Forgive thine Enemies totally, and without any Reserve of hope, that however God will revenge thee [p. 184].	*Let not the Sun* in Capricorn *go down upon thy wrath*, but write thy wrongs in Ashes. Draw the Curtain of night upon injuries, shut them up in the Tower of Oblivion, and let them be as though they had not been. To forgive our Enemies, yet hope that God will punish them, is not to forgive enough; to forgive them our selves, and not to pray God to forgive them, is a partial piece of Charity: forgive thine enemies totally, and without any reserve, that however God will revenge thee [I, 15].

The passage is an amplification of one verse in the Epistle to the Ephesians [iv. 26]: 'Be ye angry, and sin not: let not the sun go down upon your wrath.' It is a prose poem or set-piece in which, characteristically, Browne is as much concerned with precision of meaning as with rhythmic pattern. Both in *A Letter* and in *Christian Morals* he adds footnotes to ensure full comprehension: one to 'Capricorn': 'Even when the Days are shortest'; and another to 'the Tower of Oblivion': 'Alluding unto the Tower of Oblivion mentioned by Procopius, which was the name of a Tower of Imprisonment among the Persians; whoever was put therein was as it were buried alive, and it was death for any but to name him.' The last clause of the note makes the pertinence of the allusion vivid. Browne could, of course, take it for granted that his reader would recognize the Biblical quotation. The first revision, other than italicizing the quotation, is the change from *Water* to *Ashes*. One obvious reason for the change is stylistic; he gets rid of a fourth *W* and he balances the sibilant in the opening phrase 'Let not the Sun' with the sibilants in the close 'wrongs in Ashes'. But there is also an improvement in the sense. The verse in Ephesians begins: 'Be angry, and sin not....' To write in water is to make no mark; it is not to be angry at all. To write in ashes is to make a mark that can easily be obliterated; it mirrors the manner in which we can 'be angry, and sin not'. The third sentence is amplified in *Christian Morals*; the rhythm is improved, but not by mere tautology. He climbs by separate steps to total Christian forgiveness, whereas in the letter he had sprung to his conclusion. We must not hope that God will punish our enemies; more than this, we must pray for their forgiveness, and the final imperative, the same in both passages, though it adds no new thought, has been more fully prepared for. The comic effect with which Browne notes a common flaw in human forgiveness is more telling in the more magniloquent version.

My last example of detailed revision is the penultimate paragraph of *A Letter* and *Christian Morals*:

A Letter

Give no quarter unto those Vices which are of thine inward Family, and having a Root in thy Temper, plead a Right and Propriety in thee. Examine well thy complexional Inclinations. Raise early Batteries against those strong-holds built upon the Rock of Nature, and make this a great part of the Militia of thy Life. The politick Nature of Vice must be opposed by Policy, and therefore wiser Honesties project, and plot against Sin; wherein notwithstanding we are not to rest in Generals, or the trite Stratagems of Art. That may succeed with one Temper which may prove successless with another; there is no Community or Commonwealth of Virtue; every Man must study his own Œconomy, and erect these Rules unto the Figure of himself [p. 185].

Christian Morals

Bid early defiance unto those Vices which are of thine inward Family, and having a root in thy Temper plead a right and propriety in thee. Raise timely batteries against those strong holds built upon the Rock of Nature, and make this a great part of the Militia of thy life. Delude not thy self into iniquities from participation or community, which abate the sense but not the obliquity of them. To conceive sins less, or less of sins, because others also Transgress, were Morally to commit that natural fallacy of Man, to take comfort from Society, and think adversities less, because others also suffer them. The politick nature of Vice must be opposed by Policy, and therefore wiser Honesties project and plot against it; wherein notwithstanding we are not to rest in generals, or the trite Stratagems of Art. That may succeed with one which may prove successless with another: there is no community or common-weal of Virtue; every man must study his own œconomy, and adapt such rules unto the figure of himself [I, 18].

The major change here is the introduction of two new sentences expressing an idea which did not figure in the original version. (By now we can, I think, be assured that the original version is the one in *A Letter*.) These sentences interrupt the sequence of military images; the moral idea they contain is, however, important and germane to that image-pattern. The new thought could have been suggested to Browne by a clause in the last sentence of the passage in *A Letter*: 'There is no Community or Commonwealth of Virtue.' This leads naturally to the idea that we must not forgive our own vices because they are common in our society. Other changes in the paragraph are relatively minor but show, I think, careful revision. 'Give no quarter unto' becomes 'Bid early defiance unto', which introduces the importance of timeliness at the outset; in the first version it does not occur until the third sentence: 'Raise early...'. There is a small improvement in the sentence that now comes after the new material. Instead of 'and plot against sin', which changed the object of opposition from *vice* to *sin*, without any effect on meaning, Browne now writes, 'and plot against it' (*vice* being the antecedent of *it*). A similar excision of the redundant accounts for the absence, in *Christian Morals*, of the word *Temper*. 'That may succeed with one Temper which...' becomes 'That may succeed with one which...'.

Taken together, all these differences between the valedictory paragraphs in *A Letter to a Friend* and their counterpart in *Christian Morals* demonstrate alert and sensitive revision. When Browne revises, his first concern is to communicate his meaning as precisely as possible; his second is to convey it with all the vitality and elegance of which he is capable. In short, his object in revision is the same as that of any great writer—Henry James for example.

There is one more pair of paragraphs which are interesting in juxtaposition. *Christian Morals* has a counterpart in *A Letter to a Friend*; but this time Browne has totally rewritten the passage; he makes central an idea which is only latent in *A Letter*.

A Letter	*Christian Morals*
Tho humane Infirmity may betray thy heedless days into the popular ways of Extravagancy, yet let not thine own depravity, or the torrent	However thy understanding may waver in the Theories of True and False, yet fasten the Rudder of thy Will, steer strait unto good,

of vicious Times, carry thee into desperate Enormities in Opinions, Manners, or Actions. If thou hast dip'd thy foot in the River, yet venture not over Rubicon; run not into Extremities from whence there is no Regression, nor be ever so closely shut up within the holds of Vice and Iniquity, as not to find some escape by a Postern of Resipiscency [p. 183].

and fall not foul on evil. Imagination is apt to rove, and conjecture to keep no bounds. Some have run out so far, as to fancy the Stars might be but the light of the Chrystalline Heaven shot through perforations on the bodies of the Orbs. Others more ingeniously doubt whether there hath not been a vast tract of Land in the Atlantick Ocean, which Earthquakes and violent causes have long ago devoured. Speculative Misapprehensions may be innocuous, but immorality pernicious: Theoretical mistakes and Physical Deviations may condemn our Judgments, not lead us into Judgment; but perversity of Will, immoral and sinfull enormities walk with Adraste and Nemesis at their Backs, pursue us unto Judgment, and leave us viciously miserable [I, 17].

The source in *A Letter* is only just discernible in the passage from *Christian Morals.* The first image, 'the torrent of vicious Times', could have suggested 'the Rudder of thy Will, steer strait...'. But whereas the paragraph in *A Letter* is principally concerned with the threat of vicious times to *manners*, *action*, *vice* and *iniquity*, and the danger of indulgence in Enormities of Opinion is closely related to morals, in the paragraph of *Christian Morals* the central theme is the *understanding* and *theories of true and false*. The argument is that provided we 'steer strait unto good, and fall not foul on evil' intellectual error is venial or even harmless. It is a theme upon which the author of *Religio Medici* felt strongly and the passage is a clear statement of his long-considered belief.

Edward Browne's description of *Christian Morals* as a continuation of *Religio Medici* may have given rise to the belief that it was an earlier work than *A Letter*. The description is not wholly misleading; this posthumous work shows the old man reflecting upon religion and morals in the same spirit as he had done in his youth. The difference in the form of the work, however, implies a difference in the substance. *Religio Medici* was autobiographical, whereas *Christian Morals* is didactic. In the earlier work Browne is discovering his own thought; he looks back at the years of its development and describes what it now is. Every opinion reaches us as an aspect of a self-portrait. In the later work, moral ideas are presented as though from a common stock, the note of personal discovery is muted and the loss is great. In *Religio Medici* he achieved an organic form, each successive section was linked with its predecessor by some filament of personal (but recognizable) association. In *Christian Morals* Browne was, I believe, attempting to construct a suitable form; the moral ideas, probably written in notebooks from time to time, do not grow out of one another; but he endeavours to arrange them in sequences. The work is divided into three parts and presumably he intended some kind of homogeneity within each one. It is not fully achieved. In Part I each section recommends and defines a virtue; in Part II the first section continues the general moral advice; he counsels against the pursuit of pleasure: 'Punish not thy self with Pleasure; glut not thy sense with palative delights...', but this is followed by four successive sections about how scholars and writers should behave to one another. The remaining six sections in this part introduce other topics only tenuously related to one another. They could be said to be all concerned with God's providence, or how individual men may be affected by what seems to be chance or fortune. Part III is even more miscellaneous. This may mean that it contains transcripts from his notebooks and these he had not yet decided where to place in a work which was obviously unfinished when he died; occasional sequences of related sections suggest that he was endeavouring to arrange his material according to subject-matter.

Among such sequences Part II, sections 2–5 is of especial interest; each section concerns virtues appropriate to scholars and writers; Browne is here writing for those who share his own addiction to authorship.

Bring candid Eyes unto the perusal of men's works, and let not Zoilism[1] or Detraction blast well-intended labours. He that endureth no faults in men's writings must only read his own, wherein for the most part all appeareth White. Quotation mistakes, inadvertency, expedition and human Lapses, may make not only Moles but Warts in Learned Authors, who notwithstanding, being judged by the capital matter, admit not of disparagement [II, 2].

And he supports this admirable piece of good sense in excellent plain prose with examples of venial slips in the works of Cicero, Plautus, Apollinaris, Sidonius and Machiavelli.

The advice to his fellow-writers in the next section is to avoid dogmatism; advice that he has earned the right to give:

Let well-weighed Considerations, not stiff and peremptory Assumptions, guide thy discourses, Pen, and Actions. To begin or continue our works like Trismegistus of old, *Verum, certe verum, atque verissimum est*, would sound arrogantly unto present Ears in this strict enquiring Age, wherein, for the most part, *Probably* and *Perhaps*, will hardly serve to mollify the spirit of captious Contradictors. If Cardan saith that a Parrot is a beautiful Bird, Scaliger will set his Wits o' work to prove it a deformed Animal....Besides, many things are known, as some are seen, that is by Parallaxis, or at some distance from their true and proper beings, the superficial regard of things having a different aspect from their true and central Natures. And this moves sober Pens unto suspensory and timorous assertions, nor presently to obtrude them as Sybyl's leaves, which after considerations may find to be but folious apparences, and not the central and vital interiours of Truth [II, 3].

The subject amuses him and he writes of it in his arabesque style. When he is untrammelled by memories of the great didactic prose

[1] Zoilus: 'a poete, whych envied Homerus: and therefore the enviers of well lerned men are called Zoili' (Sir T. Elyot, *Dictionarie* (1538)).

writers of the past he lets his fancy roam freely and may well light on such a pun as links 'Sybyl's leaves' with 'folious apparences'.

The next section directs the reader to the just valuation of learning. It begins:

> Value the Judicious, and let not mere acquests in minor parts of Learning gain thy preexistimation. 'Tis an unjust way of compute to magnify a weak Head for some Latin abilities, and to undervalue a solid Judgment, because he knows not the genealogy of Hector,

and it ends with a sentence which tersely places book-learning: 'They do most by Books, who could do much without them, and he that chiefly ows himself unto himself is the substantial Man' [II, 4]. This is more just and more logical than the no less book-learned Milton's declaration in *Paradise Regained*,

> who reads
> Incessantly, and to his reading brings not
> A Spirit and judgment equal or superior,
> (And what he brings what needs he elsewhere seek?)
> Uncertain and unsettled still remains,
> Deep-versed in books and shallow in himself.
> [Book IV, ll. 322–7.]

Milton has (perhaps inadvertently) constructed a dissuasive from all book-learning; Browne only discourages those who cannot use it.

Indeed the next section opens with encouragement to any who have what John Donne called an 'immoderate hydroptic thirst for all humane learning', but with a warning to submit 'Thoughts and Contemplations' to the facts. This is Browne's last discourse about the relation of the New to the Old Learning. He opens the section in his character of Baconian:

> Let thy Studies be free as thy Thoughts and Contemplations, but fly not only upon the wings of Imagination; joyn Sense unto Reason, and Experiment unto Speculation, and so give life unto Embryon Truths, and Verities yet in their Chaos. There is nothing more acceptable unto the Ingenious World, than this noble Eluctation of Truth; wherein, against the tenacity of Prejudice and Prescription, this Century now

prevaileth. What Libraries of new Volumes aftertimes will behold, and in what a new World of Knowledge the eyes of our Posterity may be happy, a few Ages may joyfully declare; and is but a cold thought unto those who cannot hope to behold this Exantlation of Truth, or that obscured Virgin half out of the Pit [II, 5].

And he closes the section with characteristic homage to Aristotle, who must be revered, but whose work must not be used as a barrier against further discoveries:

Men disparage not Antiquity, who prudently exalt new Enquiries, and make not them the Judges of Truth, who were but fellow Enquirers of it. Who can but magnify the Endeavours of Aristotle, and the noble start which Learning had under him; or less than pitty the slender progression made upon such advantages, while many Centuries were lost in repetitions and transcriptions sealing up the Book of Knowledge? And therefore, rather than to swell the leaves of Learning by fruitless Repetitions, to sing the same Song in all Ages, nor adventure at Essays beyond the attempt of others, many would be content that some would write like Helmont or Paracelsus; and be willing to endure the monstrosity of some opinions, for divers singular notions requiting such aberrations [II, 5].

We find in Browne's writings, whether in his thirties or in his seventies, the same spirit of inquiry, the same respect for the pursuit of knowledge and the same homage to all who have zealously sought it. In all the various themes that turn up again in *Christian Morals* we find a basic consistency with the ideas in his earlier writings. Consistency is not always a virtue, but in Browne it is never the result of obstinately clinging to views once held. He can change his opinion about the facts; for example, he became increasingly less certain that the sun moves round the earth, and an entry in his Commonplace Books shows that he came to doubt whether those accused of witchcraft were in fact always guilty; might not some of these unfortunates be Devil-possessed?

We are no way doubtfull that there are wiches, butt have not been alwayes satisfied in the application of their wichcrafts or whether the parties accused or suffering have been guiltie of that abomination, or persons under such affliction suffered from such hands. In ancient time wee reade of many possessed and probably there are many still, butt the common crye and generall opinion of wiches hath confounded that of possession, men salving such strange effects from veneficiall[1] agents and out of the partie suffering. Many strange things have been done beyond the salvo of human reason wch might proceed as well from possession as venefication. If the man in the Gospel had now lived who would not have sayd hee had been bewiched wch few or none might then suspecte; Or who now sayeth that Saul was bewiched? Many examples may occurre of the like nature among us wherin whether possession bee not sometimes mistaken for venefication may well bee considered [Keynes, vol. v, p. 252].

It seems that this possibility had not occurred to him at the time of the witch-trial in 1665. It is likely indeed that his participation in that unhappy event prompted these later reflections. Browne is not consistent in the sense that he never changes his mind, but his interests and his moral taste remained constant. In accordance with his own idea of a man who can afford the luxury of reading, Browne continues to 'owe himself to himself'. He achieved what he recommends in *Christian Morals*: 'Swim smoothly in the stream of thy Nature and live but one Man' [III, 20]. His nature and circumstances led him, as he declared in *Religio Medici*, to accept the Christian faith; his reading caused him to admire and to learn from Pagan philosophers. In *Christian Morals* he gives the advice that had been implicit in everything he wrote concerning them:

Rest not in the high-strain'd Paradoxes of old Philosophy supported by naked Reason, and the reward of mortal Felicity, but labour in the Ethicks of Faith, built upon Heavenly assistance, and the happiness of both beings. Understand the Rules, but swear not unto the Doctrines of Zeno or Epicurus. Look beyond Antoninus, and terminate not thy Morals in Seneca or Epictetus. Let not the twelve, but the two Tables be thy Law. Let Pythagoras be thy Remembrancer, not thy textuary and final Instructor; and learn the Vanity of the World rather from Solomon than Phocylides. Sleep not in the Dogma's of the Peripatus,

[1] 'associated with witchcraft'.

Academy, or Porticus. Be a moralist of the Mount, an Epictetus in the Faith, and christianize thy Notions [III, 21].

After all the years in which the great classical moralists had been his counsellors and the Bible his storehouse of wisdom, the resonant names are his to command; they dance to his tune. His theme is the difference between reason and revelation, between the unaided will and divine grace. But he does not tell his reader to close his pagan books and it would have distressed him, as it had always done, to doubt the salvation of their authors.

Just as consistent with the man as we come to know him in all his works is the twenty-seventh section in Part III. Now he is an old man, preparing for death, and he reflects about how good men dying think about the future of the world they leave:

Though Good Men are often *taken away from the Evil to come*, though some in evil days have been glad that they were old, nor long to behold the iniquities of a wicked World, or Judgments threatened by them; yet is it no small satisfaction unto honest minds to leave the World in virtuous well temper'd times, under a prospect of good to come, and continuation of worthy ways acceptable unto God and Man. Men who dye in deplorable days, which they regretfully behold, have not their Eyes closed with the like content; while they cannot avoid the thoughts of proceeding or growing enormities, displeasing unto that Spirit unto whom they are then going, whose honour they desire in all times and throughout all generations. If Lucifer could be freed from his dismal place, he would little care though the rest were left behind. Too many there may be of Nero's mind, who, if their own turn were served, would not regard what became of others, and, when they dye themselves, care not if all perish. But good Men's wishes extend beyond their lives, for the happiness of times to come, and never to be known unto them. And therefore while so many question prayers for the dead, they charitably pray for those who are not yet alive; they are not so enviously ambitious to go to Heaven by themselves; they cannot but humbly wish, that the little Flock might be greater, the narrow Gate wider, and that, as many are called, so not a few might be chosen.

And thus he comes back to the questions that had moved him thirty years before, when he wrote *Religio Medici*; he has not outgrown the generous mind that led him, in his youth, to dally with three gracious heresies and to approve, Anglican though he was, of prayers for the dead.

For us Browne survives because he was 'a man of achievement in literature'. He wrote because he loved to write; he enjoyed using words as a painter enjoys using paint. But, in the art of writing, the medium is inseparable from the meaning; Browne used words to convey meaning. He did not think of himself as making literature. He wrote to enlighten, to inform, to clear away obstacles that impeded the road to knowledge; and even his modern reader receives light, gleans information, is guided towards ways of combating error. But for him all this is due to Browne's gifts as a writer; because of these gifts even Browne's most old-fashioned doubts or certainties retain their vitality. Everything he writes is saturated in personality; his curiosity, his sense of wonder, his amusement, his faith in the harmonious order of the universe are all mirrored in the way he uses the language. He may use it clumsily or superbly well, but he cannot use it commonly. Even when his vocabulary or his constructions are grotesque, they are grotesque in an individual way. His polysyllabic excesses may be due to what Bacon calls 'falling in love with words', but the love is often enlightened by a sense of humour. His sometimes clumsy sentence-structure is another matter: other good prose writers of his century, including Milton, tangle their sentences at times. When Browne does this, it is worth while to unravel the meaning, not because we need to know the facts, for instance, about the amphisbæna, but because it is delightful to know Sir Thomas Browne. Also, the whole response to experience that his writings convey, though so personal and even idiosyncratic, carries us back into the mid-seventeenth century. At no other period in our literature could anyone have responded just as Browne did to knowledge and morals and faith: he lived at the meeting-point between the medieval and the modern world.

SELECT LIST OF BOOKS

I. BIBLIOGRAPHY

Keynes, Sir Geoffrey. *A Bibliography of Sir Thomas Browne* (Cambridge, 1924).

2. WORKS

Sir Thomas Browne's Works including his Life and Correspondence, edited by Simon Wilkin, 4 vols. (1835–6).

The Works of Sir Thomas Browne, edited by Sir Geoffrey Keynes, 6 vols. (1928–31).

Religio Medici. Edited from the Manuscript Copies and the Early Editions, by Jean-Jacques Denonain (Cambridge, 1953).

Une Version Primitive de Religio Medici par Sir Thomas Browne. Texte inédit de la copie manuscrite au Collège de Pembroke Oxford, par J-J. Denonain (Paris, 1958).

Religio Medici, edited by Vittoria Sanna (Caligari, 1958).

3. CRITICISM AND BIOGRAPHY

Digby, Sir Kenelm. *Observations upon Religio Medici* (1643).

Ross, Alexander. *Medicus Medicatus* (1645).

Ross, Alexander. *Arcana Microcosmi* (1651).

Whitefoot, John. 'Some Minutes for the Life of Sir Thomas Browne', in Browne's *Posthumous Works* (1712).

Johnson, Samuel. 'Life of Sir Thomas Browne', in his edition of *Christian Morals* (1756).

Hazlitt, William. *Lectures on the Dramatic Literature of the Age of Elizabeth.* Lecture XI (1820).

Coleridge, S. T. *Literary Remains* (1836).

Stephen, Sir Leslie. *Hours in a Library*, Series Two (1876).

Pater, Walter. *Appreciations* (1889).

Osler, Sir William. 'The *Religio Medici*', *The Library*, Second Series, vol. VII (1906).

Strachey, Lytton. *Books and Persons* (1922).

Howell, A. C. 'Sir Thomas Browne and Seventeenth-Century Scientific Thought', *Studies in Philology*, vol. XXII (1925).

Leroy, O. *Le Chevalier Thomas Browne, sa vie, sa pensée et son art* (Paris, 1934).

Willey, Basil. *The Seventeenth Century Background* (1934).

Dunn, William P. *Browne: a Study in Religious Philosophy* (New York, 1950).

Finch, Jeremiah S. *Sir Thomas Browne. A Doctor's Life of Science and Faith* (Minneapolis, 1950).

Williamson, George. *The Senecan Amble* (1951).

Wiley, M. L. *The Subtle Knot. Creative Sceptics in Seventeenth Century England* (1952).

Wilson, F. P. *Seventeenth Century Prose* (Berkeley, 1960).

Huntley, F. L. *Sir Thomas Browne: A Biographical and Critical Study* (Ann Arbor, 1962).

INDEX

Index

Index